From the Seams of History
Essays on Indian Women

From the Seams of History

Essays on Indian Women

edited by
Bharati Ray

DELHI
OXFORD UNIVERSITY PRESS
CALCUTTA CHENNAI MUMBAI
1997

Oxford University Press, Great Clarendon Street, Oxford OX2 6DP

*Oxford New York
Athens Auckland Bangkok Calcutta
Cape Town Chennai Dar es Salaam Delhi
Florence Hong Kong Istanbul Karachi
Kuala Lumpur Madrid Melbourne Mexico City
Mumbai Nairobi Paris Singapore
Taipei Tokyo Toronto*

and associates in

Berlin Ibadan

© *Oxford University Press 1995
First published 1995
Oxford India Paperbacks 1997*

ISBN 0 19 564438 7

*Typeset by Rastrixi, New Delhi 110 070
Printed at Pauls Press, New Delhi 110 020
and published by Manzar Khan, Oxford University Press
YMCA Library Building, Jai Singh Road, New Delhi 110 001*

For
Isha, Tista, Lopa
and Jishnu

Contents

Acknowledgement		ix
Notes on Contributors		xi
Introduction		1
1.	Caste, Widow-remarriage and the Reform of Popular Culture in Colonial Bengal *Sekhar Bandyopadhyay*	8
2.	Popular Perceptions of Widow-remarriage in Haryana: Past and Present *Prem Chowdhry*	37
3.	Attired in Virtue: The Discourse on Shame (*lajja*) and Clothing of the *Bhadramahila* in Colonial Bengal *Himani Bannerji*	67
4.	The Early Muslim *Bhadramahila*: The Growth of Learning and Creativity, 1876 to 1939 *Sonia Nishat Amin*	107
5.	Conformity and Rebellion: Girls' Schools in Calcutta *Raka Ray*	149
6.	The Freedom Movement and Feminist Consciousness in Bengal, 1905–1929 *Bharati Ray*	174
7.	Women's Work in Bengal, 1880–1930: A Historical Analysis *Mukul Mukherjee*	219

8. The Role of Women in Economic Activity:
   A Study of Women in Rice-Farming Systems
   in West Bengal   253
        Bahnisikha Ghosh

   Index   289
   Illustrations following page 172

Acknowledgement

It is a pleasure to record the many kindnesses that were showered on me during the preparation of this volume. I would first like to thank the scholars whose contributions constitute this collection. I am deeply grateful to Justice Chittotosh Mukherjee, Ms Swarupa Das, Mrs Sita Ghosh, Mr Ajit Gupta, and Mrs Anuradha Gupta who generously provided me with rare photographs from their private collections and permitted me to reprint them. Ms Sonia Amin, Ms Sipra Dasgupta, Headmistress of Sakhawat Memorial Government Girls' High School, and Mr Badal Bose of Ananda Publishers have very kindly lent me some invaluable photographs for reproduction. Thanks are due to Professor Rajat Kanta Ray, Dr Basudev Chattopadhyay, Dr Suranjan Das, Mrs Pronoti Deb, Dr Tapati Basu and Ms Supriya Guha for their assistance, and to my publishers for their co-operation.

Notes on Contributors

SONIA NISHAT AMIN is Assistant Professor of History at the University of Dhaka. She is engaged in research towards her Ph.D. on Muslim women in Bengal in the late 19th and early 20th centuries. She also works for a feminist journal published from Dhaka.

SEKHAR BANDYOPADHYAY is currently a Lecturer in History at the Victoria University of Wellington. He received his MA and Ph. D. degrees in History from Calcutta University where he also taught for more than a decade. His publications include several articles on caste and society in colonial Bengal and a monograph entitled *Caste, Politics and the Raj: Bengal 1872–1937* (Calcutta, 1990).

HIMANI BANNERJI is an Associate Professor in the Department of Sociology at York University, Canada. She teaches in the areas of feminist theory, gender and colonialism, and women and development. She has been published widely, and is the author of *The Writing on the Wall* (1993). She has edited and introduced a book of essays on feminism, racism and politics *Returning the Gaze* (1993) and coedited and authored a book on feminist pedagogy *Unsettling Relations* (1991).

PREM CHOWDHRY is a UGC fellow at the Jawaharlal Nehru University, being on a sabbatical from Miranda House, Delhi University, where she is a Senior Lecturer in History. Her publications include *Punjab Politics: The Role of Sir Chhotu Ram* and *The Veiled Women: Shifting Gender Equations in Rural Haryana 1880–1990* (OUP, 1994).

BAHNISIKHA GHOSH is a Reader at the University of Kalyani, West Bengal. She has published widely on agriculture, human resource development, the role and status of women, the economics of population, and farming systems. Her book, *The Indian Population*

Problem: A Household Economic Approach (1990) has gained wide acclaim.

MUKUL MUKHERJEE is a Senior Lecturer in Economics, Maitreyi College, Delhi University. Her recent research has been on women in rice processing, female-headed households, women in agriculture in India (for the FAO) and studies on women's employment and training.

BHARATI RAY is Professor of History, and currently Pro-Vice-Chancellor for Academic Affairs of Calcutta University. She is also the Director of the Women's Studies Research Centre, at Calcutta University. Her publications include *Hyderabad and British Paramountcy* (1988), *Women's Studies in the Emergent Indian Scenario* (ed., mimeo, 1990), *Women and Science* (ed., mimeo, 1990), and *Women's Struggle: A History of the All India Women's Conference* (with Aparna Basu, 1991) and *Sekaler Narisiksha: Bamabodhini Patrika* (1994).

RAKA RAY is Assistant Professor at the Department of Sociology at the University of California at Berkeley. Her Ph.D. dissertation (University of Wisconsin, Madison) was on a comparative study of the women's movements in two major Indian cities. Her publications include 'The Contested Terrain of Reproduction: Class and Gender in Schooling in India' in the *British Journal of Sociology of Education* (1988).

Introduction

Women have long been pushed to the seams of history. The marginalization of women, both in mainstream history and in society, has been a political act. In these essays we seek to explore the overt and covert operations of gender which regulated the trajectory of politics in colonial and postcolonial India. To this extent, this anthology is, in its aim, political. The contributors, drawn from diverse disciplines and various institutions, differ in their approaches to the subject. Yet there is a leitmotif which links them together. At an elementary level they share a common concern to reclaim the realities of the lives and experiences of women. At a somewhat deeper level, they tend to move out of the constricting orbits of mainstream history which has devalued female agency in the making of history. This anthology seeks to redress this perceived imbalance in historiography and, we hope, will contribute towards 'the rewriting of history'.

This is not to state that the discipline of history should focus on women only, but to assert that the traditional criteria for historical attention need to be changed. Moreover, 'there are events that are specific to women and there are some things that concern them particularly'.[1] A central objective of this volume is to focus on these 'events' and 'things'. We will also examine the roles played by structure and agency in women's lives and investigate how women themselves acted.

Often the strength of structural barriers blind us to the fact that a conscious resistance is perceptible among women amidst the daily hardships. Yet at other times, in our zeal to celebrate this resistance, we overestimate its impact and ignore the ways in which social structures limit and shape the options available to women. Both

---

[1] Michelle Perrot, 'Introduction', in Michelle Perrot, ed., *Writing Women's History* (Oxford, 1992), p. 1.

individually and collectively, women are actors and are acted upon. If we are to better understand women's history we must be sensitive to this duality. And if we are to comprehend the place and role of women, the cultural representation of womanhood and women's self-images, we have to explore the realm of ideology and consciousness while keeping in view the constraints of politics and economy. Discussions about women have to be contextualized, and the processes which make for the political construction of gender explored.

Gender, however, is a complex phenomenon and is, by no means, amenable to simple analysis. It is socially defined in a variety of ways through cultural practices, symbolical representations, and roles — and on a plurality of sites — the home, work place, and school, pervading all hierarchies in a complex intermeshing. Indeed, as Chandra Mohanty points out, ideologies of womanhood are created as much by the realm of the sexual as by the realms of race, class and nation.[2] Gender informs every aspect of a woman's existence. But precisely because its manifestation is conditioned by local specificities, any meaningful exploration of the gendered ordering of society entails a combination of different levels of analysis.

The contributors to this volume have therefore freely pursued their own methodologies without any editorial interference. As against a tendency to universalize feminism or patriarchy as categories, we seek to posit their differential operation among different social groups and in different parts of India. In the words of Natalie Zemon Davis, 'What we are after are gender systems in all their variety'.[3]

This search for variety led our contributors to raise some significant questions. In what ways do various constellations of ideological and institutional factors help or retard social change? What are the ways in which forms of institutions may be appropriated to serve patriarchal interests? What are the forms resistance may take,

[2] Chandra Talpade Mohanty, 'Cartographies of Struggle: Third World Women and the Politics of Feminism' in Chandra Talpade Mohanty et. al., ed., *Third World Women and the Politics of Feminism* (Bloomington, 1991), *Passim.*

[3] Interview with Natalie Zemon Davis in Marho, *Visions of History* (Manchester University Press, 1983), p. 118.

and what are the limits to such resistance? What were the processes by which women became aware of their subordination? These and other related issues have been taken up for detailed investigation in the articles that follow.

The debate over the remarriage of widows serves as an appropriate entry-point to the women's question which agitated the public mind in nineteenth-century India. In colonial Bengal, as analysed by Sekhar Bandyopadhyay, the dedicated efforts of Iswar Chandra Vidyasagar failed to ensure the remarriage of Bengali widows. Unlike Rammohan Roy's fight against *sati*, Vidyasagar's crusade for the amelioration of the state of widowhood exposed the limits of state-intervention in social issues. The Act of 1856 only legalized the remarriage of widows: it could not make the procedure socially acceptable. Obviously, Vidyasagar had to fall back on social consent and it was here that his 'defeat' may be located. Bandyopadhyay does not wholly reject the traditional explanation of this failure in terms of the structural weakness of the reformist efforts. But he lays greater stress on cultural factors, since it was to the realm of culture that the issue of widow remarriage ultimately belonged. Drawing on Peter Burke's formulations on the 'reform of popular culture', Bandyopadhyay shows that in Bengal popular culture began to lose its own moorings and tended to internalize the hegemonic ideologies of the elite strata of society. And the latter was so deeply permeated by the notion of patriarchic control over women that the reform could not make any headway. Nor was it possible. Vidyasagar himself had accepted and internalized this notion, and the language in which he phrased his reform clearly revealed his concern to maintain the patriarchic control over female sexuality and family discipline. Bereft of an alternative ideology and stonewalled by a culture that refused to be reformed, the issue of widow-remarriage met its 'unavoidable defeat'.

As one turns from Bandyopadhyay's Bengal to Prem Chowdhry's Haryana, one is struck by the apparently contradictory approach to the widow-question. Chowdhry, like Bandyopadhyay, emphasizes the cultural variable in her explication of the compulsions of Jat widows within the framework of the traditionally prescribed form of leviratic remarriage. Elsewhere she has discussed in detail the role of this institution in a small peasant economy.[4] Here she examines the reflection of this phenomenon and the wider image of female sexuality in the popular culture of rural Haryana, where common law had permitted, abetted and even compelled widow remarriage. It clearly protected patriarchal interests in an agrarian economy based on the family farm. As Chowdhry shows, in such a society a widow becomes immediately anomalous and is therefore a threat; and the dire need is to control and dominate her again. An interesting point which emerges from her analysis is that widow-remarriage in Haryana was not at all confined to the lower castes. All except the Rajputs followed the custom. Reports indicate that it was followed by the Brahmins too. It is not surprising therefore that the social reform culminating in the Widow Remarriage Act of 1856 was accepted by the 'reformed' high-caste Hindus of the region. The two papers on widow-remarriage, taken together, raise some important methodological issues. If the 'reform' of popular culture under Brahminic influences sealed the fate of widows in Bengal, the very absence of similar influences arguably furthered their remarriage in Haryana. But viewed from the perspective of women's history, the social pressure for remarriage in Haryana and against it in Bengal, though apparently contradictory tendencies, were both aimed at consolidating the hold of patriarchy. The potential sexuality of young widows was sought to be defused and/or kept under patriarchal surveillance in two different modes of power. And in both, women were being treated as 'objects'. Autonomy for women was clearly never an issue.

In the reformist ideology, an image of the gentlewoman was being constructed endowed with attributes approved by the patriarchic society. For this, they had to be marked by signs of respectability which would clearly distinguish them from the 'other' women, and simultaneously be 'protected' from the unsolicited male gaze to which emancipation might subject them. In her study of the emergence of the *bhadramahila*, Himani Bannerji shows how

[4] Prem Chowdhry, 'Customs in a Peasant Economy: Women in Colonial Haryana' in Kumkum Sangari and Sudesh Vaid, eds., *Recasting Women* (Delhi, 1989).

no aspect of this construct was beyond male approval, whether in formulation of character or in appearance. Patriarchy provided the basic philosophy for the investiture of the female body: the emergence of upper-class Hindu-Brahmo women from the seclusion of the *antahpur* or *zenana* necessitated the mediation of their male patrons in the design of a new style of dress at once modest and appropriate to the new image of womanhood envisaged by the reformers of nineteenth century Bengal. This image was likewise invested with the 'virtues' of *sabhyata* (civility), *sobhanata* (propriety) and *lajja* (shame/modesty), together creating a dominant 'feminine' ethic which worked as a powerful subjective regulator of female physicality and sexuality. Bannerji concludes that in subscribing to this patriarchal icon, middle-class women capitulated far more to patriarchal stereotypes than in any other area of social change.

While Hindu and Brahmo women were stepping beyond the confines of the *antahpur*, their Muslim counterparts were denied even those restricted freedoms. This was because seclusion of women was closely tied to the notions of *izzat* and therefore of status.[5] Writing with rage against the practice of confinement Rokeya Sakhawat Hossein, a pioneer in women's education, likened seclusion to being under siege[6] and fantasized about a world which, in Natalie Zemon Davis's words, put 'women on top'.[7]

Sonia Nishat Amin's article in this volume describes the work and struggles that marked the emergence of the Muslim *bhadramahila*. Amin focuses on two complementary areas — education that nurtured the new Muslim gentlewoman, and the literary activity by means of which she asserted her new-found independent presence in society. Amin traces the contributions of early Muslim pioneers in women's education in undivided Bengal, and explores the controversial study of Bengali as against Urdu as an act of resistance and self-assertion. In her analysis of creative writing and

[5] Patricia Jeffrey and Roger Jeffrey, *Frogs in a Well* (New Delhi, 1988).
[6] Begum Rokeya Sakhawat Hossein, *Motichur*, vols. I & II (Calcutta, 1907 & 1921).
[7] Natalie Z. Davis, 'Women on Top' in Natalie Z. Davis, ed., *Society and Politics in Early Modern France* (London, 1975).

social discourse Amin highlights the tensions experienced between *'purdah'* (modesty) and *'abarodh'* (literally 'imprisonment', seclusion). She also traces the emergence of new literary themes such as romantic love, and the daring portrayal of the educated Muslim gentlewoman as a companion to her man rather than as a mere housewife.

However, while one school of thought regarded education as the magic panacea for all ills afflicting women, other viewpoints have increasingly problematized the impact of education, regarding it as a process not of liberalization but of the reification of stereotypes. In this collection, Raka Ray's study of the students of two girls' schools in contemporary Calcutta shows how education may serve to confirm and bolster existing inequalities and to create or retard self-image and aspirations. At the same time, the 'objects' of the educational process are not passive recipients. Subtle subversion of the processes of education and quiet resistance to the content characterize both sets of students, who decode social messages in different ways, depending on their position in social stratification.

In looking at the various catalytic processes such as social change and education that helped to radicalize (if not wholly ameliorate) the traditional self-image of women, one must not overlook the contribution of political consciousness and activism, both in the heady days of the nationalist movement and in the post-independence period. My contribution attempts to analyse the link between early feminism in Bengal and contemporary mainstream politics. As participants in the national movement, women emerged as active agents, no longer content to remain passive objects of social reform. Like women in other national liberation and anti-imperialist movements,[8] Bengali women in the struggle wanted more than just freedom from their colonial oppressors: they wanted freedom from male domination as well. The period was thus marked by a heightened questioning of old assumptions by some middle class women while others gave expression to the new-found aspiration.

---

[8] See, for example, some essays in Sonia Kruks, Rayna Rapp and Marilyn B. Young, eds., *Promissory Notes: Women in the Transition to Socialism* (New York, 1989).

We end with a set of analyses of the ways in which cultural and social marginalization of women is extended and aggravated into the sphere of economic activity through traditional biases in the interpretation of concepts such as 'work' and 'productivity'. The economic marginalization of women has been documented elsewhere.[9] Both government and academia have systematically failed to recognize the contributions of women to the economy, and have defined their tasks as marginal or unproductive. Two essays in this volume address this problem. Mukul Mukherjee traces the pattern of women's work in Bengal as reflected in the Censuses between 1881 and 1931, and Bahnisikha Ghosh's time allocation study in rural Bengal compares a woman's typical working day to that of a man's. The studies together serve as necessary correctives to our inherited biases about the relative values of 'masculine' and 'feminine' work. Viewed in this light these two essays supplement others in this volume. Together these will provide a clearer understanding of the operation of gender in Indian society.

Calcutta, *Bharati Ray*
August 1994.

---

[9] See, for example, Nirmala Banerjee, 'Trends in Women's Employment, 1971–1981: Some Macro Level Observations', *Economic and Political Weekly*, vol. XXIV, 29 April 1989.

1

Caste, Widow-remarriage and the Reform of Popular Culture in Colonial Bengal

Sekhar Bandyopadhyay

I

Social reforms in Bengal in the nineteenth century affected many aspects of human relations and existential realities, the most important of them being gender relations and the condition of women. Yet, towards the close of the century a large section among the latter who were widows by civil status were still being 'forced' to live celibate and austere lives, despite the reform endeavours of men like Rammohun Roy, Iswar Chandra Vidyasagar and others. As the realities stand, while the former had succeeded in achieving his goal, the latter's mission ended in what has been described as an 'unavoidable defeat'.[1] *Sati*, the eradication of which was on Rammohun's reform agenda, was abolished by Regulation XVII of 1829. Widow-burning was made a penal offence, any violation of which would immediately invite the regulating hand of the state. Rammohun could thus save widows from being immolated with the help of the constant presence of state power and the law-enforcing apparatus. But Vidyasagar failed to see many widows remarried, as in this case the Act of 1856 only legalized their marriage, but could not make it socially acceptable; nor was it possible to enforce it with the help of the police force. So

[1] Asok Sen, *Iswar Chandra Vidyasagar and His Elusive Milestones* (Calcutta, 1977), p. 6.

Vidyasagar had to depend ultimately on social consent, not on the power of the state, and it was here that his 'defeat' was quite manifest. But one might ask whether this was in fact avoidable or not.

It may also be argued that in retrospect the movement does not appear to have failed. That widow-remarriage has gained in social legitimacy to-day is partly due to this nineteenth century reform endeavour. But it may be pointed out also that this legimization has taken place only among the educated sections of the community and, even within that limited social sphere, it is not widespread. 'Everyone feels the evil and wishes that it could be removed', wrote *Hindu Patriot* in 1855, 'but the difficulty is how to meet the lion in his den . . . '.[2] Widow-remarriage remains exceptional among the educated even to-day, as it was in the nineteenth and the early twentieth centuries. And contrary to the existing stereotypes, the uneducated and the lower orders are also ardent defenders of the taboo just as their social superiors are. This compels us to re-think this reform movement as a 'defeat', since the problem was complex and not one of education alone.

The existing literature[3] seeks to explain this 'defeat' by focussing mainly on the structural weaknesses of the reformist effort, but does not adequately emphasize the power of tradition that refused to be reformed. This paper is concerned mainly with the traditional culture of the Bengali Hindus, as it was to the realm of culture that the issue of widow-remarriage ultimately belonged. Culture, according to Peter Burke, is 'a system of shared meanings, attitudes and values, and the symbolic forms . . . in which they are expressed and embodied'.[4] Forms of marriage or social organization of human sexuality and relationship are therefore to be understood in terms of their cultural connotations and imputed social meanings. But culture is also multi-layered, different social groups have different cultures. Usually, we assume a simple dichotomy between the two broad cultural traditions, the 'elite culture' and the 'popular

[2] Benoy Ghosh, ed., *Selections from English Periodicals of 19th Century Bengal* (Calcutta, 1979), vol. III, p. 116 (hereafter *Selections*).
[3] Asok Sen, *Ishwar Chandra Vidyasagar*; Amales Tripathi, *Vidyasagar, The Traditional Moderniser* (Calcutta, 1976).
[4] Peter Burke, *Popular Culture in Early Modern Europe* (London, 1978), p. xi.

culture', or to use E.P. Thompson's Marxian phraseology, between 'patrician' and 'plebeian' cultures.[5] But we need not assume a clinical disjunction between these two traditions, as there are constant interaction and overlapping, though of an unequal nature, between them. As a result of this process popular culture often accepts and internalizes the ideologies of the elites and assumes in some respects a common interface with their culture. This process of the 'reform of popular culture', which Peter Burke first talked about in relation to early modern Europe,[6] implies an imposition of certain elite cultural forms on the masses from above, rather than voluntary emulative behaviour of the socially mobile groups from below, as suggested in our familiar 'Sanskritization' discourse.[7] Martin Ingram has more recently defined the process in the following words:

> ... the world of popular culture came under attack from elite groups (clergy, nobility and some middle class groups in town and country) who gradually attenuated and transformed many aspects of social life among the mass of the people. This 'reform of popular culture' combined attempts to suppress many popular activities and to modify the behaviour of the common people, ... and the sponsoring of a new 'popular' or 'mass' culture which embodied the ideologies of the ruling elites.[8]

This concept,[9] can be a useful tool for understanding and explaining the success or failure of the reforms proposed by men like Vidyasagar. The present paper will try to show that the taboo on widow-remarriage, which was adhered to by more people than is usually

[5] E.P. Thompson, 'Patrician Society, Plebeian Culture', *Journal of Social History*, vol. VII, 1974, p. 395.

[6] Peter Burke, *Popular Culture*, pp. 207–43.

[7] See M.N. Srinivas, *Social Change In Modern India* (Bombay, 1977), pp. 1–45.

[8] Martin Ingram, 'The Reform of Popular Culture: Sex and Marriage in Early Modern England', in Barry Reay, ed., *Popular Culture in Seventeenth Century England* (London, 1988), pp. 129–30.

[9] For more details, see Barry Reay, ibid., Introduction, pp. 17–22; also David Hall, Introduction, in S.L. Kaplan, ed., *Understanding Popular Culture* (Berlin, 1984).

believed, was in itself the result of a 'reform of popular culture'. This first process of reform was so effective and of such antiquity, that the subsequent attempt at counter reform was bound to fail, given the weakness of the reform ideology and the vulnerability of the strategy to promote it.

II

One of the major contentions of the most recent feminist critique of the nineteenth-century reform movements is that the issues which had been picked up concerned mainly a small section of women. The reform endeavours therefore reflected only the paternalism of the elitist male reformers, concerned exclusively about their own class, and their eagerness to retain their patriarchal control over the private spheres of life.[10] The first premise of this feminist discourse, however, needs to be re-examined, for compulsory widow-celibacy, like many other similar customs, were more widely practised than indicated by the available cultural stereotypes, both old and recent.

In Bengal widow-remarriage was strictly forbidden among the upper castes and most of the middle ranking castes in the nineteenth century. The 1891 list of castes that forbade widow-remarriage included, apart from the Brahmans, Kayasthas and Vaidyas of the upper stratum, the various trading castes, as well as the Sadgops, Sundis, Mahishyas, Telis, Mayras and Napits.[11] It was allowed among the lower castes, but they too appear to have shared the values of their social superiors. Widow-remarriage even when permitted, was looked down upon and was disparagingly referred to as *sanga* marriage, a practice prevalent in many other parts of India as well. Among the Namasudras of Bengal, for example, the married couples of a widow-remarriage occupied a lower place in the estimation of their caste fellows and were referred to as *Krishna-Paksha* (dark fortnight after full moon), while those married in a regular

---

[10] For a comprehensive discussion of this recent critique, see Barbara N. Ramusack, 'From Symbol to Diversity: The Historical Literature on Women in India', *South Asia Research*, vol. 10, no. 2, November 1990, pp. 154ff.

[11] *Census of India*, 1891, vol. III, The Report, p. 267.

way were described as *Sukla-paksha* (bright fortnight after new moon).[12] The very use of the terms 'dark' or 'bright' indicates the respective values attached by the community to the two forms of marriage. And by the beginning of the twentieth century, they too, like many other *antyaja jatis* around them had almost completely discontinued the practice and begun to conform to the traditional upper-caste behavioural norms of widowhood.[13] At the turn of the century, therefore, it was perhaps only the lowest menial groups like the 'Doms, Boonas, Bagdis and "low people" of various kinds' and the so-called 'aborigines' who practised widow-remarriage without any stigma attached to it, while the rest of the Bengali Hindu society strictly forbade this custom.[14] Nothing can be a better indicator of the failure or 'defeat' of the reform movement to introduce widow-remarriage.

Side by side, we also come across another social phenomenon the importance of which need not be minimized. And that was the increasing social legitimacy of widow-remarriage among the educated *bhadralok* who had been constructing in the nineteenth century new 'models of womanhood' to suit the socio-psychological as well as political needs of the time.[15] Even during Vidyasagar's life time, important groups in Calcutta, in addition to Young Bengal, and a significant section of the native press, like *Hindu Patriot, Tattvabodhini Patrika, Sambad Purnachandroday* or *Bamabodhini Patrika* had lent full support to his reform movement.[16] As the *bhadralok* category kept on expanding across caste and local

---

[12] Risley Collection, Eur. MSS. E. 295, vol. 3, pp. 258–9, vol. 4, p. 95, India Office Library, London.

[13] Shyamlal Sen, *Jatitattva-Vivek* (The Caste Ethics, Barisal, 1797 Saka), p. 111.

[14] H.H. Risley, *The Tribes and Castes of Bengal* (Reprint, Calcutta, 1981), vol. I, p. lxxxiv.

[15] For details on the construction of these models, see Uma Chakraborty, 'Whatever Happened to the Vedic *Dasi*? Orientalism, Nationalism and a Script for the Past', in Kumkum Sangari and Sudesh Vaid, eds., *Recasting Women: Essays in Indian Colonial History* (New Brunswick, New Jersey, 1990), pp. 27–87.

[16] *Selections*, vol. III, p. 116; Benoy Ghosh, ed., *Samayikpatre Banglar Samajchitra* (Reflections of Bengali Society in Journals, Calcutta, 1980) (hereafter *Samajchitra*), vol. III, pp. 70–1, 166–7; vol. IV, pp. 157–66.

boundaries, this legitimacy became more and more broad-based. The Bengali *bhadralok* was never a closed status group incorporating only the members of the three traditional upper castes. In reality, as John McGuire's quantitative study has shown, in the latter half of the nineteenth century the Calcutta *bhadralok* community included individuals belonging to as many as eighteen different castes.[17] In the early twentieth century, as there was further extension of education and literacy down the caste lines,[18] there were fresh entrants into this category. As the newcomers got access to the new literate culture of the educated urban *bhadralok*, they also began to accept and imbibe the reform ideology of the latter. To them widow-marriage now appeared to be good conduct or *sadachar* while its prohibition became *kadachar* or bad conduct.[19] A symbolic acceptance of this innovation was taken as a signifier of their entrance into the new status group. Certain sections of the Sadgops, Baruis, Gandhabaniks, Jogis, Rajbansis and Namasudras therefore sought to promote widow-remarriage at least for the minors. The educated Mahishyas also advocated remarriage of widows, though only for those who would be found incapable of practising *brahmacharya* or self-abnegation. And some of the progressive Jogis and Sadgops went even beyond such oral acceptance of the reform, and actually organized a few such marriages.[20] Such symbolic actions did not however mean that the innovation had acquired popular acceptance among such communities. The newly educated sections of these communities, the recent entrants into the *bhadralok* category, shared with the old members of the group the same

[17] John McGuire, *The Making of a Colonial Mind: A Quantitative Study of the Bhadralok in Calcutta, 1857–1885* (Canberra, 1983), p. 22.

[18] *Census of India*, 1911, vol. V, Part I, p. 373, Subsidiary Table VI.

[19] Madhusudan Sarkar, 'Abar Bidhaba Bibaha Keno?' (Why Widow-Remarriage?), *Navyabharat*, vol. 25, no. 12, Chaitra, 1314 BS

[20] *Jogisakha*, Baisakh, Jaistha, Ashadh, Sraban, 1312 BS; *Bangiya Tili Samaj Patrika*, Chaitra-Baisakh 1332–3 BS, Magh-Falgun 1333 BS; *Kshatriya*, Chaitra 1332 BS; *Sadgop Patrika*, Baisakh 1330 BS, Sraban, Paush 1337 BS; *Tilir Gaurab*, Aswin 1326 BS; *Bangiya Vaisya Barujibi Sabhar Chaturdas Barshik Karya-Bibaran* (Jessore, 1915), p. 55; *Subarnabanik Samachar*, Magh 1327 BS; *Gandhabanik*, Kartik-Agrahayan 1330 BS; *Mahishya Samaj*, Falgun 1328 BS, Jaistha 1329 BS

dilemma as regards the actual practice of the reform. Since Vidyasagar himself had failed in his mission, a Sadgop rationalized his dilemma, what else could they be expected to achieve![21]

Thus as a direct legacy of the reform movement started by Vidyasagar to introduce widow-remarriage what we find during the decades immediately following his death are two parallel situations. Prohibition of widow-remarriage became a far more widely shared popular custom, while the innovation of widow-remarriage gained wider social legitimacy among the educated sections of society. But even those who had accepted the innovation refrained from practising it. This paradoxical situation constitutes a problematic that can be explained only with reference to the dynamics of popular culture in Bengal in the nineteenth and the early twentieth centuries.

III

Public control over private life as a dominant feature of Bengali Hindu society has had a long history. In this cultural milieu, marriage was not a consensual union between two individuals. It was indeed a concern of the whole community, as endogamy was one of the fundamental aspects of the caste system with a bearing on social rank. Transactional modalities, rituals and rites in a marriage were therefore parts of a public spectacle, supervised and often monitored by the community. Slightest deviation from the established norms invited public censure, while major violations meant more severe punishments, which usually took the form of social boycott of the erring families. Popular Hinduism in other words inculcated an ideology of discipline, which was enforced or maintained through a hierarchized structure of social authority that expressed itself through the idiom of caste. The caste system represented, according to a recent commentator, a cultural construction of power in Indian society.[22] That it was a system connotative only of a structure is essentially a colonial ethnographic stereotype.

[21] *Subarnabanik Samachar*, Magh 1323 BS
[22] See Nicholas B. Dirks, *The Hollow Crown: Ethnohistory of an Indian Kingdom* (Cambridge, 1990), pp. 5–7.

It was also a normative system which defined, determined and also legitimized the structure,[23] and this relationship is crucial for understanding the failure of the reform movement advocating widow-remarriage.

The *Hindu Patriot* in 1855 recognized without any reservation the rationality of the proposed reform of widow-remarriage. But for it the major problem was how 'to bring about so desirable an end as the removal of miseries of our helpless females without incurring the risk of losing caste with all its concomitant disadvantages . . . .'[24] The widow of the first proposed remarriage, who was subsequently let down by the prospective bridegroom, also complained that 'she had by such refusal lost her position in society and is now an outcast . . . .'[25] Even the observers who had participated in the first widow-remarriage ceremonies organized by Vidyasagar, 'were completely outcasted' by the large majority of *bhadralok* in Calcutta.[26] Social rebels like Dakshinaranjan Mukhopadhyay, who had committed a double sin by marrying outside his caste and by marrying a widow, also had to acquiesce ultimately to this social tyranny and had to migrate and seek refuge in a completely different and distant social environment of Awadh.[27] What appears to be crucial is the fear of 'losing caste', of being excommunicated by the society, which intimidated people into surrendering to dominant social norms. The question therefore is what were the social implications of this phenomenon of 'losing caste' and how was the terror that it generated organized.

Caste as a normative system prescribed for each group in society, according to its rank, certain codes of conduct or *jati-dharma*,[28] which every individual had to perform in real life. This performance was believed to be the chief determinant of the quality of 'body

---

[23] For a detailed discussion on this aspect, see Sekhar Bandyopadhyay, *Caste, Politics and the Raj: Bengal 1872–1937* (Calcutta, 1990), pp. 1–51.
[24] *Selections*, vol. III, p. 116.
[25] Quoted in Asok Sen, *Ishwar Chandra Vidyasagar*, p. 58.
[26] John McGuire, *The Making of a Colonial Mind*, p. 37.
[27] Ibid., p. 40.
[28] Ronald B. Inden, *Marriage and Rank in Bengali Culture* (New Delhi, 1976), pp. 14–21.

spiritual', which determined a person's ritual as well as social rank and therefore took precedence over both the 'body individual' and 'body social'. Any deviation from such codes would lead to the fall from the ascribed rank, or loss of caste, which implied the denial of interaction with the local community and sometimes even of essential social services. The codes varied from group to group, but always there was a tendency of the lower groups changing and remoulding their behavioural patterns with reference to the elite model. The process which Alfred Lyall had once described as 'the gradual Brahmanisation of the aboriginal non-Aryan or casteless tribes' had reached such a point in Bengal in the mid-1880s that Herbert Risley could not detect any variance in customs and ceremonies of the different castes, high and low. He had to adopt, therefore, the method of anthropometric measurement in order to determine the origin of the intermediary and lower castes, who could thus be separated, somewhat arbitrarily, from the upper castes, to fit into his racial model of Aryan–non-Aryan dichotomy in Hindu society.[29] The phenomenon which Lyall and Risley had observed in the nineteenth century was no doubt the reflection of the process of reform of popular culture, which had taken place apparently by volition and not by any visible application of power.

But this acculturation was not entirely voluntary; there was, as it appears, an element of compulsion in it. In order to get access to Hindu society and to move up in its status ranking scale, acceptance of its behavioural norms was mandatory. These norms were essentially based on an ideology of hierarchy that legitimized the prime position of the Brahmans who, because of their monopoly over knowledge, both used to define such normative standards of social behaviour, as also arbitrated in cases of their violation. But the maintenance of social discipline, or the actual execution of the Brahman's mandate, depended on an elaborate power structure within which every single individual had his or her own location.

---

[29] 'On the Application of Dr Toppinard's Anthropometric System to the Castes and Tribes of Bengal', by H.H. Risley, 8 March 1886, Government of Bengal, Financial (Miscellaneous) Proceedings, March 1887, pp. 83–5, West Bengal State Archives, Calcutta.

Caste, Widow-remarriage and the Reform of Popular Culture 17

The primary unit within this structure was the extended family, which was always patriarchal, as patriarchy alone corresponded to the hierarchical ethos of Hindu society. The family household, as it appears from the late nineteenth century evidence, was organized in a hierarchical structure of obedience, in which every member was situated according to age, generation and gender, the supreme position of authority being held by the eldest male member, the patriarch or the *karta*.[30]

The lowest position, in terms of entitlement to rights and resources of the family, was held by the women, who were expected only to obey their husbands. An anonymous author wrote in a popular treatise entitled *Hindudharmaniti* (Principles of Hindu Religion) in 1794 Saka: 'The wife should follow her husband like his shadow; she should be like his friend in performing all religious duties; and like his maid she should carry out all his orders ... The wife who retains her smile in spite of the harsh words and angry looks of her husband, is considered to have properly performed her sacred duties'.[31] What was thus defined as the *dharma* or the duties of an ideal wife virtually meant her unconditional surrender to the dictates of the husband, and this subjection would continue even beyond the death of the husband, as marriage was conceived to be a relationship of eternal bondage. As another pamphlet called *Hindu Narir Kartabya* (Duties of Hindu Women) noted in 1916: 'The duties of a widow are included among the duties of a wife. For marital relations among Hindus continue even beyond death'.[32] It was this eternalist concept of marriage which rationalized prohibition on widow-remarriage. But such restrictions were not applicable to the widowers. In Bengali Hindu society of the nineteenth century polyandry was unthinkable but polygamy was acceptable and in certain cases a legitimate social practice. A widower was therefore often encouraged to remarry, particularly for procreating progeny

[30] Shib Chandra Bose, *The Hindoos As They Are* (Second edition, Calcutta, 1883), pp. 2–3.
[31] Anonymous, *Hindu Dharmaniti* (The Hindu Code of Ethics, Calcutta, 1794 Saka), p. 8.
[32] Jatindramohan Gupta, *Hindu Narir Kartabya* (The Duties of Hindu Women, Calcutta, 1323 BS), p. 108.

for the patriliny. The twentieth-century Bengali literature bears ample testimony to the existence of this social mentality.[33]

In the traditional social hierarchy of the Hindus, the women and the Sudras were the two lowest categories, as both were denied access to Vedic religious rites. Later on as sections of the Sudra *jatis* became socially mobile, gained access to elite culture, and became claimants to higher ritual status, they too began to conform to the patriarchal norms of the upper caste elite families. Even the women of these castes were so deeply socialized into this essentially elite (or upper caste) and male world-view that they too accepted without any question this patriarchal standard of morality. 'Devoted wives must always follow their husbands dead or alive', wrote *Mahishya Mahila*, the journal of the Mahishya women, in 1911. 'If the husband was dead', it continued further, 'the widow, until her own death, should observe self-abnegation and should never even pronounce the name of any other man during her life time'. Because, 'it is only by serving the husband that a woman can reach the heaven'.[34] The prohibition on widow-remarriage, which thus virtually implied a total control over the mind and body of the women by their husbands during their life-time and even after, had become, as we have noted already, an almost universal practice in Bengal by the beginning of the twentieth century. This near total acceptance of the moral code of widow celibacy was not just due to an imitative urge from below. It resulted from a long drawn and often imperceptible process of the 'reform of popular culture' imposed from above.

The question that we had begun with, i.e., how were these moral behavioural codes enforced, should now be answered. At an ideological level, these codes of behaviour derived their legitimacy from the injunction of the *shastra* or scriptures as interpreted by the Brahmans, who enjoyed, till the advent of print culture, a near total monopoly over Sanskrit textual knowledge. Even when the printing

[33] Cited in Bharati Ray, 'Do we have a choice? Widows of India with Special Reference to Bengal, 1900–1956', paper presented at the Berkshire Conference of Women Historians, June 1990 and at the Seventeenth International Conference of the Historical Sciences, August–September 1990.

[34] *Mahishya Mahila*, vol. I, no. 3, 1318 BS

press allowed a broader section of the people access to the scriptures, it was not the texts as such which were taken to the people,[35] but the commentaries written by these *pundits* which became more popular and widely read. Thus paradoxically, the spread of education or literacy in Bengal had led to a further traditionalization of society. The modernizing impact of education depends on its content, or as Bernard Cohn remarked on 'what people read after they have become literate'.[36] Even a cursory glance at the list of vernacular publications in the late nineteenth and the early twentieth centuries,[37] would at once reveal that the average reading public in Bengal was more interested in the traditional lore or the knowledge of the *shastra*, than in the new secular humanistic knowledge.

The educated Bengalis' infatuation with the *shastra* was, however, due mainly to the Orientalist tradition which had attached supreme importance to scriptures for understanding Indian society. Consequently, during the debate over *sati*, the competing discourses established the 'centrality' of Brahmanic scriptures in determining the legitimacy of social customs.[38] Vidyasagar, an inheritor of this tradition and a Sanskrit scholar by training, also recognized the power of the *shastra*, from which he believed all social behavioural codes derived their legitimacy. His innovation of widow-remarriage would therefore acquire social acceptance, as his contention was, only if it could be supported by some scriptural maxims; because, as he noted, 'in this country people behaved in accordance with the dicta of the *shastra* and only the *shastra*'.[39] In his first treatise of

[35] Basumati Sahitya Mandir was one of the pioneering organizations responsible for the publication of such Smriti, Nyaya and Darshana texts published since the time of Rammohun Ray.
[36] Bernard S. Cohn, *India: The Social Anthropology of a Civilization* (New Jersey, 1971), p. 100.
[37] See for example, National Library, India, *Author Catalogue of Printed Books in Bengali Language*, vols. I–IV (Calcutta, 1959–63); also J.F. Blumhardt, ed., *Catalogue of the Library of the India Office*, vol. II, Part IV (London, 1905).
[38] For a recent and excellent discussion on this aspect, see Lata Mani, 'Contentious Traditions: The Debate on *Sati* in Colonial India', in Kumkum Sangari and Sudesh Vaid, eds., *Recasting Women*, pp. 88–126.
[39] Iswarchandra Vidyasagar, *Bidhaba-Bibaha Prachalito Haoya Uchit Kina Etadbishayak Prastab* (Should Widow-remarriage be Introduced?) in Gopal Hal-

widow-remarriage we find a massive effort to hunt for a supportive text from the available corpus of scriptural knowledge. But Vidyasagar by going according to the Orientalist tradition misunderstood his own society.

The *shastra* constituted only one element among many on the basis of which the moral-behavioural codes were constructed. The other elements were oral traditions and longstanding customary usages that gave Hinduism the character of a folklorized religion. Thus when Vidyasagar discovered in *Parasarasamhita* a maxim in support of his reform, the *Hindu Intelligencer* immediately pointed out that

> 'the views of Parasara, if they were such as have been interpreted to us by the author of the brochure under notice (i.e. Vidyasagar's first treatise on widow-remarriage), have never been adopted by the Hindus, and will continue to be discarded by the people of this country for a long time to come.[40]

Samachar Sudhabarshan also observed around the same time:

> Since the beginning of the Kali Yuga till date, the remarriage of Hindu widows has never been *heard of, nor seen*. And it is for this reason that people believe that widow-remarriage is against the *shastras* and the codes of good conduct.[41]

This statement needs to be emphasized as it implied that the popular perception that widow-remarriage did not conform to the accepted standards of moral conduct was not derived from any written tradition. It was based on hearsay knowledge or a long standing oral tradition which a citation from an obsolete text could not invalidate. To the Hindus 'established custom is law' and in this case, the age-old, often believed to be 'eternal', custom was to debar the widows from re-entering connubial relations.[42] An

---

dar, ed., *Vidyasagar Rachana Sangraha* (The Collected Works of Vidyasagar, Calcutta, 1972), vol. 2, pp. 21–2.

[40] *Hindu Intelligencer*, 12 February 1855, *Selections*, vol. III, p. 112.

[41] *Samachar Sudhabarshan*, 29.12.1855, *Samajchitra*, vol. III, p. 140.

[42] *Hindu Patriot*, 15 February, 1855, *Selections*, vol. III, p. 115; *Samachar Sudhabarshan*, 6.11.1855, *Samajchitra*, vol. III, p. 137.

editorial in *Bamabodhini Patrika*, while discussing the futility of Vidyasagar's reform endeavour, very aptly summarized this situation:

> The common people neither follow reason, nor understand *shastra*; local customs also follow more or less the established tradition. These people hate widow-remarriage as a great sin, as they find it to be alien to their tradition.[43]

Vidyasagar had also realized, though much later, the power of oral tradition and customs and admitted it in his second treatise on widow-remarriage:

> ... Most of the people in this country are ignorant of the *shastra*. Therefore when there is a debate on any issue concerning the *shastra*, they cannot evaluate the arguments of both sides to get at the actual truth.

As they remained 'slaves of local customs' or *'desachar'*, they continued to prohibit widow-remarriage and thus 'ignored the injunctions of the *shastra*'. But local customs in this country changed from time to time and therefore Vidyasagar hoped that this inhuman custom could be changed, provided there was the right type of social consciousness.[44] But he himself failed to promote this consciousness, as neither he nor his associates were able to offer a radically new ideology — and they did not challenge the power structure that sustained the old custom.

But before we go into the limitations of the reform movement, it is essential to discuss the power structure that maintained social discipline and punished the errant in Bengali society. At the primary or family level, it was the *karta* who enforced the prescribed codes of behaviour on the individual members of his family. If he failed to do so, the family as a collective was held responsible for the violation or deviation and was liable to be excommunicated or ostracized. It could also be absolved, if the violation was involuntary, through

---

[43] *Bamabodhini Patrika*, Sraban 1277 BS, *Samajchitra*, vol. III, pp. 166–7.
[44] Iswarchandra Vidyasagar, *Bidhaba Bibaha Prachalito Haoya Uchit Kina Etadbishayak Prastab: Dwitiya Pustak*, in *Vidyasagar Rachana Sangraha*, vol. 2, pp. 36, 160–1.

the performance of *prayaschitta* or penance.[45] Such matters affecting families were the concerns of their immediate larger body, the clan or *goshthi* headed by the *goshthipati* who often adjudicated, with the advice of the clan elders, in such social disputes.[46] But the more serious matters, particularly those involving the possibility of excommunication were referred to the higher authority, the caste council or the *jati panchayat*. Each caste had its own council which settled disputes relating to caste and family affairs and acted as the custodian of public morality. All these councils were however subservient to the larger *samaja*, which actually meant the hierarchy of castes living within a particular territory. In medieval Bengal, with minimum interference from the central state authority, the territorial chiefs or the *Rajas*, and below them the *Zamindars*, controlled the *samajas*. The *Raja* was the headman of his own caste council, as well as the head of all the councils in his chiefdom. He provided protection for his subjects, maintained law and order, settled caste and family disputes, and enforced the appropriate codes of social and moral behaviour. Thus, as Ronald Inden has shown, in a medieval Bengali Hindu chiefdom there existed different levels of leadership for social control. But all these levels were tied to each other in fixed vertical relationships and at the apex stood the Raja, the most powerful patron in the whole chiefdom.[47]

This medieval system of control possibly continued into the early British period, as it was present in the living memories of the Bengalis even in the early twentieth century. A social historian of Bengal wrote in 1911:

> Previously some Brahman rajas like the Raja of Nadia, the Raja of Tahirpur, the Raja of Natore or the Raja of Susung, exerted immense influence on the Bengali Hindu society. The rules which

---

[45] Bani Chakraborti, *Samaj-Sanskarak Raghunandan* (Raghunandan, A Social Reformer, Calcutta, 1970), pp. 246–8, 255, 259.

[46] Umeschandra Gupta, *Jatitattva-baridhi-dwitiya bhaag ba Ballal-Mohamudgar* (Calcutta, 1905), p. 441.

[47] Ronald Inden, 'Hindu Chiefdom in Middle Bengali Literature', in Edward C. Dimock, Jr. ed., *Bengal: Literature and History* (East Lansing, Michigan, 1967), pp. 25ff.

they prescribed, in consultation with the chief *pundits* of the country, regarding ritual and social behaviour were obeyed by everybody.[48]

This *Raja-pundit* nexus, with one group enjoying monopoly over political power and the other a monopoly over scriptural knowledge, controlled popular culture in medieval and early colonial periods. These power elites retained their control at the local level even in the nineteenth century, by adjusting themselves to the changes in the political structure of the country and in the organization of its social production. The nexus now started operating through a new institution called *dal*, which S.N. Mukherjee found to have, in the late eighteenth and the early nineteenth centuries, the same functions as those of the *samajas* in the earlier time.[49] The only difference was that while the control of the *samajas* was local or at the most territorial, that of the *dal* system was regional. Led by the absentee landlords and *Rajas* and guided by the priests and *pundits*, these *dals* operated from the colonial metropolis of Calcutta and stretched their controlling hands over the countryside. As a late nineteenth-century observer notes, the *dals* in many respects performed the functions of the *Rajas* of the pre-colonial days.[50] The caste questions, which were theoretically under the jurisdiction of the colonial courts, remained for all practical purposes the prerogative of the *dalapatis*. It was on them that the interpretation, arbitration and modification of the customary laws depended almost entirely; only, they were advised in such matters by the knowledgeable *pundits*. While the *dals* usually operated at the local level, there emerged what McGuire has called a number of *supra-dals*, which were referred to variously as *sabhas* or *samajas*. Each consisted of a number of local *dals* and thus cut across the territorial boundaries of Calcutta and linked the city to the country. This *dal* system, which was generally used by the traditionalist elites as an apparatus of control over popular culture, continued to operate till about the

---

[48] Durga Chandra Sanyal, *Banglar Samajik Itihas* (The Social History of Bengal, Calcutta, 1317 BS), p. 450.
[49] S.N. Mukherjee, *Calcutta: Myths and History* (Calcutta, 1971).
[50] Shib Chandra Bose, *The Hindoos*, p. 167.

end of the nineteenth century. Then, as McGuire has noted, it 'became increasingly more diffuse as capitalist development broke down the relationships upon which it was based. Yet this process of disintegration was long and complex'.[51]

The *dal* was gradually replaced by the various exclusive caste associations which began to emerge in Bengal in great numbers since 1905. These organizations, as recently discussed,[52] were also responsible for the process that has been described earlier as the 'reform of popular culture'. Through them more and more of upper caste behavioural norms and notions of morality found acceptance and wider currency among the people of the lower orders. The hegemonic culture set the limits for the imagination of the upwardly mobile lower caste groups, who could not think of subverting the ritual order or repudiating its moral behavioural codes. Instead of inversion, which was rare and exceptional, we usually find co-option of these groups into the hegemonic cultural order and their acceptance or appropriation of upper caste cultural symbols, which was mandatory, as we have discussed earlier, for being recognized as respectable in Hindu society. Any deviation from the prescribed norms led to the fall from the ascribed rank and this was monitored, as we have seen, through an efficient and ubiquitous control mechanism. As *Hindu Patriot* had noted in 1855: 'Conservatism forms a principal feature in the character of the Hindu . . . The slightest breach of the established rules and practices is attended with serious consequences — the rash innovator is branded with infamy and discarded from all social intercourse'.[53] It was for this innate 'conservatism' of popular culture that even those who recognized the desirability of widow-remarriage could not actually practise it.

The power structure within Hindu society, together with its normative system, both based on the concept of hierarchy and expressed through the cultural idiom of caste, operated as a 'massive chain' that kept the entire society bound together. Important changes in the socio-economic structure were accommodated, but this

[51] John McGuire, *The Making of a Colonial Mind*, pp. 30–5 (quotation from p. 35).
[52] Sekhar Bandyopadhyay, *Caste, Politics*, Chapter III.
[53] *Hindu Patriot*, 15 February 1855, *Selections*, vol. VIII, p. 116.

was a gradual or slow and long-drawn process; the Sudra *jatis*, for example, were given more and more rights towards the turn of the century. Deviations from moral behavioural codes, on the other hand, were usually dealt with individually and were often pardoned after the performance of penance. The system in other words, made piecemeal adjustments, but lacked the capacity to cushion and absorb the shock of any sudden or radical organizational reform. Like a 'massive chain', as a correspondent of the *Friend of India* had observed in the middle of the nineteenth century, 'Caste must exist in its entirety, or gradually cease altogether . . . .'[54] Destruction of any particular component of that chain would mean its losing the binding capacity and that would imply the loss of power and privilege for a traditionalist elite who had so long ruled the society and controlled popular culture. Therefore, when the prohibition of *koolin* polygamy had been proposed, a panicky 'defender' of the system wrote a letter to the editor of the *Reformer* stating that if it was dropped by authority, it would lead to 'nothing short of great confusion and breach of peace . . . .'[55] Vidyasagar himself had to call in the police a number of times so that the widow-remarriage ceremonies which he organized could pass off smoothly.[56] The conservative press at the same time continued to threaten the widows willing to remarry with the consequences of being ostracized.[57] The battle over widow-remarriage had thus become for the traditionalist elites a fight for a symbol of authority and domination. To lose the battle would mean the destruction of that 'massive chain' which had ensured their hegemony.

To fortify their position further, the traditionalist elites now began to argue that the caste system, both its structural and normative aspects taken together, was the essence of Hinduism, and so the destruction of the one would mean the annihilation of the other. In 1883, Shib Chandra Bose had observed in a cautious tone that ' . . . though in every sense of the word an anti-social institu-

[54] *Friend of India*, 5 June 1851, *Selections*, vol. III, pp. 44–5.
[55] *Reformer*, 7 April 1833, *Selections*, vol. I, p. 170.
[56] Subal Chandra Mitra, *Iswar Chandra Vidyasagar* (in Bengali) (Calcutta, 1902), p. 319.
[57] *Samachar Sudhabarshan*, 29.12.1855, *Samajchitra*, vol. III, p. 140.

tion, it (caste) is nevertheless the main support of the Hindu religion. Take away this support and you destroy the very life and vitality of that religion . . . .'[58] Within a quarter of a century this sentiment came to be shared by a wide range of people in Bengal, from Chintaharan Chattopadhyay, a Brahman *pundit* of village Sundisar in Dacca district, to Sakharam Ganesh Deuskar, the celebrated history teacher of the Bengal National school. In 1910 Deuskar wrote in a little known pamphlet: 'These days, to the people of this country, destruction of caste system has become synonymous with the destruction of Hinduism'.[59] Within a few months, Chattopadhyay noted in the same tone: 'Casteism is integrally related to Hinduism. For maintaining family life and Hindu identity, it is essential to preserve the caste system'.[60] Both of them belonged to the same elite group that was carefully building up this notion of an organic connection between caste and *Hindutva*. It was done to force people to adhere to the moral behavioural codes that legitimized the social hierarchy.

People down the ladder had also internalized this concept of hierarchy that imposed limits on their imagination. Talking about the caste feeling of the lower caste people, an early twentieth century observer had noted: 'A sort of instinctive dread of breaking caste puts the idea of doing without caste absolutely beyond the range of possibilities to their minds'.[61] Indeed, how their minds were conditioned becomes more clear from another observation of the same period:

> Each caste considers itself as only a petty member of a mighty body and it never entered into its head even in dreams to set itself in opposition to the central authority. Humble as it might be it was content to share the glory of belonging to the proud hierar-

[58] Shib Chandra Bose, *The Hindoos*, p. 163.
[59] Sakharam Ganesh Deuskar, *Bangiya Hindujati Ki Dhangsonmukh* (Is the Hindu Community in Bengal on a Path of Decline, Calcutta, 1317 BS), p. 116.
[60] Chintaharan Chattopadhyay, *Brahman* (The Brahmin, Faridpur, 1317 BS), p. 19.
[61] N. Sengupta, 'The Census and Caste', *The Dacca Review*, vol. 1, no. 6, September 1911, p. 200.

chy. A man had no place unless he belonged to a caste; everyone therefore looked upon his caste as a valuable privilege, and no one would be foolhardy enough to lose this by offending the Brahmanical authority....[62]

To lose caste would further mean losing religion, that is to say, a forced uprooting from the familiar social and cultural environment — a terrifying prospect for any individual or family. Some people braved the consequences, as there are instances of widows being converted to Islam or Christianity before actually getting remarried.[63] This meant that they had to get out of the control mechanism of Hindu society, before defying its cultural norms. But most people could not afford to do so because of the dreadful implications. *Samachar Sudhabarshan* could therefore boast: 'Widow-remarriage would mean violation of a part of the Hindu *shastras*, which we do not think most of the religious minded people would be courageous enough to risk'.[64]

IV

Vidyasagar was aware of and had consciously accepted this power structure of Hindu society and its ideology of hierarchy. In other words, he neither challenged the power structure, nor offered any radically different ideological alternative. This becomes apparent if we look at his two treatises on widow-remarriage as texts.

To some of his traditionalist contemporaries, Vidyasagar was the representative of the western educated intelligentsia. For the *Hindu Intelligencer*, he was 'the learned Principal of the Sanscrit [sic] College, who is regarded by foreigners as a man of enlarged views and deep research . . .'[65] And to the *Sambad Prabhakar*, his only achievement was the Anglicization of the Sanskrit College,

---

[62] Jatindra Chandra Guha, 'Reform in the Hindu Society', *The Dacca Review*, vol. 1, no. 9, December 1911, pp. 284–5.

[63] *Bamabodhini Patrika*, Jaistha 1277 BS, *Samajchitra*, vol. III, p. 165; *Census of India*, 1901, vol. VI, Part I, Appendix II.

[64] *Samachar Sudhabarshan*, 6.11.1855, *Samajchitra*, vol. III, p. 137.

[65] *Hindu Intelligencer*, 12 February 1855, *Selections*, vol. III, p. 112.

which was not allowed to develop in the way that would have been most appropriate for it.[66] But whatever his popular image might have been, Vidyasagar's reformist ideology was not derived from the so called 'western' concepts of rationality or equality, as opposed to the traditionalist Hindu concept of hierarchy. At the very outset, in his first treatise on widow-remarriage, he had discarded the use of reason, for he believed that people were not amenable to reason and were only governed by *shastra*. So he went on interpreting and reinterpreting the *shastra*, trying to prove that his reform had sanctions within the corpus of traditional religious texts. In this he was not perhaps doing anything qualitatively very different from what the Nabadwip and Bhatpara *pundits* did when they issued *vyavastha* on various social issues.[67] The difference was only of degree: the *vyavastha* was applicable to individual cases, while Vidyasagar's reform had implications for the entire society.

When this method of referring to *shastra* failed, Vidyasagar in his second treatise appealed for a change of the local custom or *desachar*. While doing this, he argued:

> No one can prove that there has been no change in our customs since the first day of creation . . . . If an example is cited, you will be able to realize more easily to what extent the customs have changed in our country. In olden times, if a Sudra sat with a Brahman, there would have been no end to his crime. Now those very Sudras take the higher seats, and the Brahmans like obliging servants sit below.

This was, as Vidyasagar's footnote goes, 'against the *shastra*'. So at the end of his treatise he laments: 'Oh shastra! What a misfortune has befallen you! People who live their lives by indulging in activities which you have repeatedly identified as destructive of religion and caste are hailed as wise and pious, while those who even mention, not to speak of performance, the duty which you prescribe as an

---

[66] *Sambad Prabhakar*, 21.4.1265 BS, *Samajchitra*, vol. II, p. 177.

[67] Indeed, some time before Vidyasagar wrote his first treatise, some of the *pundits* had given a *vyavastha* sanctioning the marriage of the widowed daughter of one Shyamacharan Das of Calcutta. See Iswarchandra Vidyasagar, *Bidhaba-Bibaha . . . Etadbishayak Prastab*, pp. 14–17.

appropriate *dharma* (referring to widow-remarriage) are endlessly rebuked as atheist, irreligious and unwise'.[68] There could be no clearer statement vindicating the hierarchic ethos of the traditional Hindu society. It was essentially within this discourse of hierarchy, despite occasional references to equal rights for women,[69] that Vidyasagar situated his reform proposal.

The notion of patriarchic control over women in Hindu society, as we have discussed earlier, emanated from this concept of an all encompassing hierarchy. Vidyasagar had also accepted and internalized this notion. The language in which he phrased his reform proposal clearly revealed his concern to maintain the patriarchic control over female sexuality and family discipline. What we find in his two treatises is first of all a definite and honest statement of paternalistic sympathy for the miserable plight of the widows. But side by side, what is also writ large is a concern for the falling standards of public morality and the increasing social tendency towards adultery and foeticide, all due to the unsatiated sexual appetite of widowed women. Unable to lead a life of self-denial, they indulged in illicit sex and thus put to shame all the three lineages of their husband, father and mother. So it was necessary to regulate and direct this unbridled and wayward female sexuality into a socially legitimate channel, i.e. marriage, and for this it was essential to remove the prohibition on widow-remarriage.[70] The reform, in other words, was meant to ensure social discipline and patriarchic control over women's bodies and desires.

Most of the educated contemporaries of Vidyasagar who supported his cause shared this basic hierarchic assumption of gender inequality and expressed the same concern for public morality. The growing sexual anarchy in society was attributed only to the inability of the widows to restrain their libido which, as even the more progressive *Tattvabodhini Patrika* apprehended, would affect other

[68] Iswarchandra Vidyasagar, *Bidhaba-Bibaha . . . Dwitiya Pustak*, pp. 161, 164.

[69] Iswarchandra Vidyasagar, *Ratnapariksha* in *Vidyasagar Rachana Sangraha*, vol. 2, p. 538.

[70] Iswarchandra Vidyasagar, *Bidhaba-Bibaha . . . Etadbishayak Prastab*, p. 32 and *passim*; *Bidhaba-Bibaha . . . Dwitiya Pustak*, pp. 164–5 and *passim*.

women in society and thus would completely destroy the family structure. The plea for widow-remarriage was no doubt coated in a language of equality. If men could remarry after the death of their wives, the *Patrika* asked, why could not the widows do the same? But in the same breath it also argued in a sexist language that widow-remarriage was all the more necessary, as the libidinal urge of women was eight times greater than that of men. It was for this reason that all of them could not restrain their desires and brought infamy to Bengal.[71] A biological dimension was thus added to the concept of innate gender inequality. Other proponents of the reform also shared the same concern for falling standards of public morality and believed that what had further contributed to this social disorder were the other two evil institutions of child marriage and *koolin* polygamy,[72] which were also on the nineteenth century reform agenda.

This assumption of innate and uncontrollable feminine sexuality, as James Mill had already shown, was embedded in Hindu cultural traditions.[73] And therefore, the ideology of reform as Vidyasagar and his supporters had defined it, appeared not as an alternative to but as a derivative from the ideology of hierarchy which the traditionalist elites of Hindu society had been propounding. It was natural therefore that this new reformist position would not find popular acceptance, unless sanctioned by these elites. Even those who had realized that the reform was a social necessity, could not raise their voice, as *Tattvabodhini Patrika* commented, for fear of either offending the *dalapatis* or inviting public censure.[74] This was because Vidyasagar and the other protagonists of reform, instead of trying to subvert the power structure of Hindu society, sought the patronage of both the *dalapati* and the *pundit* themselves. Vidyasagar, for example, had accepted quite resignedly, that

[71] *Tattvabodhini Patrika*, no. 140, Chaitra 1776 Saka, *Samajchitra*, vol. IV, pp. 158–62.
[72] *Sangbad Purnachandroday*, 17.6.1851, *Sarbasubhakari Patrika*, no. 1, Bhadra, 1772 Saka; *Samachar Sudhabarshan*, 31.12.1855, *Samajchitra*, vol. III, pp. 70–1, 89, 140.
[73] Uma Chakraborti, *Vedic Dasi*, p. 35.
[74] *Tattvabodhini Patrika*, p. 157.

in this country people had to behave according to the words and dictates of the great men who were the interpreters of *dharmashastra*.[75] So he went to Radhakanta Deb and his *dal* for support and appeared in a public debate to argue his case against the rival *pundits*. He won the first round and got a *shawl* and favour from the almighty *dalapati*. Victory would have been his if the situation had not changed further. But soon the other *dalapatis* approached Deb and requested him to revise his decision to promote widow-remarriage. Vidyasagar was called for a second round of debate and here he lost, or he was perhaps meant to lose. The decision of the *dalapati* was reversed[76] and with this the fate of the reform movement was also sealed. Even those *pundits*, who had earlier given a *vyavastha* in support of the marriage of the widowed daughter of Shyamacharan Das of Calcutta, now changed their mind and became opponents of widow-remarriage.[77] And the common people could hardly muster the courage to go against the *shastra* as interpreted to them by the *pundits* or defy the established customs as imposed upon them by the *dalapatis*.[78] No legislation had the power to break this massive chain.

Vidyasagar, in other words, had opted for the traditionalists' method of reforming popular culture, i.e. of initiating and imposing reform from above. Crucial for the success of this method was the support of the hegemonic power of the traditionalist elites, in which he too had reposed his faith. The movement against *koolin* polygamy was successful as it received the support of some influential leaders of Hindu society, like the Maharaja of Burdwan, the Raja of Nadia and the Raja of Dinajpur. As *Friend of India* had noted, the Raja of Nadia was 'to Hinduism what Sir Harry Inglis was to Church of England' and the Raja of Dinajpur was 'a Hindoo of Hindoos'.[79] But widow-remarriage seemed to be too exotic a devia-

---

[75] Iswarchandra Vidyasagar, *Bidhaba-Bibaha . . . Etadbishayak Prastab*, p. 16.
[76] For details, see John McGuire, *The Making of the Colonial Mind*, p. 33.
[77] Iswarchandra Vidyasagar, *Bidhaba-Bibaha . . . Etadbishayak Prastab*, pp. 15–16.
[78] *Sarbasubhakari Patrika*, no. 1, Bhadra 1772 Saka, *Samajchitra*, vol. III, pp. 82–3, 88.
[79] *Friend of India*, 17 July 1856, *Selections*, vol. III, p. 93.

tion from the established moral-behavioural codes of Hinduism to enjoy the favour of these elites. In the nineteenth century cultural stereotype it appeared as a custom that violated the *shastra*; and it was complemented by another stereotype, that it was prevalent only among the lower orders. The *Hindu Intelligencer* wrote in 1855: 'This custom no longer prevails among the natives of the higher orders, . . . but it is still followed by those of the lower grades'.[80] For the *Samachar Sudhabarshan*, it was more specifically a custom of the *'antyaja'* (low born) castes, 'prevalent only among the Hari, Methar, Dom, Chandal etc.'[81] Vidyasagar appeared to be proposing the adoption of the values of the unclean castes, who were at the bottom of the society, by the Brahmans and the clean Sudras, who were the elites among the Bengali Hindus. He was asking the *bhadralok* to adopt a social practice that the *chotolok* had been pursuing since time immemorial. This must have looked like a reform of popular culture in the reverse direction — a 'counter reform'. The elites could only be expected to resist this effort.

The only alternative now left for Vidyasagar, which indeed he had already opted for, was to rely on a higher authority, i.e. the colonial state. He had been pleading for a legislation, perhaps with the assumption that the state and social authority were the two mutually validating reflections of the same hierarchy. But this was a crucial misunderstanding of the relations of power in nineteenth-century Bengal, where the colonial state and the leaders of Hindu society still held sway over two mutually exclusive domains of power. The former occasionally tried to encroach upon the territory of the latter, but could never completely control it. Therefore, even if there was a law, there was no prospect of its being enforced without social consent. And this consent or cultural acquiescence of the people could only be ensured either through the support of the traditionalist elites or by completely breaking off what we have described as the 'massive chain' of caste. Vidyasagar was denied the first, and his mind, like that of most of his contemporaries was

---

[80] *Hindu Intelligencer*, 12 February 1855, *Selections*, vol. III, p. 113. .
[81] *Samachar Sudhabarshan*, 10 July 1855, 15 September 1855, *Samajchitra*, vol. III, pp. 134, 137.

culturally so conditioned that he could not even think of opting for the second alternative. He operated essentially within the ideological and functional boundaries imposed by the dominant power structure of Hindu society. The roots of his tragedy lay here; the reasons for the 'unavoidable defeat' of the reform movement.

V

However, as a result of Vidyasagar's campaign for reform, the question of widow-remarriage became an issue of public concern as well as a subject of controversy. This had long term implications for Bengali society, as it became a symbol for the traditionalist elites, the acceptance or rejection of which was thought to have been inversely related to the diminution or continuance of their power. By taking the issue to the legislature, Vidyasagar had renewed the conflict over definition of boundary between the two domains of power of state and society. The traditionalists had already lost the first battle when Rammohun had the custom of *sati* abolished through the intervention of the state. As the *Hindu Patriot* had observed, the practice was discontinued only because it became 'penal at law'.[82] The leaders of Hindu society were no longer prepared to concede any further ground and the result was a stubborn resistance which sometimes even lapsed into violence. This critical response to the bill pending before the Legislative Council was adequately reflected when the *Eastern Star* noted

> 'that the proposed legislative interference . . . is improper and quite uncalled for. The legislative body of the country, not being a representative assembly of the people for whom it legislates, is under the necessity of using great care and circumspection in the enactment of laws . . . . The legislative council cannot compel the natives to marry their widows, but it proposes to fix the stamp of legitimacy on the children born of Hindu widows . . . . The community will continue to look upon them as bastards, and as persons not born in lawful wedlock. The legislature cannot coerce

---

[82] *Hindu Patriot*, 15 February 1855, *Selections*, vol. III, p. 117.

the opinions of men, nor influence their social relations, at least not directly'.[83]

The statement clearly questions the legitimacy of state power within the domain of social relations, where the will of the community was held to have been the supreme authority. But this social opinion, as we have seen, was effectively manipulated by the powerful traditionalist elite group. And therefore, even when there was a law validating widow-remarriage, just as the *Samachar Darpan* had predicted four years before it was actually passed, there was no way to enforce it.[84] In the case of *sati*, what was being proposed was the abolition of an evil custom, which could be ensured through the intervention of the state. But widow-remarriage was an innovation, indeed a revolutionary one, which could not be introduced by government fiat. The law therefore remained a dead letter for several decades after Vidyasagar's death.

What was worse, widow celibacy gradually became a much more widely practised popular custom. The elites portrayed it as one of the most authentic symbols of the culture of the respectable, and the socially mobile sections of the lower orders readily appropriated it. There were some among the educated members of the lower castes who had notionally accepted the innovation, but they too shared the same patriarchal and moralist concerns[85] and refrained from practising it in real life. Neither could they popularize the reform among their respective communities, because of the obvious socio-cultural compulsions to adopt the dominant elites' behavioural codes, defined by the ideology of hierarchy. This was the on-going or the usual process through which the traditionalist elites had been extending their hegemonic control over popular culture. It was beyond the power of Vidyasagar or his reformist compatriots to make a dent into their sphere of influence. This situation continued till about the middle of the twentieth century, when the war, the famine and the Partition disrupted social bonds and

---

[83] *Eastern Star*, 8 December 1855, *Selections*, vol. III, p. 137.

[84] *Samajchitra*, vol. III, p. 71.

[85] Balaram Sarkar, *Namasudra Jnanabhandar* (About the Namasudras, Faridpur, 1911), pp. 80–3.

destroyed in many cases the structure of the patriarchal family, making way for new values and fresh adjustments within the relations of power in Bengali society.

The final point to be mentioned about this reform movement is the marginality of women in the whole process. While Vidyasagar had started his crusade out of a sense of compassion for the young widows, what followed subsequently was a battle for a cultural symbol, in which the plight of the widows had become a subsidiary concern for both the contending parties. It was never a concern for the opponents of the reform; even Vidyasagar's sympathetic self often got superseded by the orthodox social disciplinarian in him. And in the scriptural polemics, women did not even figure as objects. In the nineteenth or the early twentieth century social world of Bengal, women had not as yet emerged as conscious subjects of history, trying to assert their own rights. If *Bamabodhini Patrika* represented the only feminine voice raised in support of the reform, it too accepted in a resigned mood the futility of the endeavour.[86]

On the other hand, women at the intermediate and bottom layers of the ritual hierarchy appear to have been so thoroughly socialized into the orthodox male worldview, that they not only accepted and promoted the dominant Hindu stereotypes of womanhood, but also opposed the idea of widow-remarriage. The *Mahishya Mahila*, a monthly journal for Mahishya women, edited by Krishnabhamini Biswas, is an ideal example at hand.[87] Even the Subarnabanik Mahila Sammilani, the first ever conference of about five hundred women of the Subarnabanik caste, held in December 1925 under the supervision of the male leaders of their community, discussed strategies for the spread of female education and other issues concerning women, but did not dare to include widow-remarriage in their agenda.[88] This also explains the differential success achieved by the two reform programmes. The first reform for the

---

[86] See note 43 above.

[87] See note 34 above; for a more detailed discussion on *Mahishya Mahila*, see Chandrima Sinha, 'Mahishya Jatir Samajik Andolan O Mahishya Nari' (The Social Movement of the Mahishya Community and their Women), *Aitihasik*, vol. 3, no. 2, April–June 1981.

[88] *Subarnabanik Samachar*, Paush 1333 BS.

spread of higher education had been relatively more successful, because its proponents, Vidyasagar included, had succeeded to a large extent in mobilizing female opinion in support of it. Some of the caste associations, as that of the Subarnabaniks mentioned above, had also ensured the active participation of women in this organized drive for female education. The *Mahishya Mahila* urged its literate women readers to educate their female neighbours and thus to spread literacy among the womenfolk of their community.[89] But none of the champions of widow-remarriage ever thought of mobilizing women's opinion in favour of the reform, not to speak of involving them as active participants in the actual reform process. This explains to a large extent the failure of their reform endeavour. And individual or independent voices of women, either in support of the reform or against it, have remained totally unrecorded, confirming only their marginality in this crucial social debate in colonial Bengal.

[89] *Mahishya Mahila*, vol 1, no. 9, 1319 BS, pp. 108–12.

2
Popular Perceptions of Widow-remarriage in Haryana: Past and Present

Prem Chowdhry

ājā beṭī lele phere
yoh margyā to aur bhatere [1]
(Come daughter get married,
If this one dies, there are plenty more.)

This proverb was first recorded in nineteenth-century colonial Punjab and signifies a widespread acceptance of widow-remarriage that may go much further back into history. Yet I have heard it quoted all over Haryana to this day. Its popular usage suggests not only the continuity of the tradition but perhaps even its strengthening. Clearly, certain rural areas of northern India, especially Haryana and Punjab, have always upheld and practised widow-remarriage in sharp contrast to the high-caste Hindus elsewhere who, under the Brahmanical code, prohibited widow-remarriage completely and upheld instead the ideal of *sati* (immolation of the widow along with her husband's body).

In this paper I attempt to look at the custom of widow-remarriage in terms of the perceptions accumulated at the local level and

---

[1] W.E. Purser and H.C. Fanshawe, *Report on the Revised Land Settlement, Rohtak District, 1873–79* (Lahore, 1880), p. 53; hereafter, *Revised Land Settlement*, Rohtak.

to examine how the local populace viewed and continues to view various related aspects of social life and relationships. A dip into the reservoir of folklore and tradition reveals an acceptance and celebration of the practice of widow-remarriage, primarily restricted to its levirate form. The emphasis in the folk tradition is on the sexuality of widows, which evokes deep-rooted distrust, and on the urgent need to control and harness it. What also comes across forcefully is the sexual exploitation of women, their concomitant resentment and the female consciousness of widow-remarriage as a repressive system. The resultant attempts of widows to back out of this system and the breaches in its levirate form have also not escaped attention in the oral tradition. I have dealt comprehensively elsewhere with the underlying colonial and post-colonial socio-economic and political factors behind the perpetuation of widow-remarriage and the motivated encouragement provided by the state, both colonial and independent.[2] Although these factors are absolutely intrinsic to the widow-remarriage problematic, it is interesting to note that they hardly find a reflection at the popular folk level. Therefore, I have made an attempt to examine the perceptions of the rural populace of Haryana towards widow-remarriage in order to determine the dominant trend of ideology, attitude and behaviour to which they themselves have been giving primacy.

[2] The colonial interest in strengthening the hold of the existing peasant society over land, which the claims of widows (for partitioning their land holding and seeking permission to marry men outside the family) threatened to disrupt both economically and socio-politically, coincided with the interests of the landowning classes in Punjab-Haryana. Therefore, the colonial state, which selectively adopted customs and made them legally enforceable, was blatant in its attempts to encourage widow-remarriage through administrative and judicial agencies. For a full discussion see Prem Chowdhry, 'Customs in a Peasant Economy: Women in Colonial Haryana', in Kumkum Sangari and Sudesh Vaid, eds., *Recasting Women: Essays in Colonial History* (New Delhi, 1989), pp. 302–33. The post-colonial state has also reinforced the system of *karewa*, though indirectly and unintendedly, through present day legislation, such as inheritance law, or more directly through executive and administrative directives of later day pension and award claims. For details, see Prem Chowdhry, 'Conjugality, Law and State: Inheritance Rights as Pivot of Control in Northern India', *National Law School Journal*, Bangalore, vol. I, 1993, pp. 95–116.

I Popularity of Widow-remarriage

The colonial administrators projected the Brahmanical code as the dominant model, advocating a complete prohibition of widow-remarriage. The *sati* ideal fitted with their view of India as a 'primitive society' direly in need of being 'civilized'. Yet even they had to acknowledge the existence of widow-remarriage. According to them, it 'commonly' existed but only among the 'inferior castes'.[3] It is interesting that, in direct contradiction to their stand with respect to high-caste Hindus whom they severely condemned for not allowing their widows to remarry, the British denigrated the practice of widow-remarriage where it did exist as a 'low-caste Sudra practice'.[4] Chief among the low castes, also known as *achchut* (untouchables) or *kamins* (menials), who practised widow-remarriage were: Chamar, Dhanak, Chuhra, Kumhar, Tarkhan, Nai, Teli, Jhimar, Jogi, Chimba, Dhobi, Mirasi, Julaha, Maniar, Bharbhunja, Gadaria, Kunjara, Od, Bhatiara, Aheri (Heri), Darzi.[5] In practice, widow-remarriage was popular not only among the low castes but also among the 'agriculturist castes' so notified under the Punjab Alienation of Land Act, 1900.[6] These were, chiefly, Jat, Rajput, Pathan, Sayyad, Gujar, Ahir, Biloch, Ror, Moghal and Mali. By subsequent notifications Taga, Saini, Chauhan, Arain, Gaud-Brahmin and Qureshi were also included. All except the Rajputs and Sayyads followed the custom of widow-remarriage. Reports indicate that the custom was present among the Brahmins as well. The Brahmins of Punjab were mostly landowners who followed the dominant social custom of this region in preference to the Sanskritic model of the other Brahmins who brooked no remarriage at all.[7] Among other Hindu castes, the 'low-grade

---

[3] *Principles of Hindu and Mohammadan Law* (London, 1862), p. 62.

[4] This was repeatedly mentioned in a large number of civil judgements. See, for example, *India Cases*, vol. 166, 1937, Joginder vs. Kartara, Lahore, pp. 719–23.

[5] *Census of India, Punjab*, 1931, vol. XVII, Part II, Tables, pp. 281–302.

[6] See Alienation of Land Bill of 1900, *Gazetteer of India, 1899*, Part V.

[7] *Census of India, Punjab and Delhi, 1911*, vol. V, 17, Part I, Report, p. 219.

Khatris' also observed this practice; others like the Banias and the Kayasthas did not.[8] It is difficult to statistically calculate the number of people practising widow-remarriage, but it is clear that an overwhelming majority seemed to have allowed it.[9] This fact was ignored by the imperial rulers.

Unexpected moral support for widow-remarriage came in the nineteenth century from the social reform movements. The movements were a protest against the extremely repressive system of the high-caste Hindus which condemned widows, even child widows, to a life of living hell. Social reformers in Bengal, Maharashtra, Punjab and the South, made a virulent attack on the Brahmanical model of *sati* and advocated widow-remarriage. The Imperial Government responded by first abolishing *sati* in 1829 and then by passing the Widow Remarriage Act XV of 1856 which legitimized the practice. Although this hardly made a difference to the regional castes and classes who had been practising widow-remarriage, it did grant the legal sanction of the foreign *sarkar* and assured an acceptance by the 'reformed' high-caste Hindus. The importance of the moral support of the reformers cannot be denied. For example, the Arya Samajists in Punjab provided this practice with justification drawn from the most ancient Hindu texts and offered protection to those who accepted it.[10] In actual practice, the

---

Pauline Kolenda argues that widow-remarriage in its levirate form is not non-Sanskritic. According to her, it was an ancient north Indian practice common to all *varnas* which the higher castes gave up, rather than a 'tribal custom' that has survived sanskritization. Over the years, the Hindu law books began to advocate celibacy and even *sati* or widow immolation as preferable for the twice-born communities, while widow-remarriage was appropriate for servants, Sudras and other lower castes. This practice, therefore, has to be looked at as an alternative norm within a north Indian kinship system. For details, see Pauline Kolenda, 'Widowhood among "Untouchable" Chuhras' in Akos Ostor, Lina Fruzzetti, Steve Barnett, *Concepts of Person: Kinship, Caste and Marriage in India* (London, 1982), pp. 172–220.

[8] *Census of India, Punjab and Delhi, 1911*, vol. V, 17, Part I, Report, p. 219.

[9] The castes which did not allow widow-remarriage, viz., Bania, Rajput, Kayastha, Khatri and Sayyads numbered only 605,177 out of a total population of 3,623,743 in this region in 1931, i.e., less than 20 per cent. See *Census of India, Punjab*, 1931, vol. XVII, Part II, Tables, pp. 281–302.

[10] In fact, one of the major reasons for the popularity and acceptability of

Arya Samaj in this region emphasized the Vedic derivation of *niyog* (levirate) while widow-remarriage *per se* did not have the same importance in their reform programme.

II Popular Sanction and Celebration

The peasant ethos which maintains '*ek kanya sahansar var*'[11] (there are several bridegrooms for one bride) still celebrates this idea as it did a century ago:

tītar pānkhi bādli
bidhwā kājal rekh
wuh barse yoe ghar kare
yā main nahin bisekh [12]

(A dark-grey cloud
is bound to burst,
A widow using kohl
is bound to remarry.)

the Arya Samaj in this region was the legitimacy that it provided to the custom of widow-remarriage.

[11] Jainarayan Verma, *Haryanavi Lokoktiyan: Shastriya Vishleshan* (Hindi) (Delhi, 1972), p. 43; hereafter Verma, *Lokoktiyan*.

A great deal of oral tradition used in this paper is based upon my extensive interviews and field work in Haryana from 1986-90. Some of the oral sources used here are also drawn from the vast published collection of the Haryana government as well as certain Hindi literati and folklorists of this region, born out of their field observations. Moreover, the fact that the custom of widow-remarriage has not only remained but got strengthened in this region makes the roots of this tradition perhaps as old as the custom itself. Some of this tradition was found to be recorded in the 19th century and has been indicated as such; yet others are recalled by the people as either having existed in the past but without relevance now, or remained in popular usage because of its continued social relevance. Wherever these shades of oral opinion exist, they have been pointed out in the work. Here I wish to point out that in translating the local dialect the emphasis is on conveying the mood and the message rather than its literal meaning. I also offer my profound thanks to Omi Manchanda and Rajul Sogani for helping me with the translation.

[12] A common proverb quoted by village men as well as women. It was first recorded in the 1890s; see R. Maconachie, ed., *Selected Agricultural Proverbs of the Punjab* (Delhi, 1890), p. 46.

The spread of the acceptance of widow-remarriage in this region gave the local sayings added relevance and also wider currency. Other proverbs that describe the sexuality of widows are:

Khole kes ughāre sir, ek vidhwā nazar me āyee [13]

(A widow sighted, with head uncovered and hair undone.)

Aalas neend kisān ne khowe, chor ne khowe khānsi tkkā vyāj mool ne khowe, rānd ne khowe hānsi [14]

(Sloth ruins a farmer, A cough exposes a thief, High interest forfeits the capital, A laugh betrays a widow.)

The old folk sayings also reflect popular sanction behind the public enjoyment of the festival of Holi by widows. In fact, they seem to have celebrated it fully. Holi, the most important rural festival in northern India, ranks above other festivals like Diwali and Dussehra.[15] Holi is marked by earthiness, make-belief and laughter. The open mixing erases divisions of sex, age and status. There are mock fights between men and women characterized by bawdy horse-play, ribald singing and throwing of coloured powder, water and even cowdung. In a reversal of roles the women beat up men with *kore* (a lash or whip made of cloth laden with stones), and hurl abuse and obscenities at them. The men incite them with snatches of ribald rhymes and the use of double entendre.[16] Similar

---

[13] Cited by women in the villages Dighal and Dujjana, of the Rohtak district. Also cited in Shanker Lal Yadav, *Haryana Pradesh Ka Lok Sahitya* (Hindi) (Allahabad, 1960), p. 469; hereafter, Yadav, *Lok Sahitya*.

[14] This was found to be very popular among men. Also see Yadav, *Lok Sahitya*, p. 427.

[15] See D.P. Saxena, *Rural-Urban Migration in India: Causes and Consequences* (Bombay, 1977), p. 170. The fact was confirmed by the villagers.

[16] Such behaviour is a common sight all over Haryana and western Uttar Pradesh during the Holi festival. My own observation relates to the celebration of this festival in the village Chhara of district Rohtak. For details of Holi celebrations in Haryana, see Bhim Singh Malik, *Haryana Lok Sahitya: Sanskritic Sandarbh* (Hindi) (Pilani, Rajasthan, 1981), pp. 44–59; hereafter Malik, *Haryana Lok Sahitya*; and D.B. Miller, 'Holi-Dulhandi: Licensed Rebellion in a North Indian Village', *South Asia*, August 1973, no. 3, pp. 15–22.

celebration of Holi known as *Laṭhmar* Holi is observed in western Uttar Pradesh. McKim Marriot describes Holi as giving explicit dramatization to specific sexual relationships that otherwise would not be expressed at all.[17] Commenting upon the sexual aspect of Holi in northern India, William Crooke had written in the nineteenth century:

> Finally comes the indecency which is a distinct element in the observance (of Holi). There seems to be reason to believe that . . . promiscuous intercourse was regarded as a necessary part of the rite.[18]

In a sort of temporary freedom from social restraints, widows are accepted as full participants in the public celebration of fun and revelry at Holi. The folk observation records:

kāchchi imlī gadrāi sāvan me
rāṇḍ lugāi mustāi phāgun me [19]

(A maiden matures in the rainy season,
A widow frolics in early spring.)

Clearly, the folk tradition has symbolically accepted the sexuality of the widows, but only temporarily, as it seeks to control it through remarriage.

The ease with which society accommodates the widow emanates from the fact that she is seldom considered to be the mystical source of her husband's demise. Unlike the areas which have strong Brahmanical traditions, derived from the Smritis which portray widowhood as the predestined *karmic* product of transgression in previous

---

[17] McKim Marriott describes the Holi celebrations as reversing the given social norms and differences of power conventionally prevailing in a man-woman relationship as well as in caste and class hierarchies. See McKim Marriott, 'The Feast of Love', in Andre Beteille and T.N. Madan, eds., *Encounter and Experience: Personal Account of Field Work* (Delhi, 1975), pp. 83–98.

[18] For a full account see William Crooke, *An Introduction to the Popular Religion and Folk-lore of Northern India* (Allahabad, 1894), pp. 387–92; hereafter Crooke, *Folklore*.

[19] A very common proverb used both by men and women. Also recorded in Malik, *Haryana Lok Sahitya*, p. 57.

lives,[20] the rural areas of Haryana and Punjab, where there is a clear lack of Brahmanical influence, culturally and ideologically attribute it loosely to *kismat* (fate), *aise karam the* (such was the destiny), of the man rather than the woman.[21]

As early as the 1930, M.L. Darling, an eminent scholar civilian of Punjab, observed that widows were looked upon as victims of misfortune rather than of sin.[22] The women married again and any stigma associated with widowhood ceased to persist. Significantly, the tradition of observing *karva chauth*, when a wife fasts in order to ensure the long life of her husband, though widespread in the whole of present-day Punjab and in most of Uttar Pradesh, does not exist in the rural areas of Haryana.[23] A woman of Haryana does not pray to die before her husband. Instead, the women observe *komai ka varat*,[24] a fast observed as a prayer for the long lives of their sons. This tradition is undoubtedly associated with widow-remarriage and, as one would expect, gives primacy to the son instead of the husband. More recently, however, some of the women of peasant castes specially among rural rich and those who live on the periphery of urban centres have started to observe *karva-chauth*.[25]

[20] Kumkum Sangari, 'Mirabai and the Spiritual Economy of Bhakti', *Economic and Political Weekly*, 7 July 1990, vol. XXV, no. 27, pp. 1464–75; and 14 July 1990, vol. XXV, no. 28, pp. 1537–52; also see Milred Stroop Luschinsky, 'The Impact of some recent Indian Government Legislation on the women of an Indian village', *Asian Survey*, 1963, vol. 3, pp. 573–83.

[21] This was the general consensus of opinion among rural women of Haryana, in the villages that I visited in the course of my field work.

[22] *Darling Papers*, Cambridge, South Asian Centre, Box No. II, see diary, 1930–1, p. 218.

[23] McKim Marriott, 'Little Communities in an Indigenous Civilization', in M. Marriott, ed., *Village India: Studies in the Little Community* (Chicago, 1955), pp. 171–222.

[24] Personal interview with Vidya Vati, Delhi, 24 December 1987. Born 1918, married to Hardwari Lal, a prominent educationist and politician of long standing, she has kept in very close touch with rural life despite having lived in different urban centres from the age of sixteen.

[25] Mohran Devi of village Jhojho Chamani, district Bhiwani, and Chhotu Devi of village Dujjana, district Rohtak, as well as other villagers disclosed the growing popularity of the *Karva Chauth* and *Santoshi Mata ka vrat* (fast). In an

III Deep-rooted Suspicion: Sexuality and the Widow

The deep distrust of the widowed condition, even in an old woman, can be seen in the abuse *susri rāṇḍ* ('widowed mother-in-law'). In fact, widows of all ages have been known to remarry. Some cynicism is not absent, as the following saying illustrates:

nāni khasam kare
dhewati duṅd bhare [26]

(The grandmother takes over a husband,
The granddaughter pays the price.)

Nevertheless, the remarriage of elderly widows is not altogether unacceptable. The explicit advice to widows is to remarry. A folk song mentions this by showing the rewards of marriage:

biyāhe biyāhe rāj kāreṅge
rāṅḍoṅ kā parmesar [27]

(The married ones will reign as queens,
The widows will be left to God.)

Indeed, a widow who does not remarry, becomes an object of suspicion. This region abounds in innumerable folk sayings, very popular, which show a deep sexual distrust of the widow.

To cite one example:

jāt, berāgi, naṭwā, chauthe widhwā naar
yeh chāroṅ bhūkhe bhale, dhāpe kare bigāṛ [28]

---

interesting reversal some of the urban women are observing *Komai ka vrat*, a fast kept for the sons. Mohran Devi, born 1925, wife of Mange Ram, an ex-armyman, owner of 60 bighas of land in the dry belt of Haryana. Personal interview with her, 7 January 1990. Chhotu Devi, born 1921; her late husband was a big landowner in Dujjana. Personal interview with her, 6 June 1986.

[26] A general observation considered to be not so unusual. Also recorded by Verma, *Lokoktiyan*, p. 116.

[27] Yadav, *Lok Sahitya*, pp. 263–4.

[28] Ibid., p. 421. A popularly quoted proverb in the villages with a lot of variations.

(A Jat, Beragi, Natwa and a widow,
are best left hungry, if satiated they inflict harm.)

This proverb and many others depict widows as totally faithless, self-seeking and covetous, and best avoided, as their company is certain to bring disaster. Obviously in the nature of warnings, these proverbs are used to express the threat and danger which the sexuality of widows poses to men, especially single men. It may be noted that widow-remarriage entails an alliance which can never be as worthy as the *biah* (religious wedding) and the bridegrooms are invariably 'deficient' in some way.[29] A bachelor's marriage to a widow, unless it is within the folds of a levirate marriage is frowned upon and in many cases is known to lead to violence.[30] Societal suspicion as reflected in the proverbs works as a double-edged weapon. On the one hand, it greatly circumscribes the widow's activities by declaring her dangerous until she comes under a man's control again; and, on the other, it restricts the choice of remarriage to certain partners.

A clue to this deep suspicion is indicated in the similarity of the words *rāṅd* (widow) and *raṅḍi* (prostitute). Though a widow's sexuality is highly suspect, the sexuality of a married woman is not denied. In fact, the rural women accept their own sexuality and even celebrate it.[31] There are innumerable folk songs and folk tales

---

[29] Personal interview with Ram Chander, village Bandh, district Karnal, 20–21 August 1987. Along with his two brothers, he has a joint holding of 33 bighas of land. Ram Chander opined that some compromise regarding the boy's looks, economic status, or marital and social standing has invariably to be made in such cases.

[30] Ram Chander's bachelor nephew, Gyanendra Singh, married a young widow with two small children in 1986. The family continues to disown him and so far he has remained disinherited. Violence and threats of disinheritance of the male spouse are common reactions in such cases.

[31] A fully grown girl is unable to contain her passion and requests her father to get her married. The folk song goes as follows:

bābal, yo joban din chaar ke
bājigar ka khel bābal
chhiṅke dharuṅ to dhe pare
tale dharuṅ to billāye khāye

spun around it; the joys of sex are related with a directness and simplicity of language that is easily comprehensible, sometimes in terms which would be called 'indecent' in the so called 'civilized' society, both colonial and post-colonial. For example, the famous female folk dance of *loor* and *ghumer*, popular in this region, are accompanied by a song in which the bride asks for different gifts from her husband in exchange for making love.[32] Also, the *swang* (an all male folk-theatre of Haryana) or *sang*, as it is locally known, not infrequently has the sexual escapades of a married women as an explicit central theme.[33] The same sexuality becomes suspect and a source of menace once the controlling hand of her husband is removed. However, it is strictly sexuality within the fold of marriage

---

(My youth is short-lived, father,
How long will it last?
I fear I may go astray, father,
Or be lured away.)

Yadav, *Loksahitya*, p. 322.

[32] The folk song goes as follows:

*merā dāman simā de ho, ho nandi ke bēra
meri chuṅdri maṅgā de ho, ho nandi ke bēra
tanne hyuṅ ghuṅghaṭ meiṅ rākhe ho, ho nandi ke bēra.*

(Get me a long skirt, O husband
Get me a veil, O husband
Then alone shall I be yours, O husband.)

Government of Haryana, *Gazetteer of Bhiwani District, Haryana, 1980*, Chandigarh, 1982, p. 80.

[33] *Chandra De ka Kissa*, shows the extra-marital affair of a married woman. Her husband having come to know of this throws her out of the house. Chandra succeeds in outwitting her husband and goes back to live with him happily ever after. Narrated by Anand Balmiki, son of late Ram Phal, a well known *sangi* from Haryana, who had settled in Calcutta about 30 years ago. Anand carries on with his father's work.
Interview with Anand Balmiki, Calcutta, 21st July 1988. Admittedly, there are also themes like that of *'Nal-Damyanti'* and *'Sati-Savitri'* and *'Parvati-ka-vivaha'*, with the central theme of a chaste woman, as a part of the *sang* repertoire, but these are liberally interspersed by the kind cited above.

which is accepted and celebrated.[34] For, as a widow, she is autonomous and in a position to make her own decisions about her sexual life, just as a prostitute is. It is, therefore, a short shift from the position of a *rand* to *randi*, both being commonly used as terms of abuse.

Significantly, the widow's sorrow after her husband's death is believed to be based on sexual deprivation. A folk song in the form of a widow's lament addressed to her mother-in-law reveals her unfulfilled desire and sexual loneliness:

ae sāsu jab dhasuṅ suṅ maiṅ dari bichhonā soonā
kuchh ek din ki nā sai mujhe sāre janam kā roṇā
are yānni thi jab rahi baap ke mujehe soch samajh kuchh nā thā
ib kyoṅ kaṭe din raat, kuchh ek dinā ki nā sai . . .[35]

(I shall be alone in my bed, O mother-in-law, and not just for a few days;
Immature before marriage, I was totally inexperienced;
Now, how will I spend my nights and days alone?)

Sexual deprivation not withstanding, widows, 'bereft of any control', are always perceived by women to improve in health and wealth.[36] Therefore, there is consciousness of the repressive nature

---

[34] One short example may suffice:

jo me aisee jaanu nand hatoli hogi
nandan ke veera setti kadiye ne sotti
jib sotti jib karvaṭ leti
nainā to nainā lagan na deti
chhati te chhati bhiran na deti

(Had I known my incorrigible *nanad*, (husband's sister)
Never would I have slept with her brother,
Or else I would have kept my distance,
And not allowed him to have his way.)

Yadav, *Lok Sahitya*, p. 137.

[35] Yadav, *Lok Sahitya*, p. 331.

[36] Vidya Vati, Delhi, 27 September 1988. This view was widely confirmed by rural women. Significantly, the widow has always exercised limited control over land. This control was turned into an absolute right of ownership under the Hindu Succession Act of 1956.

of the husband's control. For different reasons, male opinion also acknowledges a widow's heightened attraction, but considers it to be fatal to rural society. A *rand* is considered more demanding, almost inhuman in her desire and passion, and hard to restrain. The remedy is to put her quickly under the control of a husband again in order to curb her wayward and even destructive sexuality. The local term *'besharm rāṇḍ sai'* (shameless widow), used to describe bold and aggressive women, has arisen from the fact of the widow being generally considered shameless in her sexual desire and appetite. In fact, the general rural belief equates a *churel*[37] (the ghost of an unsatiated woman) with a *rand*. Sexually unsatiated women, whether they are dead *suhāgan* (married women) or living *rand*, turn into *churel*. The *churel* and *rand* are both seducers of young men, particularly if they are good-looking. Both operate at night. Just as the *churel* is believed to carry the youth to her own twilight kingdom and keep him there till he loses his manly beauty and send him back as a withered old man, the *rand* also lures men for her physical needs. The term of abuse *rāṇḍiā* has its origin in this belief; used for a man dominated by his wife, it means a widow's sexual slave. The myth of the sexual prowess of widows and its inherent dangers has the effect of limiting her freedom; it keeps her necessarily confined to the dictates of the males of her family.

In fact, the status of a widow directly confronts the deep-rooted ideology of dependency and control which operates on a woman right from her childhood. This was very perceptibly observed and recorded in 1910 by E. Joseph, a British district official:

> A female, minor or adult, is always under guardianship; while single she is under the guardianship of her father, if he be dead, of other relatives, in the order given — (all male members) so too when married until her *muklawa*, when she comes under the guardianship of her husband; on his death till remarriage she is under the guardianship of his family, whether she be minor or major.[38]

[37] Crooke, *Folklore*, pp. 168–71.
[38] E. Joseph, *Customary Law of the Rohtak District* (Lahore, 1911), pp. 54–5; hereafter, Joseph, *Rohtak Customary Law*.

The operation and relevance of this ideology today is visible in the manner in which rural women are still known largely in terms of their familial relationships with males. For example, a woman may be called 'Girdhari *ki chhori*' (daughter), Nanku *ki lugāi* (wife), 'Ram Chander *ki bahu*' (daughter-in-law) or 'Kishan *ki mā*' (mother).[39] In such a society, a widow immediately becomes anomalous and is therefore a threat, the dire need is to control and dominate her again. The popular saying *rāṇḍ kā sāṇḍ* (offspring of a widow, literally a stud bull), describing an uncontrollable male, emanates from the basic characteristic associated with widowhood. During the Emergency period (June 1975 to March 1977), it was not uncommon for rural Haryanavis to ascribe the seemingly inexplicable actions of the then Prime Minister, Indira Gandhi, to her being a *rand*, a widow gone berserk. Her son, Sanjay Gandhi, had equally suddenly started to be identified as *rāṇḍ kā sāṇḍ*.

IV Widow-remarriage: Preference to its Levirate Form

The custom of widow-remarriage as traditionally followed has special features of its own. Known as *karewā*, *karāo* or *chaddar andāzi*, it is a throwback to the old Rig-Vedic custom of *niyog* (levirate marriage), which was prevalent in the geographical region of Haryana and Punjab associated with the early Vedic Aryan settlements.[40] The *karewa*, a white sheet coloured at the corners, was thrown by the man over the widow's head, signifying his acceptance of her as his wife. Symbolically this gesture of male protection extended once again to a woman who had become autonomous.

[39] Yadav, *Lok Sahitya*, p. 435.

[40] *Niyog* was the practice of levirate marriage. Later, as during the Mahabharata times, *niyog* came to signify cohabitation by the wife with men other than her husband under certain specific conditions like impotence of the husband and the 'moral' and 'religious duty' to beget sons to continue the family line, such as in the case of Kunti. Eventually, *niyog* was given up as being inconsistent with increasingly pristine and Brahmanized standards for marital chastity and devotion. The increasing tendency in the late Dharma Sutras was to prescribe such practices. For details see Gail Hinich Sutherland, '*Bija* (seed) and *Kshetra* (field): Male Surrogacy or *Niyog* in the Mahabharata', *Contributions to Indian Sociology* (NS), vol. 24, no. 1, Jan–June 1990, pp. 77–103.

Popular Perceptions of Widow-remarriage in Haryana 51

The man also bestowed colour (red being the auspicious hue associated with matrimony) upon the woman and, through this custom, established social consent for cohabitation. There could be certain variations to it.[41] For example, it could take the form of either placing *churris* (glass bangles) on the widow's wrist, or sometimes even a gold *nath* (nose-ring) on her nose and a red sheet over her head with a rupee tied in one of its corners, before a full assembly. This would be followed by the distribution of *gur* (molasses) or sweets. This custom is followed to this day. Significantly, this form of remarriage is not accompanied by any kind of religious ceremony, as no woman can be customarily married, i.e. go through the ceremony of *biah* twice. The widow after *karewa* merely resumes wearing the jewels and brightly coloured clothes which she had put away on her husband's death. In colonial times, mere cohabitation was sufficient to confer all the rights of a valid marriage. However, for cohabitation to be accepted as remarriage it had to be cohabitation in the man's house. Visits to women in their own homes were considered 'adulterous'.[42]

Karewa, as a rule, has always been primarily a levirate marriage in which the widow is accepted as wife by one of the younger brothers of the deceased husband; failing him, the husband's elder brother; failing him, his agnatic first cousin, and so on. In fact, the persons eligible to marry a widow were not only severely restricted, but the marriage could be settled only by her late husband's family. And although the widow could not be compelled to remarry, she was not free to marry without their consent. So complete was the control over women and the question of their remarriage that it was freely admitted that the widow was often practically forced to yield to their wishes.[43] The situation has not changed. Levirate or the practice of marriage with the *dewar* or younger brother-in-law is amply reflected in folk lore, freely and jocularly cited among women of all ages and their younger brothers-in-law.

---

[41] For details, see C.L. Tupper, *The Punjab Customary Law*, vol. II (Calcutta, 1881), pp. 93, 123; also see Joseph, *Rohtak Customary Law*, p. 45.
[42] Joseph, *Rohtak Customary Law*, p. 46.
[43] Ibid., p. 45.

dewar bhābhī ka pyār ho sai
is me kai takrār ho sai

(The love between *dewar* and *bhabhi* is unquestioned,
There are no two ways about it.)

A more telling but somewhat restrained voice is:

rānd ke ghar me dewar maulā [44]

(The *dewar* lords in a widow's house.)

A popular folk tale has the custom of levirate marriage as its central theme:

A king had two sons. Both used to go to the forest. One day the younger brother, in order to wed his *bhābhī*, killed his elder brother and left him in the forest. He returned back alone. This aroused the suspicion of his *bhābhī* who inquired about her husband. The *dewar* replied that his brother was still hunting.

The *bhābhī* went to look for her husband in the forest where she saw vultures hovering around a dead being. The *dewar* dismissed it as a dead animal and advised her not to go near it. The *bhābhī* nevertheless did and found her husband's dead body. After having given instructions for the performance of her husband's last rites, she cursed her *dewar* by saying:

dewar tanne keere parne chāhiyen tanne apne bhāi kā ghar ujār ker apnā basāyā hai.[45]

(May you rot forever, brother-in-law. You have ruined your brother's house to set up your own.)

The oral tradition of this region is rich in such *dewar-bhābhī* songs and stories. Their popularity has obviously been reinforced by the continuing form of levirate remarriage.

[44] Heard in village Asodha Todran, district Rohtak, but mainly among men. Also recorded by Yadav, *Loksahitya*, p. 263.

[45] Narrated by Dheer Singh of village Asodha Todran, district Rohtak, 21–27 December 1988; born 1938; has 10 bighas of land in this village. The same story may be found in Madan Hariyanavi, *Haryana Lokgeet Sangrah* (Delhi, 1962), pp. 129–31; hereafter Hariyanavi, *Lokgeet.*

V Sexual Exploitation and Remarriage

For a brother, whether *dewar* or *jeṭh* (husband's elder brother), marrying his dead brother's widow was often the formalization of an existing relationship. British administrators who noted the practice since the early twentieth century recorded that even when there was only one married brother, the other brothers had free access to his wife.[46] Folk tales from Uttar Pradesh and Haryana reveal the prevalence of this practice among poor Brahmins, for example, when two brothers are shown to share a low-caste wife.[47] Darling, writing about this custom in Punjab, identified it as 'polyandry'.[48] The older generation of Haryanavis remember the sharing of women among brothers to be a common phenomenon in the 1920s and 1930s. Several similar cases in different villages were cited from memory.[49] There is no evidence forthcoming about the continua-

---

[46] P.J. Fagan, writing in 1904, observed: 'It is not uncommon among Jats and lower castes for a woman to be shared in common by several brothers, though she's recognised as the wife of only the eldest of them'. See Government of Punjab, *Hissar District Gazetteer, 1904* (Lahore, 1908), p. 65; also see M.L. Darling, *The Punjab Peasant in Prosperity and Debt* (First edition, 1925; Reprint, New Delhi, 1978), p. 51.

[47] See *William Crooke Collection*, Museum of Mankind, London, MS. 124, tale recorded by a teacher of the Baharaich district. Also recounted as an old tale by K.L. Rathi, Delhi, 24 May 1986. Born in 1912, village Rajlugarhi, district Sonepat, he is currently practising law in the Supreme Court. He and his wife have kept in close contact with their village and with their other family members living in different villages of Haryana.

[48] For the entire debate around polyandry and whether it can be broadly taken to mean a relationship in which a number of brothers hold common sexual rights in a single woman, married to just one of them, see Paul Hershman, *Punjabi Kinship and Marriage* (Delhi, 1981), pp. 176–88; hereafter Hershman, *Punjabi Kinship*; also K.P. Singh, 'Polyandry among the Jat Sikhs of Punjab, in Manis Kumar Raha, ed., *Polyandry in India* (Delhi, 1987), pp. 233–43.

[49] K.L. Rathi, New Delhi, 24 May 1986. R.M. Hooda was also of the same opinion. He saw the stark poverty of the region as responsible for this practice. Personal interview with R.M. Hooda, Rohtak, 1 June 1986; born 1938, village Makranti-Kalan, district Rohtak, B.A., L.L.B., Jat College Rohtak, practising law since 1962 at the district level, has ancestral land in the village.

tion of this practice in Haryana; even academically this aspect remains unearthed. In Punjab, however, Joyce Pettigrew, Paul Hershman and K.P. Singh have shown its continuation, especially among Jat Sikhs.[50]

The folk tradition however emphasizes the sharing of women among brothers to be a common phenomenon in colonial Haryana. A popular story from colonial days which is till jocularly related shows what a marital association entailed in the past:

> A new bride had four or five *jeth* or *dewar*. All of them had free sexual access to her. After fifteen or twenty days of her marriage, the bride requested her mother-in-law to identify her husband from among them. Upon this, the mother-in-law came out in the *gali* (street) and started to howl loudly; when asked about it, she replied: It is difficult for me to live in this house any more. I have been married for forty years, yet even now I have never asked anyone to determine the identity of my husband. This fifteen-day-old bride is already asking about hers.[51]

Although narrated to me by a woman, the story is said to be popular among men alone. The authorial voice which we can clearly discern is a male one, deriding feminine intelligence as well as speaking of female sexual appetite. The story gives us a glimpse into the popular perception of sexual exploitation as it existed at the time — the fact that it was common knowledge and widely accepted.

Women's awareness of this exploitation is highlighted even more directly and in a very perceptive manner in a *lok geet* (folk song) which is not commonly heard these days. Sung by a young bride it catalogues the many tasks she has to tackle in her marital home:

---

[50] Joyce Pettigrew, *Robber Nobleman: A Study of the Political System of the Sikh Jats* (London, 1975), p. 53; Hershman, *Punjabi Kinship*, pp. 176–88; Singh, 'Polyandry', as in f.n. 48.

[51] Narrated by Chhotu Devi, Village Dujjana, 6 June 1986. The same story was recorded by M.L. Darling in the diary of his tours of 1937. See *Darling Papers*, Box LXI, diary dated 30 Nov. 1937, p. 106 which also shows extensive polyandry being practised by the Sikhs of Punjab (caste not given).

maar koot ke main pāpan geri
dewar kar liyā ghar ka
main to māri ho gai he Rām
dhandhā kar ke is ghar ka [52]

(Beaten and forced to live
with my brother-in-law in sin,
Unending house work
has emaciated me, oh God!)

Incidentally, the current perceptions of those women still in the ambit of this practice, the remnants of which can still be found in Punjab, is also the same. Considered utterly humiliating and degrading, one of the involved women condemned it as 'an animal life' where she had to sexually 'satisfy three men'.[53]

In another *ragini* (song), used for enacting a *sang*, the theme revolves around the unwelcome advances of the *jeth* who forces himself on his sister-in-law and refuses to take no for an answer. It goes as follows:

Jeth aur Bahū

Jeth:	chandrmā si shān dekh pari tere mahal me āgyā
Bahū:	bāpā bargā jeth jale kayuṅ karan ughāi lāgyā
Jeth:	bhāi merā perdes gayā din kaṭe kis ke sahāre
Bahū:	pāṅch saat din me ājyā jale matnā boli māre
Jeth:	tu mewā ki pāki dāli main khāluṅ ban subāre
Bahū:	matnā choṅch lagāiye pāpi bhar rākhayā zahar chhuhāre
Jeth:	āshik baṅda māsukoṅ ke phal tor tor ke khāgyā
Bahū:	jis ne chedi beer birāni, turaṅt natijā pāgyā
Jeth:	mere kamre me chāle ne gori tu baṭuwā si
Bahū:	sou mārungi joot oot ke ker rahā badmāsi
Jeth:	joot maar chāhe paag taar le chāhe tuḍwāde phāṅsi
Bahū:	kāli nāgan beer parāie matnā samjhe hāṅsi [54]

[52] This folk song was remembered almost exclusively by the older generation of women in the village of Bandh in Karnal district. Also see Hariyanavi, *Lokgeet*, pp. 17–18.

[53] K.P. Singh, 'Polyandry', as in f.n. 48.

[54] Narrated by Khem Chand of village Govad, district Sonepat, a 65 years

(*Jeṭh* and *Bahū*

Jeṭh:	I am drawn to your house by your moonlike beauty.
Bahū:	Such advances don't become you, for you are like my father.
Jeṭh:	My brother is away, how do you spend your days?
Bahū:	He'll be back soon enough, rascal, don't you dare covet me.
Jeṭh:	You are a luscious fruit, let me taste of you.
Bahū:	Keep away, you sinner, this fruit is full of poison.
Jeṭh:	A fruit is meant to be eaten, a beloved meant to be possessed.
Bahū:	One who seduces another's wife gets the punishment at once.
Jeṭh:	Come to my room, my fair one, be mine, my little one.
Bahū:	With a shoe I'll beat you up, you scoundrel.
Jeṭh:	Beat me or humiliate me or hang me, if you like.
Bahū:	Another's wife is a deadly viper, don't trifle with her.)

The ardent wooing and the exposure of male desire, though thwarted by his own sister-in-law, is meant clearly to titillate the male audience. Yet, at the same time it shows an almost seductive wooing by the brother-in-law in a social milieu which sanctioned such alliances. The high moral tone of the sister-in-law is more in keeping with a concept of chastity and monogamy which is belied by the ideological and actual reality. The double voice which comes across assumes importance as it projects two attitudes with a touch of irony at the expense of both. Yet, in a curious way it does underline the woman's protest, her self-assertion and attempt to establish her self-esteem, identity and ability to say 'no' even within the given norms.

There is also a saying, very commonly heard all over northern India with minor linguistic variations, which maintains:

kamzor ki lugāi sabh ki bhābhi

---

old *sangi* (singer of local folk songs). Also see Pandit Lakshmi Chand, *Sangiyon Ke Lachchhe, Haryana Ka Asli Sangeet* (Delhi, n.d.), pp. 17–18.

(A weak man's wife is everyone's *bhābhi.*)

The proverb originates from the same practice. The sexual liberty which gave brothers-in-law sexual access was sought to be justified by giving the example of the Mahabharata: *'pānch pānduon ke bhi to ek thi Draupadi'*[55] (the five Pandavas had only one Draupadi). This is now unmentionable. The children born of similar liaisons were regarded as those of the husband. Interestingly, this attitude was reflected in the contemporary published folk literature. For example, in the *Betal Pacheesee*, a compilation of fables about a demon and Raja Vikramaditya of Ujjain published in Hindi, Gurmukhi and Urdu in the mid-nineteenth century from Lahore, Delhi, Agra and Meerut, among other publishing centres, has a story which deals with this theme.[56] The 'true father' of a child is declared by Raja Vikramaditya to be not the lover of the princess by whom she had conceived, but her husband. Elaborating on his verdict, the Raja declared that no one was certain by whom the woman had conceived, but every one knew who she was married to, i.e., the first was only conjecture but the latter an established fact. Therefore, the child belonged to its mother's husband and not to any elusive lover. It is significant that this story no longer features in any of the *Betal Pacheesee* available now.

The daughter-in-law was not above sexual exploitation by even her father-in-law. The customary practice of such relations was recorded by British officials in the late nineteenth century:

> Certain villages which need not be named, have the evil reputation of deliberately getting girls older than their boy husbands in order that the father of the latter may have illicit enjoyment of them.[57]

In fact, colonial Punjab and Haryana witnessed instances of the father-in-law moving the court to claim *karewa* marriage with the

---

[55] R.M. Hooda, Rohtak, 1 June 1986.
[56] India Office Records: *Vernacular Tracts*, no. 13 of 1874, see story no. 14 entitled *Betal Pacheesee* or The Stories of a Demon, published by Lala Piyare Lal of Manveya Heen Press (Delhi, 1871).
[57] See Joseph, *Rohtak Customary Law*, p. 19.

widowed daughter-in-law in the mid-30s.[58] The validity of such marriages was dubious. They were disputed and challenged among those very caste groups which otherwise accepted widow-remarriage.[59] In fact such claims may very well have been attempts to legitimize an existing relationship which had possibly left the widowed *bahu* (daughter-in-law) pregnant. This aspect of sexual exploitation also found its way into the oral tradition. An old tale highlights this:

> A widowed daughter-in-law was pregnant by her *susra* (father-in-law). She was deeply embarrassed about what people were going to say. The father-in-law reacted by asking her to stitch him a quilt full of patches. He wrapped it around himself and sat in the front courtyard of his house. All the men and women who saw him laughed at him and commented on his patched quilt. After a few days they stopped, having got used to him and his quilt. It is then that the old man said: 'Look here, woman, now it's all over. People take just a few days to get used to a thing'.[60]

The story illustrates the repressive elements of the gender-power relationship and helps us to understand how the word *susra* became a word of abuse. This is interesting because the relationship of father-in-law and daughter-in-law as signified in the observance of *purdah* and other rules of behaviour and etiquette has always been and still remains one of strict avoidance. Although these relationships are known to exist nowadays, either clandestinely or recognized by a few, and which are even individually condoned, or subjected to much speculation and whispering, yet socially and publicly they are widely condemned.[61] Incest even when tolerated

---

[58] W.M. Rattigan, *A Digest of Civil Law for the Punjab Chiefly Based on the Customary Law as at Present Ascertained*, revised by Harbans Lal Sarin and Kundan Lal Pandit (first edition, 1880) (Allahabad, 1966), p. 82.

[59] See, for example, *Indian Law Reports*, Lahore Series, 1934, vol. XV, Joghar Singh and Chattar Singh vs Sadhu Ram, pp. 688–93; *India Cases*, 1937, vol. 166, Joginder Singh vs. Kartara, pp. 719–23.

[60] Narrated by Vidya Vati, Delhi, 24 December 1987.

[61] Several such cases were narrated to me in confidence. For similar liaisons in Punjab, see Hershman, *Punjabi Kinship*, pp. 185–6.

is not accepted unlike the levirate form of remarriage. Protest against such relationships has always existed. Even in the past, there were women who protested against such sexual demands, as illustrated in the *ragini* cited above. But such women were known to get 'packed-off' to their parents' home; an act which was considered to be a matter of 'ultimate shame' for the natal family of the women in question.[62]

The onus, then, has always been on the young widow who is held guilty of arousing the lust of an old father-in-law. This is the significance of a proverb recorded in the nineteenth century:

jawān rānḍ, burhe sānḍ[63]

(The young widows make old men lusty.)

There is a deep suspicion of women's sexuality:

*aurat rahe to āp se
nahīn jae sage bāp se*[64]

(A woman is chaste of her own accord,
Or else she would seduce even her father.)

The predatory nature of female sexuality is described here—the strength of female desire is shown as socially subversive and disruptive. By emphasizing the 'seductive' nature of women, the onus of guilt in incestuous relationships is placed squarely on the women.

VI Female Consciousness: Levirate as a Repressive System

The social sanction behind the control of female sexuality, specially that of the widow, through *karewa* led to many mismatched alliances between women and much younger *dewars*. This factor high-

---

[62] R.M. Hooda, Rohtak, 1 June 1986.
[63] S.W. Fallon, *A Dictionary of Hindustani Proverbs* (Benares, 1886), p. 15; hereafter Fallon, *Hindustani Proverbs*.
[64] Personal interview with Daya Kaur, Sonepat, 12 Oct. 1988; born 1929, her three sons are employed in various government services. They also have land in the village. Also given in Fallon, *Hindustani Proverbs*, p. 115.

lights one of the most repressive aspects of widow-remarriage. The folk tradition attempted to make a virtue of this:

> *baḍī bahu baḍe bhāg*
> *chhoṭā bandṛā ghaṇe suhāg* [65]
>
> (An older or a taller wife brings good fortune,
> As also a younger or shorter bridegroom.)

This practice was also made fun of, for example in children's popular nonsense rhyme:

> *goṛ gaḍi bhāi goṛ gaḍi*
> *baṇṇa chhoṭṭa bahu baḍi* [66]
>
> (Oh what fun!
> The bridegroom is younger than the bride.)

The generally accepted practice of bringing a young daughter-in-law, who may be 'moulded' according to the family's needs, had clearly been inverted. Here, it may be noted that this practice was relevant not only for *karewa* marriages but also *biah*, where the bride's age and height were disregarded. There are, in fact, a large number of folk sayings which depict a mature woman married to an infant or a very young boy. In a peasant economy, the physical strength and stamina of a wife or daughter-in-law was a valuable asset on the family farm. An older girl could not only provide greater labour in agricultural and domestic work but would also be able to help in the rearing of her child-husband. In any case, patriarchy triumphed.

The plight of a physically mature wife with a child-husband is described in the following folk song.

> *ḍhunḍhā ḍhunḍhā ri baigeniā se chhoṭā*
> *paani ko jāyuṅ mere sāth sāth jāve*
> *rove rove ri yeh to neju pakaṛ kai*
> *rovo mat bāle saiṅyāṅ, jhiko mat bāle saiṅyāṅ*
> *duṅgi duṅgi ji tumhe phuliyā mangāi kai*

[65] This is a very commonly used proverb. Also see Verma, *Lokoktiyan*, p. 43.
[66] Commonly heard in the villages; also recorded by Yadav *Lok Sahitya*, p. 452.

Popular Perceptions of Widow-remarriage in Haryana 61

sone ko jāuṅ, mere sāth sāth jāve
rove rove ri ammā ammā ker kai
rovo mat bāle saiṅyāṅ, jhiko mat bāle saiṅyāṅ
duṅgi duṅgi ji tumhe guḍiyā mangāye kai [67]

(I am married to a mere child,
He follows me when I go to fetch water,
Crying and clinging he follows.
Cry not, my little beloved, don't be vexed my little beloved,
I'll get you sweets to eat.
He follows me when I go to sleep,
Mother, mother, he cries,
Don't cry my little beloved, don't be vexed my little beloved,
I'll get you a doll to play with.)

Such marriages, where the *dewar* was a mere child, are remembered by many in the rural areas as having taken place in their own families during colonial times. Ram Chander from village Bandh of Karnal district, for example, recalled that his grandmother as an eighteen-year-old widow was married to his grandfather, her *dewar*, who was merely three years old at the time. She literally brought him up and then raised her own family.[68] Many such cases are cited by people from memory. Although there may not be much of a difference in the ages of a groom and a bride, it is still considered not uncommon for the *karewa* wife to be older by anything between two to ten years. The given folk tradition, somewhat exaggerated though it may be, has been kept alive and relevant by such examples. A lot of these cases concern those widows who have been a casualty of India's extensive military engagements in the post-colonial period. This fact stands amply confirmed from army sources as well.[69] Veena Das's study similarly shows how after the Indo-Pakis-

---

[67] Ibid., p. 331. The folk song cited above was almost exclusive to women. Narrated by women of village Bandh, district Karnal. Also see Yadav, *Lok Sahitya*, p. 331.

[68] Ram Chander, village Bandh, district Karnal, 20–21 Aug. 1988.

[69] Lt. General B.T. Pandit, who served as Corps Commander of Punjab, 1989–90, recounted how a 30-year-old widow had come to him with an appeal to stop her forcible marriage with her 14-year-old brother-in-law. In this

tan war of 1971 many widows in Punjab were forced to stay on with their parents-in-law till their husband's younger brothers grew up to a marriageable age.[70] Many such remarriages have resulted in the *karewa* women running away either with older men of the same family or with outsiders.[71] The untouchable Chuhras of a village in western Uttar Pradesh who follow a similar widow-remarriage custom have been studied by the anthropologist Pauline Kolenda. She discloses a parallel pattern of remarried widows who run away to escape the repressive nature of this unequal alliance.[72]

Compulsion of widows to perform *levirate* is not uncommon.[73] In case of refusal, their marriage to others is made difficult if not impossible.[74] Yet the evidence available suggests that resistance is

---

instance, he recalled having put pressure upon the Panchayat to withhold this marriage by threatening action as a minor was involved. But he commented that the village and family elders generally got away. His observation was that it was a fairly widespread practice. Personal interview, Lt. General B.T. Pandit, Adjutant-General, Adjutant-General's Branch, Army Headquarters, New Delhi, 1 April, 1991.

[70] Veena Das, 'Marriage Among the Hindus', in Devaki Jain, ed., *Indian Women* (New Delhi, 1975), pp. 76–86.

More recently there are instances of the widows of the 1984 riots in Delhi involving forcible remarriages of widows to their brothers-in-law, some of them aged 13 to 14 years. Personal communication from Uma Chakravarty based on unpublished interviews with women activists dealing with the post-1984 riots. Also see Veena Das, 'Our Work to Cry, Your Work to Listen', in her edited work, *Mirrors of Violence: Communities Riots and Survivors in South Asia* (New Delhi, 1990), pp. 345–98.

[71] A number of cases were cited by Chhotu Devi of village Dujjana, and Mohran Devi of Village Jhojho Chamani.

[72] Pauline Kolenda, 'Widowhood among "Untouchable" Chuhras', as in f.n. 7.

[73] Cases of unwilling widows with several children being forced to cohabit with married brothers-in-law are not unknown even in Rajasthan; observation recorded by Bina Aggarwal, 'Who Sows? Who Reaps?: Women and Land Rights in India', *The Journal of Peasant Studies*, vol. 15, no. 4, July 1988, pp. 531–81.

[74] In village Asaudha, district Rohtak, Asha, a 19-year-old girl, became a widow. Her in-laws wished her to marry her much older *jeth* (estimated to be about fifty years of age) with a wife and three children. This was not accepted by her and her father who settled her marriage elsewhere. Her in-laws, however, refused to allow this and a caste Panchayat had to be called. The Panchayat gave

steadily growing. Even in the past, widows had not always given in easily to levirate marriage. They had resisted the culture of remarriage designed to retain them within the families of their deceased husbands. The district officials of the colonial administration received many petitions from young widows seeking sanction to marry men of their own choice.[75] Many widows denied that *karewa* had taken place.[76] In the former case, for reasons of their own which I have discussed elsewhere,[77] the officials turned down the petitions, and in the latter, it was very difficult to prove the contrary for, as pointed out earlier, even cohabitation could be and was recognized as *karewa*.

An act of real revolt and the only true release from this system was and still is a runaway remarriage. This phenomenon is reflected in the popular expressions that associates the very act of running away with widows.[78] *'Rāṇḍ bhāg gai'* (the widow has run away) is popularly used now not only for widows but for all runaway women. The local proverbs that speak of runaway women include:

ughlatiyāṅ nai kise kasār [79]

(A runaway woman gets no traditional farewell.)

---

sanction to her marriage elsewhere. But at a crucial juncture, the wedding ceremony was forcibly stopped by the in-laws. Even the Panchayat decision was not honoured. Asha remains single. Narrated by Dheer Singh, village Asaudha Todran, district Rohtak, 8–10 August 1990. Similar cases of resistance are available from other villages.

[75] The instructions sent to the district officials read:

Often a young widow will present a petition to the Deputy Commissioner for sanction to marry a man of her choice, but with such applications he is wise to have nothing to do.

See Govt. of Punjab, *Rohtak District Gazetteer*, 1910, III-A, Lahore, *Civil and Military Gazette*, 1911, p. 90.

[76] *Census of India, Punjab and Delhi*, 1921, XV, Part 1, Report, p. 244.

[77] For details, see Prem Chowdhry, 'Customs in a Peasant Economy', as in f.n. 2.

[78] Personal interview with Ram Singh, an Arya Samaj *updeshik* (preacher), village Bhaproda, district Rohtak, 12 August 1988.

[79] Confined mostly to men; narrated by R.M. Hooda, Rohtak, 1 June 1986. Also see Verma, *Lokoktiyan*, p. 96.

Yet another one chides those who lament the loss of such a woman:

ghar tiriyā sai lekho mānge
bhoo sukrai sowe
keh Ghāghā ji teen chūtiyā
ughal gai nai rowe [80]

(Fools are they, says Ghagha ji,
Who ask the wife for an account,
Who sleep on the floor,
Who mourn a runaway woman.)

The increasing incidence of widows running away succeeded in enlarging the scope of widow-remarriage. Consequently, it is no longer confined to its levirate form but has been enlarged to *punar-vivah*, which is literally remarriage. *Punar-vivah* also indicates that the remarriage is no longer the sole concern of the widow's late husband's family. It brings her natal family back into the picture, as they may find a second husband for her in case she refuses to accept *karewa*. In fact, in recent years, breaches in levirate have grown more common. Young childless widows often go back to their parents and are married again. The *punar-vivah*, generally arranged by the brother, has also found its reflection in folk tales and local proverbs. A short folk tale titled *'Rand kaun'*[81] ('Who's a widow'), delineates the role of a brother in a widow's remarriage. It portrays a woman whose son and brother are both held for having committed a major crime. The king pronounces the death sentence on both of them but asks the woman to choose the one she wants to save. The woman opts for her brother and observes that once he is dead, it will be impossible to get back a brother. But with her brother alive she could get married again and also beget a son. A popular proverb also emphasizes the primacy of the brother-sister tie:

---

[80] Narrated by K.L. Rathi, New Delhi, 24 May 1986. Also see Yadav, *Lok Sahitya*, p. 446.

[81] Narrated by Chhotu Devi, village Dujjana, 6 June 1986. Also given in Malik, *Haryana Lok Sahitya*, p. 131.

*Rāṇḍ te va jis ke merjāṇ bhāi
khāsam te aur bhi ker le* [82]

(A woman is truly widowed if her brother is dead,
For a husband can be got again.)

Significantly, in the simplicity of the rituals, the two forms of remarriage, *karewa* and *punar-vivah* resemble each other very closely. The important ceremony in the latter involves the exchange of *jaimalas* (garlands) by the bride and the groom and not the *phera* (a core ritual) ceremony of *biah*.[83] Also, male control over a woman's choice of marriage partner, both in *karewa* as well as *punar-vivah*, remains intact. Her own choice is not countenanced; if made, it has to be an elopement.

Conclusion

Interestingly, for a variety of reasons which are outside the scope of this paper, the custom of widow-remarriage in both its forms, that is *karewa* and *punar-vivah* especially the former, is being increasingly accepted among those groups who traditionally disapproved of this practice, such as the Rajputs and the Banias. Referring to these castes, a recent district gazetteer of Haryana (1980) points out:

> When none of the brothers accept their widowed sister-in-law as wife, *Punar-vivah* is performed anywhere in their caste.[84]

Widow-remarriages have become so common in this region that one estimate is that among widows of 'marriageable age' only one in a thousand is left out.[85] The statistical calculations are also not

---

[82] Commonly known among both men and women. Also see Malik, *Haryana Lok Sahitya*, p. 131.

[83] The Banias alone are known to marry off a young issueless widow 'who has not lived with her husband' with the usual ceremonies. The *phera* ceremony, unless the widow is a 'virgin', is prohibited. See Govt. of Haryana, *Gazetteer of Bhiwani District, Haryana, 1980* (Chandigarh, 1982), p. 67.

[84] Ibid., p. 67.

[85] Personal interview with Raghbir Singh, village Singhpura, district Rohtak,

too far from this estimate. The 1981 census shows that among the rural women of Haryana between the 'marriageable age' of 16 and 44 years only 0.77 per cent were widows.[86] This wider acceptance is not only an officially recorded fact but can also be perceived at the popular level when a proverb like '*ājā beṭi lele phere, yo margayā to aur bhatere*', is no longer quoted in the derogatory sense,[87] but merely illustrates an accepted practice.

6–7 August 1988; 65 years; an ex-*sarpanch* of his village, he is currently the President of the Singhpura Gurukul and an active Arya Samajist.

[86] *Census of India, 1981, Haryana*, Series 6, Part IV-A, Social and Cultural Tables (New Delhi, 1986), p. 46.

[87] *Revised Land Settlement*, Rohtak, p. 53.

3

*Attired in Virtue: The Discourse on Shame (lajja) and Clothing of the Bhadramahila in Colonial Bengal**

Himani Bannerji

> In those days there was a particular rule for women. Whoever became a *bou* (bride/daughter-in-law) was to veil herself for an arm's length or so, and not speak to anybody. That's what made a good *bou*. Clothes then, unlike now, were not made of such fine fabric, but were rather coarse and heavy. I used to wear that piece of heavy cloth, and veil myself down to my chest, and do all those chores. And I never talked to anyone. My eyes never looked out from within that cloth enclosure, as though I were blindfolded like the bullocks of the oilpresser. Sight did not travel further than my feet.
>
> Rashasundari Dasi, *Amar Jiban* (My Life), 1987.

> The starting point of these reflections was usually a feeling of impatience at the sight of the naturalness with which newspapers, art and commonsense constantly dresses up a reality which even though it is the one we live in, is undoubtedly determined by history. I resented seeing Nature and History confused at every turn, and I wanted to track down, in the decorative display of what-goes-without-saying, the ideological abuse which, in my view, is hidden there.
>
> Roland Barthes, *Mythologies*

* This paper is one of a series that I have undertaken to write in order to display the gender organization of class, and the ideological construction of

Introduction

Judging by the moral and legal preoccupations of the colonial state and the wholly male indigenous intellectual elite, the nineteenth century in Bengal could be called the Age of Social Reform.[1] The rapid process of colonization, the type of colonialism brought into India by the English, and new class formations in Bengal gave rise to a radical sense of disjunction and changes in existing social relations and values, precipitating a sense of social and moral crisis.[2] Questions ranging from religious to everyday life, inclusive of sexuality, gender relations and the family, erupted in

---

subjectivities and agencies of/for women implied in the social reform projects in colonial Bengal. This project has been very kindly sponsored by the School of Women's Studies, Jadavpur University, Calcutta, which has offered me the most vital necessities for research, namely encouragement and an access to original material. I must especially thank Abhijit Sen of the School, who has most painstakingly and discerningly copied out by hand articles from magazines which are literally on the verge of extinction. I should also take the opportunity of thanking Professor Jasodhara Bagchi, the Director of the School, herself a scholar in the area, for her unflagging support for the project and the valuable discussions we had. All translations within the text are by myself.

[1] Themes of social reform and social change in various ways dominate studies on nineteenth century social and cultural history of Bengal. Books as diverse as S.C. Sarkar, *On the Bengal Renaissance* (Calcutta, 1979); V.C. Joshi, ed., *Rammohan Roy and the Process of Modernization in India* (New Delhi, 1975); M. Borthwick, *The Changing Role of Women in Bengal 1849–1905* (Princeton, 1984); S. Sarkar, *A Critique of Colonial India* (Calcutta, 1985); T. Raychaudhuri, *Europe Reconsidered* (New Delhi, 1988); A. Sen, *Ishwar Chandra Vidyasagar and His Elusive Milestones* (Calcutta, 1977), among numerous others, speak of these topics with different social analyses and interpretations.

[2] T. Raychaudhuri, *Europe Reconsidered*, Preface, pp. ix-xvi. 'But whether the change was introduced by self-conscious effort or impersonal influences, one notes an all-pervasive concern, almost obsessive, in their social and intellectual life — an anxiety to assess European culture in the widest sense of the term as something to be emulated or rejected.' p. xi. The terms and forms of this assessment are considered in their complexities and contradictions by S. Sarkar in *A Critique of Colonial India*. See also Jasodhara Bagchi, 'Positivism and Nationalism: Womanhood and Crisis in Nationalist Fiction — Bankimchandra's *Anandmath*,' *Economic and Political Weekly*, vol. 20, no. 43, and Geraldine Forbes, *Positivism in Bengal* (Calcutta, 1975).

endless public discussions, debates and disclosures. Persistent and vigorous attempts at social legislation and institutionalization, for example of education, accompanied these intellectual efforts at reorganizing and reconceptualizing the new social relations, values and their practical demands. These moral utterances and social projects of the Bengali middle-class intelligentsia did not form a monolithic whole, but rather consisted of ideological-discursive strands which converged, competed with and contradicted each other.[3]

Interestingly enough, the bulk of these reforms and discussions were aimed at women and gender relations prevailing in the family, thus seeking to reorganize many of the existing social forms and functions. The heart of the social project was 'the degradation and the decadence' of society, typified by the state in which Bengali women and families of the propertied classes existed.[4] Tanika Sarkar, for example, has commented that the Bengali male intelligentsia's interest in women's 'improvement' bordered on the obsessive.[5]

---

[3] H. Bannerji, 'Fashioning a Self: Educational Proposals for and by Women in Popular Magazines in Colonial Bengal' in *Economic and Political Weekly*, vol. 26, no. 43, 1991: WS 50–62. 'The social location of the significational aspects of ideology supply multiplicity of meanings, fissures, the openings and closures (always semiotically signalling out), which even the most thought out ideological formulation cannot escape.' It should also be noted that 'writers on ideological formations in nineteenth century Bengal are, not surprisingly, preoccupied therefore in dealing with 'shifts and slides', 'liminality' and so on — pointing to a multidimensionality within one ideological position or its class articulation.' p. WS 52.

[4] The assessment of the state of Bengali society and 'civilization' by judging the condition of women from a European/Christian standpoint, for example, is pervasive in missionary literature. Also Mrinalini Sinha, in her unpublished essay 'The Age of Consent Act: The Ideal of Masculinity and Colonial Ideology in Nineteenth Century Bengal', undated, speaks of the overall English colonial disposition to 'Victorian sexual ideology' and 'specific gender identities' and their imposition on an 'alien culture inextricably linked to the pursuit of colonial economic and political power . . . .' pp. 2–3. This ruling and condemnatory design is also spoken of by K. Ballhatchet in *Race, Sex and Class under the Raj: Imperial Attitudes and Politics and their Critics, 1793–1905* (London, 1980).

[5] T. Sarkar, 'Hindu Conjugality and Nationalism in the Late Nineteenth Century Bengal', in *Indian Women: Myth and Reality*, National Seminar Papers,

But to ameliorate the living conditions of Bengali (middle class) women, to improve their minds and morality, to regulate their conjugal and household roles, signified a concern for the upliftment of Bengali society as a whole. The 'natural' constitution of the female mind, it was felt, along with women's social condition, needed a serious 're-casting'.[6]

Constructed through the colonial discourse on 'civilization' (later 'improvement' or 'progress'), used both by the 'enlightened' or westernized middle-class Hindus and their reformed, non-idolatrous counterparts, the Brahmos, 'the woman question' emerged as a highly controversial one. The idea was to bring the women members of the propertied classes within the purview of 'civilization', 'progress' and utility. Tracts, plays, farces, novels and even poetry on domesticity, conjugality, moral and practical education for women swamped the printing presses. This process, however, was not a unilinear move of submission to colonization or 'westernization'. Attempts at understanding what is 'civilization' and how to achieve it contained thorough searches of and reflections on both indigenous and European practices and values. Ambiguity and criticism regarding both marked most of the attempts at synthesizing and imitating.[7]

1989. '... subjection for most sections of the [male] intelligentsia meant loss, albeit with some potential for progress. Against this fundamental and all-encompassing loss of self-hood, the only sphere of autonomy, of free will, was located within the Hindu family: to be more precise, with the Hindu woman, her position within an authentic Hindu marriage system and the ritual surrounding the deployment of her body ... there was a thorough examination of every aspect of the problem.' p. 1.

[6] The criteria for social reform, though not strictly an expression of or an agenda for colonizing the Bengali mind, are evolved in the colonial context and in relation to colonial content as well. The *Autobiography* of Shibnath Shastri, for example, provides an excellent sense of what is entailed in such social reform, while a book such as *Re-casting Women: Essays in Colonial History*, edited by K. Sangari and S. Vaid (New Delhi, 1989), offers a feminist reading for such attempts at 'reforming' or 're-casting'. See the Introduction of this anthology, which takes its name from Koilashchandra Bose's statement 'On the Education of Hindu Females', 1846: 'She must be refined, reorganized, recast, regenerated'.

[7] See H. Bannerji, 'The Mirror of Class: Class Subjectivity and Politics in Nineteenth CenturyBengal', *Economic and Political Weekly* May 13, 1989. 'The

In any case, a strand of the Bengali male intelligentsia, whose consciousness had a formative and positive relationship with European thought, took on the role of Pygmalion and sought to fashion for itself a Galatea. This was to be a moral or discursive portrait of the ideal feminine, otherwise known as *bhadramahila* (the gentlewoman). The moral-cultural configuration of this discursive image or sign was embedded in, and endowed with, duties, pleasures and graces appropriate to the cultural commonsense of the 'westernized' sections of the middle classes. No aspect of this construct was beyond (male) utterance, both in formulation of character (moral-domestic) and in appearance (moral-erotic/aesthetic). Men sought to become experts in all matters pertaining to women, flouting existing social proprieties deeply grounded in a sexual/cultural division of labour.[8]

A signal example of this ideological-aesthetic meddlesomeness was the attempt by 'enlightened' Hindu and Brahmo men to 'redress' the women of their own classes. The image was to simultaneously express and construct their overall class culture, that is, also their morality. Sartorial experiments on captive household females provided a concretization of reform aspirations, as we see in Swarnakumari Debi's 'Sekele Katha' (Story of Old Times), the scope of which entailed a basic change within the everyday life of the household. The need for a sartorial change was initially contexted

---

project of the creation of a new social identity or a new common sense is only partially a planned one. Its complex nature is not accounted for by the correspondence theory of base and superstructure, but rather it is various, disparate and *ad hoc*, and often in the colonial case, one of an acute and quick response. Imitation, reaction absorption and recreation were all ingredients in this social response'. p. 1042. See also P. Chatterji, *Nationalist Thought, A Derivative Discourse* (U.K., 1986), and P. Addy and Azzad, 'Politics and Culture in Bengal' *New Left Review*, 79.

[8] See the introduction to *Recasting Women*, for a discussion of the class agenda of social reform. 'Middle class reforms undertaken on behalf of women are tied up with the self-definition of the class, with a new division of the public from the private sphere, and of course with a cultural nationalism.' p. 9. See also H. Bannerji, 'Mothers and Teachers: Gender and Class in Educational Proposals for and by Women in Colonial Bengal', *Journal of Historical Sociology*, vol. 5, no. 1, 1992.

to the entry of non-kin males within the 'inner quarters' of the household. The move came in several steps, building the sartorial project into the social-moral life of women and the household.

> At the time of this new improvement of our household/home, Keshab babu became a disciple of my esteemed father. Into the inner quarters, impenetrable to the rays of the sun [a hyberbolic metaphor to signify its aristocratic honour], he was the first unrelated man, who was greeted like a close relative and welcomed to enter. Many people marvelled at this great act of courage. But that my venerable, sage-like father, who forsook friends and relatives for the sake of the right religious conduct [*dharma*], who did not hesitate to give up all earthly comforts, would receive Keshab babu (who was an outcaste of his home for converting to the true religion, seeking refuge with his wife, as a disciple) into his own home with a father's affection, was not a matter of surprise.[9]

Next came another male, both a teacher for the girls and women, and a disciple of her father, Debendranath Tagore, the founder of Brahmo Samaj, a form of ecumenical reformed Hinduism.

> My esteemed father was disappointed in the education supplied [to the women of the household] by 'mems' [white governesses]. The new preacher of the Adi Brahmo Samaj, Strijukta Ayodhyanath Pakrashi, was employed to teach in the inner quarters.[10]

Several women and girls were to study with him. Both events occasioned an 'improvement' in clothing appropriate to the notion of feminine civility.

> On this occasion clothes of the denizens of the women's quarters were reformed, [due to the fact] that it was impossible to appear in front of men [non-kin] in the Bengali women's usual garb of only a *sari*. My older sister, maternal aunt and sisters-in-law used to come to the study in a kind of civil and refined outfit of a

[9] Swarnakumari Debi, 'Sekele Katha' (Story of Old Times) *Bharati*, vol. 39 (*BS Chaitra*, 1322), 1916, p. 3.
[10] Ibid., p. 5.

peshawaj [outfit of aristocratic Muslim women] and a shawl. My esteemed father always had a distaste for the clothing of Bengali women, and deeply desired to reform it. He did not stint in effort to realize this wish, at times on my *Didis* [elder sisters], but tirelessly on the infant daughters. In those days, the youngest children in our household wore clothes similar to the girls and boys of Muslim aristocratic families. After we grew up a little, we wore a new type of clothing everyday. My father looked through a large number of paintings and ordered new designs. The tailor attended him everyday and so did we.[11]

Even though the vagaries of styles and the moral dimensions of these 'reforming' experiments elicited ridicule from the anti-reformist middle-class Hindu male faction, the situation as a whole revealed the general male preoccupation with the question of an appropriate social subjectivity for women.[12] They all postulated a relationship between the inner and outer self of women and saw her clothing as a moral signifier of her social role and thus of what they saw as the culture of their *samaj* (society) or class. The covering and uncovering of her body, the particular parts which were to be hidden or disclosed, and the style/manner in which this was done, were contested grounds for moral and aesthetic visions among males.[13]

[11] Ibid., pp. 30–1.
[12] The plethora of literature on women's social subjectivity and the family is too large for selective citation, but from Bankimchandra Chattopadhyay, the conservative thinker on women, to Rabindranath Tagore, a liberal, the same preoccupation is shared. The names of a few 'improving' texts are cited below: Manomohan Basu, *Hindur Achar Vyavahar* (Hindu Customs, Calcutta, 1887); *Garhasthya* (Domesticity, Calcutta, 1884); Iswarchandra Basu, *Nariniti* (Woman's Conduct, Calcutta, 1884); Chandranath Basu, *Hindutwa* (Hinduism, Calcutta, 1892), and *Stridiger Prati Upadesh* (Advice to women, Calcutta, 1901); Taraknath Biswas, *Bangya Mahila* (The Bengali Woman, Calcutta, 1886); Girija Prasanna Raychoudhury, *Grihalaxmi* (The Goddess Laxmi of the Hearth, Calcutta, 1884).
[13] This is also noted in the European colonial racist-sexist context. For example, Sander Gilman's essay, 'Black Bodies, White Bodies: Toward an Iconography of Female Sexuality in Late Nineteenth Century Art, Medicine and Literature' in H. Gates Jr., ed., *Race, Writing and Difference* (Chicago and

This male monopoly on the aesthetic form and moral content of ideal femininity came to an end in the last decades of the century. Even though the social context remained the same, and patriarchy provided the basic philosophy for the appropriate investiture of the female body, educated middle class women of 'enlightened' homes themselves had much to do and say regarding both the discursive-ideological and actualization processes. Summoned into education and cultural activities by the hegemonic agenda of their classes, informed by the moral and intellectual atmosphere generated by male reformers, middle-class women stepped into the world of public utterance approximately from the 1870s and added to the existing discourse of 'reform'. Through various journals and magazines, this rudimentary women intelligentsia participated actively in fashioning their own subjectivities as expressed in the sign called *bhadramahila* or the gentlewoman. One has to remember, that Debendranath Tagore's moral-sartorial dream was finally fulfilled by a woman, his daughter-in-law, Gyanada Nandini Debi. As his daughter Swarnakumari Debi puts it:

> But he could not settle on a costume/attire after so much experimentation. His dissatisfaction came to an end when [my] middle sister-in-law returned from Bombay, dressed in a civil and elegant attire in imitation of Gujrati women. This attire, an integral combination of indigenousness, decorum and modesty, was just what he had wanted. It suited what he desired and removed a fundamental deprivation of the daughters of Bengal.[14]

Malavika Karlekar, in her book *Voices from Within*, remarks on this negotiated self-making, showing how women both compromised with and pushed the boundaries of the class-patriarchy of the Bengali middle class.[15]

A long discussion ensued among educated middle-class women through magazines such as *Bamabodhini, Bharati, Sahitya, Pradip,*

London, 1985), remarks on the nature of the body—both female and black—as a signifier for colonial and other forms of domination and an ideological repository or re-presentation, as well as a site of moral hegemony.

[14] Swarnakumari Debi, 'Sekele Katha', pp. 31–2.
[15] Malavika Karlekar, *Voices from Within* (New Delhi, 1991).

Mukul, and *Sakha*.[16] The discussion was a serious attempt to think through what an 'appropriate reformed female' subjectivity, coded as *bhadramahila*, should be, and how that should be projected as a visual-moral sign. The notion of 'appropriateness' was conceived with reference to gender and family relations in the new context of the colonially inflected, respectable middle classes. Appearance, in the sense of body-self presentation through clothing, was a particularly important theme. The morality of the *bhadramahila* or gentlewoman was to be translucent in the self-composition through clothes, and this theme of self-composition, along with that of the body, provided the discursive organization for the women's texts. In spite of the fact that the women reformers came into a pre-organized moral-discursive space, their own discourse on women, femininity and clothing was tempered with a recognition of the power of gender roles. Even though they did not fashion it in its entirety, they substantially inflected the sign of *bhadramahila* — the moral/aesthetic/erotic configuration of women of propertied classes in Bengal.

This paper examines the discursive organization of sartorial morality as put forward by some of the women writers of major Bengali magazines, especially with respect to forms of class subjectivities they propose for Bengali women. The concentration here is minimally on fashions or styles, but rather on the emergence of a social morality which seeks to serve, to some extent does serve, as an unofficial form of moral regulation created by the civil society. This demarcates at the level of proposals or ideology social spaces, personal interactions between men and women, and the kind of moral personality a *bhadramahila* should have. Attitudes towards the female body and sexuality are all a part of this insignia of virtue and vice. The clothes are meant to propose a definitive relationship between the women and their class and social status.

[16] Meredith Borthwick, in her *The Changing Role of Women in Bengal, 1849–1905* (Princeton, 1984), gives us an overview of the world of middle class Bengali women, especially with regard to their educational project, as put forward in women's magazines of the time. She lists the women's magazines and approximates their circulation, claiming a large readership in Dhaka, in Calcutta and its suburbs, in small towns and even villages, both among men and women.

Significations of the moral and the immoral, the sexual and the social (posed as asexual and therefore virtuous) are never kept out of sight. In fact the position that the sexual and the social are in some ways antithetical, captures a process and a project of profound privatization of sexuality which in reality is publicly and discursively constructed. Here we need to remember Michel Foucault's response to S. Marcus's *The Other Victorians*, where he challenges Marcus's 'Repressive Hypothesis', and points out the public, discursive nature of the very project of privatization of sexuality in nineteenth-century western Europe. Hearing the bubble/babble of voices on morality and the notion of the appropriately 'feminine' (an euphemism for female sexual conduct), we cannot but ask Foucault's questions with regard to social reform in nineteenth-century Bengal:

> Why has sexuality been so widely discussed, and what has been said about it? What were the effects of power generated by what was said? What are the links between these discourses, these effects of power, and the pleasures that were invested by them? What knowledge was formed as a result of this linkage? The object in short is to define the regime of power-knowledge-pleasure that sustains the discourse on human sexuality [in our parts of the world].[17]

The emphasis on covering a woman's body in fact served to highlight her sexual potentialities, and this became central to the sartorial project for the gentlewoman. These essays by the women writers, full of rich descriptions, critical comments and exhortations, allow us to provide a semiology and ideology of culture and class in a concretely embodied and engendered fashion. And we can begin, as Foucault suggests, to question and situate our sources and voices,

> ... To account for the fact that [sexuality in various names] is spoken about, to discover who does the speaking, the positions and viewpoints from which they speak, the institutions which prompt people to speak about it and which store and distribute

[17] M. Foucault, *The History of Sexuality, Volume 1: An Introduction*, trans. by R. Hurley (Vintage, 1980), p. 11.

the things that are said. What is at issue, briefly, is the 'over-all discursive fact', the way in which sex is 'put into discourse'.[18]

Clothing as Embodiment or Sign

Are there objects which are *inevitably* a source of suggestiveness as Baudelaire suggested about Woman? Certainly not . . . *for it is human history which converts reality into speech, and it alone rules the life and the death of mythical language. Ancient or not, mythology can only have an historical foundation, for mythology is a type of speech chosen by history; it can not possibly evolve from the 'nature' of things.*

Speech of this kind is a message. It is therefore by no means confined to oral speech. It can consist of modes of writing or of representations. [italics mine]

Roland Barthes, 'Myth Today,' *Mythologies.*

In order to treat proposals and images for women's clothing as historical and ideological constructs or signs, we should explore the particular relationship displayed in them between bodies of women (of the middle classes) and their clothes, thus aiming towards the spatio-social meaning of the location of these bodies. Thus clothes are to be seen as forms of moral investiture. As the editor of the magazine *Antahpur*, Hemantakumari Choudhuri remarks, clothes are to be seen as a sign of progress, marking moments in moral/cultural advancement from primitivity to civilization.

What are clothes and why are they necessary? Only those are clothes, wearing which the body may be fully covered, and which cover/prevent shame. It is known from reading the history of the most primitive stage of humanity that humankind then had no clothes to wear. Tree barks, leaves, animal fur or leather covered the bodies of different groups/peoples. The proof of this is to be found today among savage deep-forest or mountain dwellers. The ancient Aryans, when they first arrived in India, dwelt in the

[18] Ibid., p. 11.

forests near the Himalaya mountains. Initially they felt the need of clothes in order to prevent themselves from feeling the cold .... But as humans became more civilized they used their intelligence to fashion material fit for covering their bodies .... And God has always given to women a love of beauty and a sense of modesty.[19]

This version of the evolution of clothes claims that the human body itself has to be always understood as a vehicle which is capable of signifying a moral and historical stage (of civilization), and the case of women as special within that.

The essays on clothing in the magazines and other texts[20] support a similar evaluative perspective on human and female bodies. This perspective, however, makes little sense unless contexted to the notion of class, understood in its broadest and ordinary sense of social relations of mental and manual division of labour, inclusive of sexual division and thus extending 'class' into both areas of social production and reproduction. These magazines and tracts make it clear that the female body of the propertied classes is not to be seen directly in terms of its potentialities for reproduction or social labour (as befitting for non-labouring classes as a whole). The kind of social reproductive activity or labour which involves middle class women is primarily viewed through the lens of morality, of the ideologically class-gendered notions of appropriate behaviour or decorum, such as *sabhyata* (civility), *sobhanata* (decorum/propriety/decency), and *lajja* (shame/modesty). Of the three, the first two, understood as civilized behaviour or refinement, are applicable for both males and females of the middle classes, though inflected in an appropriately patriarchal way, implying an overall moral unity of the civilizing project with gendered differentiation. But the concept of *lajja*, which is also a morally judgemental term, and should translate more as 'shame' than 'shyness' or modesty, governs or underlies all references to civilized 'proper' behaviour when applied to girls and women. This is so central a notion that Kumari Soudamini, among

[19] *Antahpur*, no. 6, 1901 (*BS Ashad* 1308), pp. 137–40.
[20] For example, autobiographies of women printed in the last century or reprinted more recently, such as Rashasundari Debi, *Amar Jiban* (My Life, 1987).

others, writes in *Bamabodhini Patrika* a small treatise on *lajja*. In tackling this topic she instantly applies it to women in a manner which straddles both the realms of manners and morals.

> Shame is of two types. Of these one prevents human beings from sinful deeds, the other is peculiar to women. This essay is about the kind pertinent to women. There is no race/people on earth that deny that 'women should have a sense of shame'. Shame resides in the hearts of women in every country. There is only one difference, that some have more of it in their hearts than others. According to social customs, it is expressed differently in different countries. Whatever is regarded as a sign of shame in one country, in another may be considered a sign of shamelessness....
>
> Another name for real sense of shame is modesty, and those women who are really possessed of a sense of shame, are also 'modest'.
>
> ... one cannot be truly modest (possess a sense of shame) simply by veiling one's face and not speaking to anyone. In fact not speaking to people might express pride. Those who are truly modest cannot have hearts which contain pride or insolence, they are adorned by gentleness, politeness, good manners, tranquility, etc.[21]

It is to be noted that Kumari Soudamini repeatedly speaks of shame as an internal quality, links it with innocence along with refinement, delinks it from hypocrisy and distinguishes it from 'savage', i.e. uncivil or impolite behaviour.

> Those who are truly possessed of modesty/sense of shame can never be hypocritical. Their hearts are adorned with the virtue of innocence, and their behaviour/manners express this sense of true modesty/sense of shame.
>
> ... One should not behave like an uncivilized person to show modesty/sense of shame. That gives it a grotesque look. Many

---

[21] Kumari Soudamini, 'Lajja', *Bamabodhini Patrika*, vol. 7, no. 95, 1872 (*BS Ashad* 1278), pp. 99–100.

women of Bengal are in the thrall of this grotesque type of shame/modesty.[22]

She firmly establishes this sense of shame as a behaviour particularly appropriate to male-female relations, and as a way of undercutting female provocation of male sexuality and of initiation of sexual response on her own part. The following passage shows the link she establishes between shame, exposure and covering of the female body, and passionate enactments and utterances, and further clarifies the sexual theme, though the writer's own sense of shame/modesty prevents her from blatantly stating that.

> They [upper class women] wear very fine [transparent] clothing and appear at ease in front of their male and female servants. Some women veil themselves but scream ugly things and carry on a fight with someone. That person who has never seen her face can [however] hear the crude words which emit from her mouth.[23]

Her concern about the sexual implication of the exposed female body and uncensored behaviour becomes explicit when she offers a 'civilizing' suggestion to counteract women's current bathing practices.

> Bathing, rubbing down of bodies [of women], etc., are done in places which can be seen. Therefore there should be a rule that male or female servants won't enter anywhere without permission, and bathing etc. will take place in privacy or secrecy.[24]

Sexuality permeates every corner of the social atmosphere she creates where possibilities of 'indecencies' are always present. From clothes to conversation, all must be ruled by 'shame'.

> However one should converse in such a way that it does not give rise to any untoward [bad/sexual] thoughts in the minds of [the male] interlocutors.[25]

[22] Ibid.
[23] Ibid.
[24] Ibid.
[25] Ibid.

Thus the colonial notion of civilization, with propriety, gentility and refinement as corollaries, to which only the new propertied classes aspired, can be always extended to sexuality, to which can also be associated the custom of enclosure for feudal, pre-British aristocracy. To be civilized is to have a sense of shame, and is the antithesis of sexual provocation brought on by explicit sexual display or seduction, and this is indicated in terms of clothing by the degree of exposure of the female body. Revealing and hiding it selectively thus works both as a lure and a deterrent to male lust, and confers on it the status of a significant and fetish object in the context of the social morality of the new propertied classes.

The overall discourse on/of shame or *lajja* is a curious blend of indigenous and colonial values regarding women, nature and the body. Here misogyny blends with a rejection of the natural or physical in any form. The female body and sexuality are read through the notions of the primitive and the savage. In essays such as 'Sindur' (Vermilion), all ornaments and colour decorations on the body are despised as savage and sexual, and women are portrayed as savages within 'civilization'.

> With the improvement in education and growth of civilization bad popular customs slowly disappear. Savages do not pay attention to the beauty of [their] mind, but rather adopt ways to enhance their physical beauty. They draw designs on their bodies, use vermilion in their hair, and pierce their ears and noses to wear ornaments. Since these bad popular customs of this country are associated with religion, their persistence is more severe. Piercing ears, nose and wearing vermilion by women of Bengal are the foremost among these. The Hindu scriptures enjoin: 'only those may be considered as good wives who colour their bodies with turmeric powder, use antimony or mascara and vermilion'. But among our women readers, whose minds have been minimally enlightened by knowledge, there has developed a profound disgust for female customs and superstitions.[26]

---

[26] Anon., 'Sindur' (Vermilion), *Bamabodhini Patrika*, vol. 4, no. 63, 1869 (*BS Kartik* 1275), pp. 121–3.

Certain behaviours, therefore, are classified as 'lower types' of body-behaviour, and contrasted to higher, intellectual-moral, or civilized ones of Europe. 'Exposure' and physicality also provide the hinge on which turn the themes of 'civilization' and 'savagery' or 'barbarism'. Hiranmayee Debi's essay, 'Sutikagrihey Banaratwa' (Apishness in the Nursery), further builds into it the relevant element of social Darwinism.[27]

Hemantakumari Choudhuri, in her essay on women's clothing, 'Striloker Paricchhad' (Women's Attire), states: 'The more civilized humans became, the more clothes they made', marking the stages of civilization from body to mind, paralleled by going from nakedness to wearing clothes, valorizing the mental over the manual and the physically reproductive.[28] The civilized man or woman is well covered and plain, unadorned by ornaments, which she considers, as do the Christian missionaries, clearly as fetishes. The plainly clothed English gentlewoman or the low church preacher, for example, as ideal female and male images, are contrasted to the well-adorned florid Bengali babu, who is 'effeminate', and his female sexually provocative counterpart, the bibi, who is pagan hedonism/decadence incarnate.[29]

---

[27] Hiranmayee Debi, 'Sutikagrihey Banaratwa', *Bharati O Balak*, vol. 15, 1892 (*BS Paush* 1298), pp. 483–91. In this essay the idea of animality is securely linked with children and savages, and associated with any kind of physicality among adult men and women. It marks stages in the development of civilization through social stages and life stages, the goals of both being the suppression of the physical or the 'natural/emotional', and elevation of the non-physical/rational. Social Darwinism's 'scientific' support for misogyny remains a field to be explored in the Bengali colonial context.

[28] Hemantakumari Choudhuri, 'Striloker Paricchhad', *Antahpur*, no. 6, 1901 (*BS Ashad* 1308), pp. 137–40.

[29] For the notion of the effeminate babu and his female counterpart, see Sumanta Bannerji, *The Parlour and the Streets: Elite and Popular Culture in Nineteenth Century Calcutta* (Calcutta, 1989), or *Keyabat Meye* (Bravo, Woman!, Calcutta, 1988); also nineteenth-century satirical journalism such as Kaliprasanna Sinha, *Hutom Penchar Naksha* (The Owl's Skits, Calcutta), or Tekchand Thakur, *Alader Gharer Dulal* (Spoilt Darling of the Worthless Rich, Calcutta, 1841). See also M. Sinha, 'Age of Consent Act', pp. 6 and 21, where she states: 'The suspicion against the Bengali middle class found expression in the popularity of the racial and cultural stereotype of the "effeminate Bengali Babu".'

The project of essays on shame or decency, as characteristic traits of the *bhadramahila*, is to render the upper class/caste women's body and physical life invisible, attempting to rarify and ideologize as far as possible the actual everyday life of women and all their bodily functions. The *bhadramahila*, which is no more or no less than the sign of genteel womanhood, is thus the interpellating device for middle class women, whose lives must illustrate particular gender-class relations of their time. Thus shame is 'an adornment of women', an especially commendable feminine virtue which both displaces the upper class/caste woman from her body, as well as identifies her with it. Going beyond the sense of common social decency, *lajja*, as applied to women, also incorporates within it a keen awareness of sexual possibilities, infusing elements of denial, forbiddenness and guilt within female sexuality. As a concept it subsumes all kinds of physical and social needs and functions within a sexual discourse, enclosed in a general imperative of self-censorship. Essays such as Krishnabhabini Das's 'Strilok O Purush' (Women and Men), or articles in *Bamabodhini*, situate shame as a central concept in 'femininity' and explicitly connect it with 'civilization', which implies both a de-sexualization and a de-physicalization. Opinions vary as to whether as an emotion it is learned or innate, but all the writers agree on creating a social ethics of denial and repression. A transparent homology is established between the body, sexuality and savagery or primitivity. Discounting both the long existence of public and common bathing as a daily practice in villages, or of ritual occasions, the writers emphasize sexual possibilities inherent in it. The women bathers are seen as 'whores', though this word is carefully avoided as a 'bad' or 'indecent' expression. The adjective *jaghanya* (repulsive/abhorrent) is endlessly repeated through the text, particularly with regard to visibility of the female body. Accepting that civilization means the denial of the body and the female body in particular, the theme of

---

'The Victorian Anglo-Indian generally considered Bengali society to be steeped in sensuality. They were constantly appalled by open discussion of sexual matters in the Hindu household. The *Pioneer* found the talk of sex "too odious for description in a newspaper read in respectable households".'

shame becomes a way of defining and institutionalizing virtue and vice. Virtue is unphysical and thus unfemale, and also not the prerogative of those who engage in physical production. It is not connected with anything biological or manual in nature. It is non-reproductive and intellectual,[30] and proposes a new type of segregation which is maintained by self-surveillance.

The female body is invested in different ways in private and public spaces and in terms of the onlooker. Her clothes and presence thus possess a set of architectural and social correlates coded as *andarmahal* (inner quarters) and *griha* (home/hearth), and as 'home' and 'the world'. This spacial organization is imbued with moral-cultural imperatives which are embedded in a specific social reproduction entailing its own sexual division of labour. With the proposal for change (only partially actualized) in the organization of social reproduction, where the 'inner quarters' give space to the notion of 'home/hearth', in which the household is a joint enterprise of men and women with 'free mixing', there arises the idea of women's 'emergence' from the inner quarters to the presence of non-kin males. The necessity and the origin of the sartorial innovations and renovations are always referred back to this notion of 'emergence' and the presence of male company, and connected to 'civilization'.

> The kind of clothing women wear here [in Bengal] is not considered reprehensible because it is customary. But upon even a slight consideration it will become apparent that it is slightly better than remaining naked by throwing a piece of cloth [over the body].
>
> . . .
>
> How perfunctory clothing may be, can be seen among women of this place. This may indicate a lack of show/pride, but it can not protect one from the winter's wind or allow one to

---

[30] This makes us rethink the whole notion of motherhood as found in Bengal, which seems to function as an antidote to women's sexual being. This may have been a way to redeem the physical and the reproductive without any undertone of or overt sexuality. All allusions to motherhood are posed antithetically to female sexuality.

> maintain civility, both major criteria of clothing. In no civilized country is there a custom of this kind of clothing, many laugh upon seeing it.
>
> ...
>
> Any civilized nation is against the kind of clothing in use in the present time among women [literally, 'weak ones'] of our country. Indeed it is a sign of shamelessness. Educated men [lit. those who have mastered knowledge] have been greatly agitated about it, almost everyone wishes for another kind of civilized clothing.
>
> ...
>
> There is a custom here of [women] wearing fine and transparent clothing, which reveals the whole body. Such shameless attire in no way allows one to frequent civilized company. If it happens that there is wise counsel being offered about religion/proper conduct, it may so happen that we cannot attend to those wise words because of the clothes around. This shows how such clothes can stand in the way of our [moral] improvement.[31]

The phenomenon of 'emergence' is noted by Swarnakumari Debi in the context of her own sister-in-law's experience.

> My middle older brother returned from England in 1864, and his service began in 1865. In those days the enclosure [of women] in the inner quarters was fully alive. Then women had to go in covered palanquins, with guards running beside it, even to go from one house to the next within the same compound. If mother got the permission to bathe in the Ganges after much pleading, they plunged her in the river along with the palanquin. When middle older brother was taking his wife to Bombay, [even then] he could not make her walk through the front yard. It was such a shameful deed for the daughter-in-law [of a good family] that everyone expressed particular disapproval. Therefore she had to get into the ship in a palanquin.[32]

---

[31] Soudamini Khastagiri, 'Striloker Paricchhad' (Women's Clothes), *Bamabodhini Patrika*, no. 97, vol. 8, 1872 (*BS Bhadra* 1278), pp. 148–52.

[32] Swarnakumari Debi, 'Sekele Katha', p. 37.

But times moved inexorably.

> Two years later when middle older brother came home with his wife, then no one could ask the daughter-in-law/bride to come into the house in a palanquin. But the tragedy that was enacted by witnessing the bride of the family descend from the carriage in front of the house [in public] like a white woman, is indescribable.[33]

Hemantakumari Choudhuri expands on the theme of Bengali women's clothes by speaking of a need for change in the attitudes of women towards their own bodies.

> Indian women, imitating the Begams [wives] of the Nawabs, started using very fine or transparent clothes. As a result of this, wives of Bengali homes felt no shame in going to bathe in the Ganges, or attending invitations. But finally many have begun to realize the bad taste involved in the custom of wearing one transparent/fine piece of cloth.[34]

These statements imply a basic change both in reality to some extent, and certainly ideologically, in the social context of female presence in Bengal. Reproductive labour carried on primarily by women within the household, outside of male participation, in large joint family structures, gives place to a reorganized emotional-moral space approximating the model of a nuclear family, at least conceptually and morally. Women writers such as Nagendrabala Mustafi decried the old arrangement, calling it an 'enclosure' and speaking of the horrible degeneracy among women as a result.

> We are trapped like birds in a cage of enclosure, our mental capacities are gradually becoming sluggish, our hearts are not able to blossom in the light of knowledge.[35]

The 'emergence', then, contrasted to 'enclosure' or 'seclusion', came to be seen as *stri swadhinata* (women's freedom), a goal of social

---

[33] Ibid., p. 37.
[34] Hemantakumari Choudhuri, 'Striloker Paricchhad'.
[35] Nagendrabala Mustafi, *Bamabodhini*, 1895 (*BS Vaisakh* 1302), pp. 30–1.

reform and an indicator of social 'progress'. But depending on the ideological stance of social critics, this could also mean an inversion of the desirable social/moral order (noted as *ghor kali*, or a fallen age).

The discursive organization of physical exposure, including veiling or leaving bare the face, is created by the usual mixture of colonial and pre-colonial moral categories for social reform applicable to all aspects of social life. They are posed as moral binary terms:

> civilization/barbarism
> modern/traditional
> spiritual/physical
> rational/irrational
> decent/indecent
> virtuous/sexual or sensual[36]

They form a moral and interpretive cluster and pose a constitutive relation between sexuality and society. They inscribe the (female) body with distinct sexual-social meanings. Accordingly, this body and its sexuality enter the realm of morality, both at the level of action and of desire. This creates a basis for both an everyday and institutional administration of sexuality in general and female sexuality in particular. The formal/sartorial presentation of the female body in particular becomes a powerful signifier of the success and failure of a moral regulation and offers a scope of controlled sexual expression as much as of suppression. It maps out the moral boundaries of the propertied classes, and subsumes within them the question of practicality of desire.

This regulatory construction of sexuality, with a manipulation, fear and negation of the body, expresses the notion of sexuality among the upper classes. It reveals at the same moment the social relations between, the ideological positions on, mental and manual labour. The relationship of the body or 'nakedness' to 'civilization',

---

[36] See D. Sayer, *Marx, Weber and Modernity*, and also R. Inden, *Imagining India*, where he traces the emergence of these concepts and applies them to the European construction of India.

expressed as sexuality versus rationality, and visualized as clothing, encodes the evaluation of, and power relations between, mental and manual labour. It typically valorizes the mind (and its functions) over the body or nakedness (and its functions). *Lajja* or physical shame (this does and does not approximate the Christian notion of guilt) becomes a pro-rationalist moral measuring concept which establishes the criteria for 'civilization'. It calls for privileging the domination of nature, body and passion or 'irrationality' by various 'higher' mental capacities. The control of the female body through the moral mechanism of *lajja* or 'shame' becomes an expression of contempt, control and fear of female sexuality and a perception of the body as quintessentially physical or 'natural'. This misogynistic and controlling attitude is most blatantly expressed in an anonymous piece on women's public bathing. 'Civilization' provides the focal point of judgement from which the bathers are viewed. The unsigned piece deserves to be quoted at length.

> Education helps to change many disgusting/revolting habits. As people become more civilized, they engage in civilized customs and practices, as befitting of the times. But habit has such an overwhelming power that people continue to nurture many disgusting practices because of it. Women's bathing customs in this country are one of these highly disgusting matters.
>
> How it is that civilized and educated people engage to this day in this disgusting/revolting custom I can not tell! No doubt habit is the cause. But if they are not vigilant about such disgusting/revolting things they will become obstacles for women's improvement.
>
> ...
>
> Genteel/civilized, as well as uncivilized women of villages bathe without any reservation together with men. This is not a matter of little disgust! And bathing [here] does not simply mean returning home after a dip. If only that were the case, even that would be no small matter of disgust. But [instead] women, eschewing all shame, stand next to men and clean their body parts in a most revolting manner .... On top of that, the kind of fine [clothing] material they wear is not fit to go out in society, and when that material becomes wet and clings to the body, then

there is no difference between being naked and dressed. Many a time a decent man hesitates to get out of the pond in such clothes, but women, displaying remarkable ease, get out of the pond and walk home in their wet clothes.

. . .

Finally, it is respectfully submitted to women that they do not engage in such a disgusting activity. It is far better to go for a week without a bath, or even to go to the pond at dawn. Yet it is never reasonable to wash the body or clothes that are on, in front of men. I don't know when you will learn the real use of shame!![37]

It is evident that this discourse and the actual principle at work in the designing of the attire are both obsessively centred on control through the segregation, obscuring and obstruction of movement of the female body.

Woman's Body: Enclosure and Exposure

The sense of crisis that we have mentioned before came to be crystallized in the theme of women's 'emergence' into the public/male domain and the entrance of men into the household. Ideological consideration of this social crisis pivoted on the theme of women's transgression and the permissiveness of progressive men. The conservative literature of the time echoed with fear and anger about women's public presence. But scrutiny reveals that it is not the presence of women in the public space as such, which created this fear and anger, but rather the type and context of the space and presence.[38] The earlier public activities by women did not challenge the established sexual division of labour and the relatively stable and segregated domains of social reproduction. Therefore, it

---

[37] 'Strilokganer Snan Pranali' (Women's Bathing Customs), unsigned, *Bamabodhini Patrika*, vol. 5, no. 72, 1871 (*BS Sraban* 1276), pp. 71–3.

[38] Articles in the magazines allude to the common presence of large numbers of upper and lower class women in public spaces for reasons of pilgrimage and other religious as well as social rituals, or for practical reasons such as that of bathing, washing clothes or fetching water, long before the 'emergence'.

is not just the spatial transgression which upset the anti-reformists.[39] It is rather the 'unnaturalness' of their social presence in the capacity of intellectual interlocutors of men, as students, and as actual and potential professionals, such as teachers or doctors, which produced an ideological/moral response of managing the crisis.[40]

If this was the 'conservative' concern, the male reformers' concerns were no less anxious, and acute. The female body and its moral-social-functional implications in the context of changing social reproduction overwhelmed them just as much. While advocating an education for women, and their 'emergence' from the 'inner' domain, they sought just as anxiously to curb any possibility of gender destabilization or any real autonomy for women. Thus the attempts to re-dress them in 'civilized attire' may have had less to do with the fact that they wore a single piece of unstitched cloth in the women's quarters than with the fact that they were feared to be found where they should not have been, doing 'what men do'. This is not to say that there was no resistance to a regular form of exposure, or an advancement of the inner quarters or the *andarmahal* as a woman's 'natural' place. Even a writer like Krishnabhabini Das, who felt that economic independence was a positive gain or at times a necessity for women, in her essay, 'Striloker Kaj ar Purusher Kaj' (Woman's Work and Man's Work), put forward this division of labour normatively. This 'natural' labour was as much about appropriate activities as about the placement of the female body or where such activities should take place. She should 'naturally' be found at 'home, keeping out of men's way, not competing with them and leaving the public space at their disposal.

[39] It is not an accident that much of the satire against 'modern women' was levelled at 'educated' women, who were very well covered in an asexual and virtuous manner. These women attracted more ridicule and venom from the satirists than prostitutes, as disguised prostitutes and home-breaking 'masculine' viragos.

[40] See satires against 'educated' women, who are seen as 'masculine', and their husbands as 'feminine'. This 'unnatural' social presence was caricatured and castigated in images and written texts. The thesis about this inversion indicating the end of an aeon, going through a fallen stage, is expressed in the notion of *kali yuga*, the age of doom.

The sartorial re-casting, therefore, meant much more than an introduction of women's fashion or style in clothing, but was a proposal to re-cast both at an ideological/moral and a social/practical level a prevalent social organization. Anxiety, signified by new experiments at dressing, reflected an anxiety over the possibility of a loss of patriarchal power in a new form of social organization. Articulating in diverse ideological propositions the actual and possible shift in social relations created by colonialism, the male reformers also sought to shape or direct these changes. Thus women 'emerged' in a new moral and social regalia, which sought to counteract any threat to patriarchy. The clothing project meant the investiture of the female body in a new enclosure — a sartorial enclosure.[41]

This problem posed by the female body and its relative exposure was curious, since Bengali men lived with both in life and art until well into the British rule.[42] Suddenly we are reminded of the 'uncivilized' appearance of women in their 'traditional' garment of an 'unstitched' piece of cloth, lacking undergarments to conceal their breasts and lower bodies. This new awareness could only have been due to the recognition that the prevailing patriarchal social organization would undergo a shock in the new context. The possibilities of male-female relations no longer regulated through appropriate kinship conduct and established modes of biological-social reproduction occasioned much speculation and articulation of moral strategies. Tanika Sarkar addresses this very issue when she says:

[41] Regarding *griha*, (The Home) see H. Bannerji, 'Mothers and Teachers'.

[42] It is obvious that Bengali men and women lived with each other with the kind of clothing that they later repudiated as 'savage' or 'uncivilized', without any violation of ethics and aesthetics. In her popular journalism about Indian women's clothes and ornaments, Chitra Deb, for example, brings out a basic change in erotic aesthetics and ethics between pre- and early colonial times and the later nineteenth century among the propertied classes. See *Abarane Abharane Bharatya Nari* (Women in Clothes and Ornaments, Calcutta, 1989). Two English women visitors in India, Eliza Fay and Fanny Burney, also leave us with descriptions which do not show any negativity among the Bengali households as to what women or men wore.

When we look at the nineteenth century household manuals and contrast them with the ancient, . . . we find that the real point of departure in our material relates not so much to the strategies of control but to unprecedented possibilities in the conditions of the women's existence.[43]

But Tanika Sarkar makes a mistake in not seeing the reform project as building in control in the very texture of how possibilities are conceived. The situation contained a special problem of signification in continuing and reorganizing patriarchy. A discourse on shame and attempts to practicalize it through clothes and other moral imperatives restrained and incorporated 'possibilities' of women's fuller subjectivities within a patriarchal class project.

The attempted reconstruction was therefore a re-construction through both older and newer ideological and social norms and forms. The 'emergence' was also a continuation of the 'enclosure', a continuation of control of women's bodies, labour and sexuality into the new phase of colonial middle class formation. As such, in the matter of appearance, which provides us, as do all visual signs, with a more flexible and spacious signifier, the enclosure/emergence opposition undergoes a formal and moral elision. Even though the icon/sign signals to what may be called *new* possibilities, it also signals *new* restraints. The new image incorporates much of the old enclosure through a formal and an ideological reshaping. The attempt is re-presented as 'virtue', as a consciously designed textile-moral contraption. The woman of the 'enlightened' middle class Bengali home was to present herself as the sign called *bhadramahila*, attired in virtue.

Lajja, National Culture and Women's Clothing

The social meaning of the body goes beyond what is functionally understood by sexual reproduction. It relates to the social organization as a whole, and involves a general morality and politics not exclusive of sexuality. The importance of physical appearance with appropriate signifiers for cultural representations is obvious in the

[43] Tanika Sarkar, 'Hindu Conjugality', p. 3.

context of Bengal's nationalism. This national culture implies and aspires to a certain kind of morality and constructs the Bengali women's ideal sexuality, and projects this as the sign of *bhadramahila*. *Lajja*, or a sense of shame, is integral to this construct of femininity, in nationalist terms, and the sartorial project consists of designing a 'national' visual form. As cultural nationalism gained momentum from the 1860s onward, European women's clothes were not seen as just 'alien' or 'foreign', but actually 'shameful', in the national context. The question of direct imitation always gave place to attempts of construction. A minuscule section among the elite wore gowns, while saris were being experimented with. But it is interesting to note that saris won the day. The reason for this outcome is the elision between feminine shame/modesty and *deshiata*, or 'nationalist' cultural authenticity which includes a restrained female sexuality. Writer after writer in the women's magazines creates a transparency between a proper female sexual morality and a national apparel. As Soudamini Khastagiri puts it:

> Relatively speaking [relative to wearing one piece cloth] clothes of nations such as those of the English may be better. But in some aspects they are a thousand times worse than ours. Therefore, if we seek to imitate them, we get rid of some faults only to embrace their deficiencies.[44]

She states that such clothes are a betrayal of national identity and what is culturally appropriate femininity for 'us'. It is hypocritical and artificial for Indians to wear western clothes, and by so doing, they become marginalized in both societies. An anonymous writer quotes approvingly from another woman, Rajlakshmi Sen:

> Therefore whatever preserves national culture, and enables all to identify [one] as a woman of Bengali homes and covers the body thoroughly, and is appropriate for both the rich and the poor, allowing at the same a free movement of the body, should be worn.[45]

[44] Soudamini Khastagiri, 'Striloker Parichhad'.
[45] 'Attire of Women of Bengal', *Bamabodhini*, vol. 8, no. 99, 1872 (*BS Kartik* 1278), p. 2.

An essay by Jyotirmayee Gangopadhyay written many years later echoes exactly the same sentiment: 'There was a time when the new promoters of women's emancipation, both male and female, adorned themselves in western clothes . . . . They adopted these clothes as an expression or symbol of their views.'[46] But she also stated:

> We have many proofs of the fact that educated men and women did not wish to wear western clothes, since they conveyed an anti-nationalist mentality. Most educated women, and it is not an exaggeration to claim about 99 per cent, do not consider gowns as tasteful as saris.[47]

The same sentiment is echoed by Soudamini Debi:

> It is never as enjoyable to imitate clothes of other nations, as to create one from one's imagination, and which is suited to both *national characteristics* and is also *civilized*. And besides, there is a sense of artificiality if Bengalis wear the clothing of English or any other nation. They are considered of that culture and are treated as such. If a Bengali person dresses like the English and frequents their society, they engage in reviling the Bengalis in front of him, which he has to listen to with patience. Such clothes also deprive one of full acceptance among one's own people.[48]

Or further:

> It is a duty to keep characteristics/signs of one's nation/culture in people's clothing or manners. Therefore it is not fit to imitate other nations wholly, this expresses lowness in status. We will accept the good things about religion and conduct [moral character] of other countries, but there is no need to imitate them in matters of appearance. Even when the [female] attires of the English, or Northern or Western Indians, or Muslims or the Chinese may be beautiful, Bengali women should not wear them.

---

[46] Jyotirmayee Gangopadhyay, 'Gown O Sari' (Gown or Sari), *Bharati*, 1922 (*BS Aswin* 1330), p. 1055.
[47] Ibid., p. 1056.
[48] Soudamini Khastagiri, 'Striloker Parichhad'.

> The duty consists of wearing clothing which shows one's national culture, covers one's body fully and which indicates instantly that one is a woman of Bengal.[49]

As we saw in Swarnakumari Debi's description of her reformer father Debendranath's sartorial experiments, a combination of 'shame/modesty' and a patriarchal nationalist aesthetic have always provided the bases of new designs. Sarala Debi's essay, 'Swadeshi Poshak' (Nationalist Clothing), is also a good example of what is meant by a national cultural identity. Concepts such as *shobhanata* (appropriateness/decorum), *shalinata* (decency) or *shilata* (courtesy), are shown to be the moral underpinnings of the fashion design of nationalism. This 'national' and sexually moral apparel also marks out the good from the bad woman, and advocates a complete sexual repression and sartorial segregation for widows. This is also the opinion of Soudamini Khastagiri, who states:

> Nowadays some women wear *kamij* [a type of long shirt with long sleeves], jacket, sari and shoes. That is fine, but even some bad/loose women of this country wear them. For this reason one should use a shawl covering from head to toe, which especially hides the upper body. This will indicate a daughter of a respectable family.... And one should also adopt a way of distinguishing married women from widows.[50]

She and others suggest a recipe for dressing in ways signifying respectability (class, national culture and shame/modesty). For wearing at home, an *ijar* (bloomers or drawers), *piran* (a short-sleeved shirt) and a sari, or a long *piran* and a sari. For going out, an *ijar*, a *piran*, a sari, pyjamas, shoes and socks, though the latter are optional, female 'shame' not residing in the feet. The experiment is obviously never complete and always on the verge of a collapse under scrutiny, and even this figure of modesty, national culture and 'good' class is not considered 'authentically national' or modest by a large section of Hindu conservative society. It is still considered

[49] Ibid.
[50] Ibid.

'anglicized' and 'masculine' both in morality and form, and ridiculed in the caricatures of the street painters of Kalighat.

Lajja, put forward as a major female ethic, projecting a high social status and an indication of national authenticity, serves as a subjective regulator of female physicality or sexuality. As an internalized censor, uplifted to virtue, it becomes the most personal, therefore moral, way of controlling women. A good example is the portrait of Krishnabhabini Das in a Hindu widow's garb, after her rejection of western clothes. It is an act and an image through which she redeems herself in the eyes of her previous critics through her acceptance of a garb of purity signifying sexual self-effacement and self-sacrifice.

> Almost everyday at the mall I saw a woman well-dressed in European clothes. It surprised me a little, because even though she was dressed in European clothes, the expression on her face was sweet and gentle . . . .
>
> . . .
>
> Where was that woman dressed in English costume now? This was a widow of Hindu homes in front of me! She was worth being worshipped. She knew of no good qualities to boast of in herself, nor had she any temptation in that direction. She never wanted to be famous. Becoming one with the very earth in humility, she carried on her tasks. Her white and pure attire of a widow created such a sense of respect and awe [towards her].[51]

In keeping with her image of white purity is her personal morality.

> After becoming a widow she gave up all kinds of comfort. She never slept in a bedstead anymore, but rather made a bed on the floor. Never ate anything good, such as fruits or sweets. She gave up everything.[52]

By discarding the European garb of her former married state and the definition of herself as an individual, with limited self-interests, she enters simultaneously into the orbit of shame and

---

[51] Sarojkumari Debi, 'Krishnabhabini Das', *Bharati*, vol. 46, 1922 (*BS Agrahayan* 1329), pp. 737–42.
[52] Ibid.

cultural national authenticity. Her portrait serves as a radiant icon of female purity, which reaches its climax with widowhood. Sexuality can now be erased completely both in the name of virtue and national culture.

An obsessive concern for well-coveredness of the female body and the visual projection of purity are the negative signifiers for female sexuality — a perpetual reminder of what lies within and what a woman must not disclose — except at the risk of being outcast both personally and politically. A passive sexuality is thus established for middle-or upper-class women, where lacking the volition of exposure or disclosure, she becomes a contained but persistent zone for activating male sexuality. The cover of clothing is presented as the future promise of un-covering by an outside agent. Unveiling her, or 'freeing' her from a fabricated encasement, becomes a male prerogative and pleasure. The passivity of the construct called *bhadramahila* is ensured by the fact that her *bhadra-ness* (gentility or modesty or class status) is dependent upon her desexualization. She must be constantly aware of male gaze and avoid being or doing anything sexually provocative. From this point of view 'shame' becomes the ideological construct on which pornography (not the same as erotic literature) is hinged. Nineteenth-century male reforming literature is full of indirect allusions or moralizing on what is forbidden or hidden. Thus shame, or decency, while considering female clothing, supersedes discussions on beauty, or is equated with it.

Sartorial moral philosophy of Bengal, whether produced by women or men, implies an invisible and constant male gaze at women. The purpose of this gaze, or rather its origin/occasion, is domination, to create an ideological object, a sexually circumscribed 'other'. Women themselves, through their own subscription to the same discourse of 'shame and civilization', participated in the same enterprise. Their construct of femininity is thus not only opposed to the masculine, through sharing the premise of gentility, but also self-divided and self-censoring. It consists of the moral notion of appropriately gendered 'goodness', 'otherizing' her own sexuality from herself through patriarchal prescriptions. The antithesis of this female goodness is the bad woman, epitomized in the notion of the prostitute.[53] This self-division is reflected in the divide among women themselves, towards other women, and regarding the attitude towards their own body and eroticism. And it should be noted that the ideology of 'proper clothes' designed for women of the urban propertied classes is held out as a typology to all others, and is a part of a general hegemonic design. Its 'naturalization' as appropriate aspiration for gentility creates a mythology, a system of signs, which encodes a reconstructed morality of a nationalist but anglicized section of the urban propertied classes.

The nature of this new morality as indicated by *lajja* for women cannot be understood outside of Bengal's colonial context. The sense of crisis that filled the air manifested itself as much in idealizing/ideologizing the collapse of the older organization of social spaces, as in attempts of reprivatization and in directing the course of change, particularly as regards women and the family. It contains a colonial response, both in an anger towards and a submission to European judgement on the decadence/savagery of Indians both male and female.[54] The prescription for female sexuality, con-

---

[53] In an unpublished paper, 'The Queen's Daughters: Prostitutes as Outcast Group in Colonial India' (1991), Ratnabali Chattopadhyay discusses the iconography of the 'bad woman' or the prostitute and the referential relationship between this construct and that of *sati*, or the chaste good woman, or the *bhadramahila* with her refined moral purity. 'In a number of moral tracts the chaste wife (*patibrata stree*) and the prostitute (*beshya*) are constructed into visible signs.' p. 29. Chattopadhyay also quotes a few lines from an anonymous tract entitled 'Stridiger Prati Upadesh' (Advice to Women, Calcutta 1874), 'The good wife, *patibrata*, is shy, silent, does her duty and is totally undemanding, stays away from men, keeps her whole body covered and does not wear flashy clothes', while the '*beshya* is loudmouthed, always restless, bares special parts of her body, falls on men, demands jewellery and continuously wears revealing clothes.' Chattopadhyay p. 29. This distinction was so widely touted, and morally organized, that it is not surprising that it formed a part of the consciousness of middle class educated women, who were particularly sensitive regarding their respectability or *bhadrata* and wanted no confusion between their own project of emancipation and the 'freeness' of 'bad/loose' *itar* women.

[54] Many authors, both Indian and western, have commented on British preoccupation with Indian moral degeneracy and savagery, particularly with regard to sexual morality and women. For example, Major C.A. McMohan writes: 'Native public opinion would not go with us in an attempt to put a stop

structed within a colonial context, shifts from being direct, to that of a repressed Victorian Christian ladyhood. This becomes clear if a contrast is established between the icon of the de-sexualized gentlewoman and the pre-anglicized version of female sexuality in eighteenth-century Bengal, when a woman's sexual initiative is portrayed with respect and frankness by male poets such as Bharatchandra. In this epic poetry from the eighteenth century, the woman is not an 'object' of male desire, as is to happen later, when this very male desire is circumscribed by a general ideology of desexualization of the human body through a narrative of vice.[55] The much advocated serene, unsexual moral female image, which is only nuanced by indirect and repressed physicality, is a sign of 'femininity' rather than of womanhood or femaleness. It also desexualizes or contains male sexuality, or rather is an expression of its containment, since it is at its most 'feminine' form in a passive state, and does not solicit a directly sexual male attention.

The colonially inflected patriarchal world view of the middle classes of Bengal, however, should be understood as being both local and foreign. The sign of the *bhadramahila* is a great example of this reconstruction of consciousness. It is in a sense a re-worked or anglicized version of the older Bengali *sati* (the chaste woman-wife). In its current phase of a gentlewoman the direct physical

---

to professional prostitution. The mind of a native is no more shocked at the thought that a girl should be born to prostitute than that a man should be born to be blacksmiths and carpenters. Prostitution is an institution the history of which in India at all events is lost in the mist of ages. Prostitutes danced before Yudishthir and Rama and in the guise of dancing girls and singers they are a necessary part of most domestic ceremonies today.' (Home Judicial File No. 48, p. 1143, 7th June 1872, to C.M. Riwarzi Esq. Officiating Undersecretary to the Government of Punjab quoted by M. Sinha). See also Tejaswini Niranjana, 'Translation, Colonialism and the Rise of English', *Economic and Political Weekly*, vol. 25, no. 15, 1990, as well as Shibaji Bandyopadhyay, *Gopal-Rakhal Dwanda Samas: Upanibeshbad O Bangla Shishu Sahitya* (An Elision of Gopal-Rakhal: Colonialism and Bengali Children's Literature, Calcutta, 1991).

[55] See K. Ballhatchet, *Race, Sex and Class*. Also R. Chattopadhyay, 'The Queen's Daughters': 'The main focus of the missionary narrative rested on recreating the atmosphere of vice. This was done to show the exact division of space that existed between the rulers and the ruled.' p. 17.

control and violence of patriarchy has been domesticized, and substituted by an ideological encirclement of clothing and other forms or morality which mix chastity and sacrifice with the moral code of a utilitarian Christian lady. After the first half of the nineteenth century, 'the feminine' emerges as a notion among the western educated population in Bengal. It is found everywhere — from education to clothes. It is not surprising therefore, that many women, in search of a direct agency and strength, turned to the colonial-nationalist myth of the Aryan Woman or notions of the mother goddess. If we compare women's and men's use of the construct of the Aryan Woman, we find that women are attracted to the myth in search of notions such as dynamism and clothing designed for public and open spaces, while men to the Aryan Woman's moral qualities which are passive, such as constancy, chastity and sacrifice.

> The clothes worn by Aryan women in ancient times bear no resemblance with the present time. In those days women had freedom. Women frequented war zones and courts freely. In many cases wives or sisters had to ride on horses with their husbands or brothers. This is why it was not suitable for them to wear just beautiful clothes. There was a great similarity between male and female clothing.[56]

The same may be said of the typology of English and American women used by Krishnabhabini Das, Hiranmayee Debi and others, who represent freedom, agency and self-sufficiency, without fully displacing women from the private or domestic sphere.

Conclusion

These essays by women on civilization, shame, the body and clothing both organize and express the consciousness of a significant strand of the developing 'westernized', reforming middle classes of Bengal. They display the commonsense of classes created on a colonial terrain which also contain competitive 'national' aspira-

---

[56] Hemantakumari Choudhuri, 'Striloker Paricchhad'.

tions. In the case of the garb of the *bhadramahila*, however, much more so than in the area of education, for example, the colonial context and content overdetermine the hegemonic forms of these classes. This sartorial-moral enterprise is profoundly English and nineteenth century in its ethos. Fundamentally distinct from pre-colonial, feudal notions of grandeur or status, this attire is an intrinsic response to and an absorption within a colonial influence. The ideology of Victorian femininity provides the lens through which is perceived and configurated the indigenous dominant ideology about womanhood.

The *bhadramahila*, both in form and content, is the Bengali males' response to European accusations of their barbarism. The configuration here depends on a particular set of social relations which express the gender organization of the propertied classes. Here we have multiple but coherent discourses of patriarchy in so far as local and colonial elements of gender and class ideologies converge into an overall misogyny and a general rejection of the physical. As we noted before, class, in the sense of division and valorization of mental over manual labour, extends into a positive hatred of the body and sexuality as embodied by women as 'nature' and 'the primitive'. Racism itself is concretized with patriarchy and classism in the European stereotypes of animality and sensuality of Bengali/pagan women in particular, but also men.[57]

If this seems like an exaggerated way of stating the colonial ideological design, we need to only look at Kenneth Ballhatchet's book on racism and sex in the Raj, which gave the 'Hindoos' and their women in particular, a savage, evil and corrupting role with regard to Europeans. Accusations of barbaric sensuality and

[57] See the account of Rev. James Ward, excerpted by Sumanta Bannerji in *The Parlour and the Streets*:

> 'Before two o'clock the place was cleared . . . when the doors of the area were thrown open, and a vast crowd of natives rushed in, almost treading one upon another, among whom were the vocal singers . . . who entertained their guests with filthy songs and danced in indecent attitudes before the goddess, holding up their hands, turning around, putting forward their heads towards the image, every now and then bending their bodies and almost tearing their throats with their vociferations.' p. 154.

primitivity fill the pages of Mill's *History of British India*, missionary tracts, letters, travelogues and drawings of Europeans in India/Bengal.[58] Rationality, or access to reason, is seen as a far away dream for Indians, so close are they supposed to be in religion and everyday life to sensuality and nature. Their spirituality or literary creation itself is seen at best as a product of a sensual, distorted imagination, rather than of spiritual transcendence.[59] And if the Indian/Bengali society as a whole, characterized in terms of its males, is such a natural excrescence, then how much more so must be the Bengali women, whose identity with nature has not been ruptured by any rational interruption. The European enlightenment's moral-social schema, which rests on 'civilization versus barbarism/moral decay' of Indian males, or an ambivalence towards 'tradition', expresses itself in a man-to-man condemnation of Indian males (as sensualists and females manque) as oppressors of 'their women', and confers on the colonial (male) rulers the role of protectors or reformers of Indian women. For Indian males, vying for the same status of reformer-protector, this means a combination of self-hatred (for being 'female/effete') acquired in the colonial context, and a hatred of women (for being natural, uncivilized, etc.) which is both colonial and pre-colonial. The project of social reform for women therefore allows for externalizing or displacing their views of the self and self hatred onto society at large and women in particular. It also calls for curbing 'naturality' (femaleness) in themselves. In the same sexually repressive configurated design aimed at women, morally-sartorially, the project of self-improvement is collapsed with self-repression for men. Thus domination of nature as embodied by women could be projected as social reform, offering examples of rationality (therefore true masculinity a la old Brahmanism and European enlightenment/utilitarianism) on the part

[58] See, among numerous sources, Anil Chandra Dasgupta, comp. & ed., *The Days of John Company: Selections from Calcutta Gazette 1824–32* (Calcutta, 1959); J.R. Martin, *Notes on the Medical Topography of Calcutta* (Calcutta, 1837); Rev. J. Long, *Calcutta in the Olden Times*, reprinted in *Nineteenth Century Studies*, vol. 5; J.C. Marshman, *Life and Times of Carey, Marshman and Ward* (London, 1859); Mary Carpenter, *Six Months in India* (London, 1968).

[59] See R. Inden, *Imagining India*.

of Bengali male intelligentsia. Indians such as Rajnarayan Bose (and many others) expressed just this conjuncture when their reforming zeal was expressed in terms of 'she must be refined, reorganized, recast and regenerated'. This introjected colonial judgement, along with a reorganized older patriarchy, provided much of the middle classes' hegemonic self-definition. It could therefore be said that the clothes designed for the *bhadramahila* inscribed on women's body the moral-political agenda of the same classes. Krishnabhabini Das and Swarnakumari Debi, describing changes in the social organization of a household, speak of growing male control over all aspects of women's lives. Much of their own writing aims to establish a relative autonomy for women while maintaining a somewhat differentiated social domain.

The virtuous attire designed for the gentlewoman of Bengal is a reworking of existing and incoming social and cultural forms. This convergence, negotiation and fusion on grounds of cultural commonsense and ideology between colonial and indigenous patriarchal class values can only happen because the European forms and norms are not dissimilar to those prevailing in Bengal. The intelligibility of colonial, foreign notions actually rests on prior social organization in Bengal or India. A highly evolved division of labour as expressed in the caste system and forms of class, valorization of mental production by placing Brahmins (priest-scholars) at the head of the society, depriving women (even of the Brahmins) and low caste physical-manual producers of intellectual prerogatives, all contain a basic similarity to European social organization in terms of gender and class organization. The pre-existing social organization thus provides enough ground for weaving in or reworking colonial misogyny, elitism and racism. Fundamentally patriarchal, Brahminical rationalism and asceticism is also characterized by a basic hatred and contempt towards women (as natural, physical entities) and the lower castes/classes as unreconstructed body or nature, and thus collapses the woman and the *sudra* (low caste).[60] This predisposition could not have been inimical to

---

[60] Sukumari Bhattacharji, a scholar on ancient India, as well as Uma Chakravarti, have done much work on the status of women in ancient India, challenging the Aryan myth. The physical status of women is evident, according to

colonial-capitalist class distinctions, protestant Christianity, utilitarianism and Cartesian rationalism, all of which were fundamentally anti-woman, anti-physical/manual producer and racist. Franz Fanon has written about the colonial discourse as a discourse of Cartesian masculinity, in which the colonizer/conqueror is the sole male or intellectual subject, and the colonized is an object, a body, an animality and by extension a femaleness.[61] The equation of women with nature, with the reproduction of physical life, womb and instinct, and expandedly, with feelings and primitivity, was equally well-known to both India and Britain. This is why the woman of India and the savage, and the Indian/Bengali woman as the quintessentially savage, must be reformed and clothed or re-clothed. This is not to say that the European attitude towards European women was any different or better. European contempt (and hatred) for females of the conquered species was disguised as paternalistic charity. This charity, mediated through notions of civilization and progress, offered both an indictment of Indian society and a legitimacy for colonial rule.

The women writers of the magazines share to a great extent, in spite of their nationalism, the colonial view of themselves and their society. They adopt the same trajectory of historiography originating from James Mill, starting with the golden age of the Aryans, moving through the dark ages of Muslim rule to the present moral and intellectual decay, to the English era of enlightenment which

---

Bhattacharji, from the settled agricultural period, by her deprivation of education and control over her body (and its fruits) by men. 'The wife had no property rights, nor had she any right over her body (Satapatha Brahmana IV:4:2:13). If she refused to oblige the husband sexually she should first be coaxed and cajoled, then bribed and 'brought over (cf. avakriniyat) with gifts; if she still refused, he should beat her with his palm or with a rod into submission' (Brhadaranyaka Upanishad VI:4:7)'. From Bhattacharji, 'Laws on Women: Judaism, Christianity and Hinduism' in *Indian Women: Myth and Reality.*

[61] Franz Fanon, *The Wretched of the Earth* (New York, 1963), pp. 35–43. Fanon points out the physicality/body status attributed to the colonized and the rationalist essentialism of the European colonizer 'self'. This shares the same ground with patriarchy in so far as women are seen as 'nature' or 'body' and equated with a reproductive self, qualitatively a different consciousness, and incapable of rationality.

calls for social reform.[62] These sartorial innovations therefore represent a recovering of a higher, intellectual-moral self, a disguising and a muting of the 'natural', through consciously eliminating sensuality/sexuality signalled by hiding of the female body. If nothing else, through the reform attempts the basically reproductive natural femaleness is tempered with virtue, taming sexuality and animality into sweet sentimentality and mothering. The colonially preferred image of the Victorian, Christian middle-class woman which overshadows this sartorial project, less the grand lady than the helpmate of missionaries and social reformers, represents the icon of a civilized society, while holding forth the possibility of moral improvement to a section of Bengali women.

Much more so than in education, where the feminist thrust of the women's self-improvement project is strident in spite of subscription to norms of a class-patriarchy, it is in the area of clothing and the body that a guilt-ridden, shameful, indigenous-cum-colonial patriarchy holds women in thrall. While the same women are unashamedly demanding in acquisition of intellect and reason, they are held in place by 'shame' in the matter of their body, sensuality and sexuality. It is with 'shame' that middle-class women are most inexorably riveted to patriarchy. The life of Krishnabhabini Das is a prime example of this situation. It shows what suspicions she had to allay for going to England, being educated and independent, what she traded off, in order to gain a morally correct image. That white-robed icon of the Hindu widow which hides her femaleness in a heavy garb of coarse cloth, which mutes all expressions and potentiality of sexuality, which tempts no male, is her uniform of legitimacy for being a 'modern' woman and advocating women's emancipation and education. Only attired in virtue can she fully expiate her past of transgressions. So even she, critical and strident as she is, a tireless promoter of reason and knowledge, subscribes to the same discourse of shame, to the triumph of male Brahminical-colonial rationality over the female mind and body.

---

[62] For the myth of the Aryan woman and its implications for nationalism, and nationalism's influence on social reform for women, see Uma Chakravarti, 'Whatever Happened to the Vedic Dasi?' in *Recasting Women*.

If we are to consider the issues of subjectivity and agency of women in nineteenth-century Bengal, it becomes apparent through this sartorial-moral project that middle-class women are held hostage between colonialism and nationalism, patriarchal class subjectivity and their resistance to it.[63] In helping to create an icon and sign for the emerging aspirations of a Bengali culture and Bengali nationalism, women capitulated far more to a patriarchal fashioning of themselves than in any other area of social change and development. The values they represent sartorially are in no way contrary to those of men, and in fact the more 'enlightened' they are, the more they compensate by sacrificing their social-sexual agency, for their encroachment in the male domain of reason and public service.

In the end, we might say that though middle class Bengali women 'come out' or 'emerge' by overstepping the boundaries of an earlier 'inner quarters' (in terms of location in space and an earlier division of labour), their sartorial morality indicates an object-subject ideological status, which they themselves are active in bringing forth. As active relegated agents for constructing an objectified subjectivity, they enter a textile prison, fashioned by male tailors and fathers of Bengal's social reform. This prison is constructed from lace, linen, cotton and silk, and from the sober and sombre tints of shame and guilt adding up to virtue.

---

[63] On this notion of divided subjectivity of women caught in the interpellation of class and patriarchy, see H. Bannerji, 'Fashioning a Self': '. . . it can be said that women class members were "summoned" both by Bengal's urban propertied classes' formative agenda and Bengali nationalism's "emancipatory" calls to become "social actors", and hence their presence in the stage of education. This amounts to "dominant ideology" interpellating women to function as class subjects, while that subjectivity itself is sought to be contained, managed, truncated and unauthenticated by the repression of their full social being through patriarchy.' p. WS 51.

4

The Early Muslim Bhadramahila: The Growth of Learning and Creativity, 1876 to 1939

Sonia Nishat Amin

Bengali society witnessed the emergence of a new type of person towards the end of the nineteenth century. This was the early Muslim *bhadramahila*. Out of what did she emerge? And how did she make her presence felt in society? These are the questions explored in this essay. It has two themes. One is the growth of the new learning — the instrument that engineered the Muslim gentlewoman. The other is the growth of creative literary activity — the means by which she asserted her independent presence in society. Education acted as the mediator between the private sphere in which middle-class women lived their lives, and the public domain belonging to men. These factors together with other social and economic forces led, in the course of time, to a cultural restructuring of the Muslim community in Bengal. Borthwick has argued that the emerging *bhadramahila* class of enlightened middle-class women was the key to women's modernization in late nineteenth-century Bengal. But of course the term '*bhadramahila*' as applied to Muslim women gives rise to certain problems which need to be dealt with. Though Borthwick has used it, various questions have been raised on this issue.

May we call the women of the educated Muslim urban middle class, *bhadramahila*? If so, on what grounds? Once this set of questions is answered, we are compelled to ask, when did the '*bhadramahila*' come into being, or what was the course of her emergence? The answer to the first question would depend largely on the extent to which we accept the applicability of the term *bhadralok* to the enlightened emergent Western-educated Muslim urban middle class. A scrutiny of contemporary literature reveals that the non-Muslim community, Hindu and Brahmo in the main, did not refer to their Muslim counterpart as *bhadralok*, the term being apparently reserved for their own kind. The Muslims did, however, occasionally refer to themselves as *bhadralok*. There is frequent occurrence of such nomenclature in the Muslim periodicals and writings. That leaves one with a valuable clue as to how the Western-educated Bengali Muslim middle-class professional gentry referred to themselves. Obviously the word *lok* (man) would not suffice, so they wrote *bhadralok*. There seems to be no other Bengali equivalent, and the Persian/Urdu terms (*sharif, buzurgu, miah, janab*) were less popular in middle-class Bengal. This leads us to the entire problematic of Bengal Muslim identity which I shall address briefly in this paper. What I suggest is that till a more historically appropriate term is discovered *bhadralok* did and does include the Muslims from the nineteenth century onwards. This claim is based on a similarity of certain core class, cultural and educational traits, shared by the middle-class professional gentry of both communities. Given this, one can move on to the question of *bhadramahilas*. The same logic may be applied here and a comparison made of traits/characteristics between the Brahmo women who had emerged from the *antahpur* (inner quarters) and the Muslim women of the *andarmahal* (inner quarters) who participated in the process of modernization in order to justify the application of the term *bhadramahila*.

This brings us to yet another concept — 'the Muslim women's awakening' (*Muslim nari jagoron*) which, seen from the viewpoint of the present piece of research, is a subset of the late nineteenth-century 'Muslim awakening',[1] which in its turn formed part of the

[1] For details of the Muslim awakening in Bengal, see: Anisuzzaman, *Muslim Manas o Bangla Sahitya* (Muslim Thoughts and Bengali Literature, Dhaka, 1964); Wakil Ahmed, *Unish Shataker Bangali Musulmaner Chinta Chetanar Dhara* (The Thoughts of Bengali Muslims in the Nineteenth Century, Dhaka, 1983); Rashid Al Faruqi, *Muslim Manas Sanghat o Pratikriya* (Conflict and

greater 'Bengal awakening'. Contemporary women have referred to their age as a period of women's awakening (for example, Rokeya and Shamsunnahar). Among present-day scholars, Maleka Begum in *Banglar Nari Andolan* refers to the late nineteenth century as a period of women's awakening and the early twentieth as one which saw the birth of the women's movement in Bengal.

Once these analytic tools are applied and categories accepted, the similarities between a Brahmo woman of 1900, and her Muslim counterpart, are more visible as are perhaps the differences. The similarities, however, cut across community and culture, the differences are culture and religion specific. Mankumari Bose, Sarala Debi, Swarnakumari Debi, Sarojini Naidu, Kadambini Ganguly on one hand, and Rokeya Sakhawat Hossein, Shamsunnahar Mahmud, Mamlukul Fatema or Nurunnessa Khatun on the other, had much in common. They wore the same style of dress; they wrote and published; their husbands/fathers or brothers were in some kind of professional service mostly under the British government; they read many of the same kind of books. It should be noted however that sometimes their readings would not match and whereas the latter group had some acquaintance with the Ramayana-Mahabharata tales, it is doubtful if the former group were equally acquainted with the stories of Ayesha, Khadija or Rabeya though they probably knew of Mughal ladies such as Jahanara or Nurjahan. They had partaken of a similar kind of education in that many of them had attended a formal educational institution for some years; they were trained to play similar roles, (wife, mother, companion), held many aspirations and hopes in common and, quite significantly, shared similar values. Fortunately, most of the women we focus on, in both the Brahmo and Muslim communities, wrote and their stories have reached us through the works they have left behind. Their preferred genres were similar too: short stories, memoirs, poems and essays. Thus, while education was a mediator between their private and public spheres, literature was the vehicle of their thoughts. As in the case of the

---

Reaction in Muslim Mind, Dhaka, 1989); and Abdul Wadud, *Banglar Jagaran* (The Awakening of Bengal, Calcutta, 1952).

preceding generation of Brahmo women, the tale of the Muslim *bhadramahila*'s emergence, a process that spanned the last two decades of the nineteenth and the early decades of the twentieth centuries, may be pieced together with the help of these writings.

By the end of the nineteenth century, the Muslim community of Bengal began to emerge as a socio-economic force. The 'awakening' in colonial Bengal which had infused new life into the Hindu/Brahmo community also had profound implications for Muslim society. The movement led by liberal reformers such as Syed Ahmed Khan in Aligarh, Thanawi in Deoband, Abdul Lateef, Ameer Ali and others in Bengal contained simultaneously liberal and conservative strands of thought, which deeply affected the Muslim *manas* or mentality of Bengali Muslims.

Women's issues (such as, *sati*, widow remarriage, *kulinpratha*, *purdah*, education) formed a central strand of the reform movement led by Rammohan, Vidyasagar, Keshab Chandra, the Tagores and other Brahmo reformers in Bengal. Reformers of a colonized Bengal, face to face with a different cultural and intellectual order and divested of crucial elements of their public selves, turned their gaze inward to the private sphere (the home and the family, the space inhabited by women, children and servants). When a similar process set in among the Muslims it was not surprising then that here too, the woman question became a central issue. Looking back, one finds that the early decades of the twentieth century witnessed a gradual process of social change that may be termed the Muslim women's awakening.[2] This has been generally believed to have been largely initiated by the new generation of Muslim men who had received Western/liberal education in some measure, broken away from the old way of life and familial structure of the landed gentry, and were engaged in some form of government employment under the Raj. But it is becoming more apparent as research on the matter progresses that, in many instances, the women themselves were

---

[2] Maleka Begum, in her *Banglar Nari Andolan* (Women's Movement in Bengal, Dhaka, 1989), views the late nineteenth century as a period of *jagaran* or awakening, and the early twentieth as the period that gave birth to the women's movement.

active agents in the process of social change. The term *bhadramahila* has been given academic currency by Meredith Borthwick who describes the changing role of women of the *bhadralok* households.[3] Both Borthwick and Murshid refer to the fact that they have dealt with the Brahmo/Hindu *bhadramahila* only, leaving the Muslim *bhadramahila* to future research.[4]

The sources for the reconstruction of this hitherto bypassed area of Bengal history — the making of the Muslim *bhadramahila* — are rich and varied, contrary to popular notion. This essay relies to a great extent on the words of the women themselves as recorded in their own writing — memoirs, letters, essays and addresses, biographies as well as fictional work (novels, short stories, fantasies). It is fortunate for us that many of the early generation of Muslim women who 'responded to modernization' took up the pen. In fact, literature and education were the first arenas where the woman's question (as framed by the women as well as the men), publicly manifests itself. Many of the women were self-taught, or tutored at home, and few had had access to a formal school. This did not halt their pens, or inhibit their ambition or intellect, as the writings they have left behind testify. Their writings have been culled from periodicals, contemporary texts and their reprints (e.g., *Rupjalal*), and compilations (for example, *Rokeya Rachanabali*).

The question of educating Muslim women generated much discussion, from which it is possible to distinguish two main strands of thought. For instance, in 1867, the issue of educating Muslim girls was raised at an assembly of the Bengal Social Science Association. Maulvi Abdul Hakim of the Calcutta Madrassah summarily dismissed the idea, maintaining that the education provided at home was adequate. On the other hand, Syed Ameer Ali stated at the All Indian Muslim Education Conference in 1891 that female education should advance at the same pace as male education. It was in such an ambience that Faizunnessa, the pioneer of Muslim

---

[3] See Meredith Borthwick, *The Changing Role of Women in Bengal 1849–1905* (Princeton, 1984). See also Ghulam Murshid, *The Reluctant Debutante: Response of Bengali Women to Modernization 1849–1905* (Rajshahi, 1983).

[4] Meredith Borthwick, *The Changing Role of Women in Bengal*, Preface, p. xiii.

female education in Bengal, had to proceed. By the early twentieth century, a host of papers and periodicals edited by Muslims which adopted a liberal stand on women's education appeared on the scene. These included the *Mussulman, Nabanoor, Mohammadi, Al-Eslam, Sadhana, Bulbul,* and *Saugat.* These papers not only supported female education, but provided a first platform for the women writers we shall discuss. The question now was not whether women should be educated, but the nature and purpose of their education. These discourses, both orthodox and liberal, played a key role in the emergence of the Muslim *bhadramahila* during the late nineteenth and the early twentieth centuries.

I Learning

From Andarmahal to High School

Traditionally Muslim women received the rudiments of education within the strict privacy of the *andarmahal* (*zenana* or women's quarters). *Sharif* or upper-class Muslim families found it inconceivable that the women of their households should go outside in violation of *purdah*, for any education.

Women would be 'put in purdah' from the age of seven or so, within the *andarmahal*, a state Rokeya referred to as *abarodh* (literally siege), the worst kind of seclusion, tantamount to imprisonment. These *abarodh-basini*s or dwellers in seclusion received some elementary education, mostly of a religious nature if the family had the mind and means for it. *Ustadnis* or female tutors were kept to teach girls how to read the Quran, some Urdu and Persian, and some basic accounting skills, to equip them for their future roles as housewives. Women who grew up in the 1920s and 1930s in Dhaka referred to the 'ustad ammas' and '*mem*-teachers' of their childhood in their interviews with the author. Such instructresses were part of the Dhaka *andarmahal* scene, going from home to home teaching young girls Arabic, Persian and Urdu and in some cases English. Bengali, hitherto discouraged, was just coming into vogue. Bengali Muslim girls of the upper class were taught to recite the Holy Quran and in exceptional cases to read a few primers in

Urdu, the language of the Muslim elite in northern India, mostly concerned with ideal female conduct. Reading and writing of Bengali, the language of Bengal, was discouraged.[5] Elite families (such as the Dhaka Nawabs), in imitation of Victorian England, kept governesses for their girls, who were often skilled in various languages including English, sewing and embroidery, and even horse riding.[6] Of course, this was not representative of average Bengali girls in middle-class families. For the greater part, life behind *abarodh* was stifling, but that it was spoken of as being so was itself a sign of changing times.

Priscilla Chapman in her book, *Hindu Female Education* (London, 1839) was perhaps the only writer who referred to early nineteenth century attempts at the education of Muslim females. In 1822, when the Muslim men of Calcutta city shunned Western education, a Muslim lady of Shyambazar came forward to aid Miss Cook in the latter's campaign for women's education. This lady, whose identity has not been established, went from door to door, like Rokeya a hundred years after her, to recruit girls for the schools she helped set up in Shyambazar, Entally, Janbazar, and Mirzapur.[7] Sporadic efforts were made in Calcutta (and Dhaka) but the schools were short-lived. In 1897, residents of the city set up the Calcutta Girls' Madrassah with the patronage of Murshidabad's Nawab Firdaus Mahal who donated a large sum of money for the Madrassah from her treasury. Isolated incidents of education among Muslim girls are recorded; for instance, about 160 girls, mostly Muslims, studied at the twelve schools conducted by the Ladies' Association (a missionary enterprise) in 1827. The *Bamabodhini Patrika* of May 1896 (no. 376) mentions a Muslim lady, Latifunnessa, who passed the final examination of the Campbell Medical School in 1896, securing the second place among fifty-five students. Little is known

---

[5] Roushan Jahan, in her Introduction to *Inside Seclusion: The Abarodhbasini of Rokeya Sakhawat Hossein* (Dhaka, 1981), p. 3.

[6] Interviews with Mrs Sarwar Murshed and Mrs Aji Sadruddin, descendants of the Dhaka Nawab family, provided information on education for girls in an elite family.

[7] See Benoy Ghose, *Vidyasagar o Bangali Samaj* (Vidyasagar and Bengali Society, Calcutta, 1973).

about her except that she was a resident of Shahzadpur. In 1909, Khujasta Akhter Bano founded the Suhrawardiya Girls' School in Calcutta.

Muslim Suhrid Sammelani

The year 1883 was a memorable year for the women of Bengal, Hindu and Muslim. In Calcutta, Chandramukhi Bose and Kadambini Bose (Ganguly) received their B.A. degrees from Calcutta University — the first Bengali women to obtain that degree. In Dhaka, a group of young male progressives, mostly students of Dhaka College, Abdul Majed, Fazlul Karim, Bazlur Rahim, Hemayetuddin and Abdul Aziz, founded the Muslim Suhrid Sammelani (also known as the Anjuman-i-Ahbabiya-i-Islam). The avowed aim of the Sammelani was the 'regeneration of Muslim society', but in its annual report for 1883 it was stated 'for the time being this association will devote itself to the spread and development of female education in the Muslim community'.[8] The association embarked on a 'liberal' campaign for the education of girls, bearing in mind the community's extreme regard for purdah. It drew up a scheme whereby girls could study the courses for classes I–V at home and take the regular examinations as 'private' candidates. This led to the spread and popularity of modern education in several Muslim homes where girls took advantage of the scheme while remaining in the *antahpur/andarmahal*. A total of twenty-three girls from Dhaka, Barisal, Mymensingh and Calcutta took examinations in Bengali while fourteen appeared in Urdu. However, it is interesting to note that the liberal *bhadralok* of Muslim society found it necessary to preserve the tradition of purdah in their scheme for women's education in the late nineteenth century.

Faizunnessa's Pioneering Work

The credit for being the pioneer in formal education for Muslim women in Bengal goes to Nawab Faizunnessa Chaudhurani

---

[8] Cited by Muntasir Mamun, 'Unis Shatake Purba Banger Sabha Samiti' (The Associations of Nineteenth Century East Bengal), *Dhaka Viswavidyalay Patrika* (December, 1983), p. 101.

(1834?–1903) of Paschimgaon in Comilla. She lived in the post-1857 period in which Muslims turned their back on Western education and retreated into dreams of past glory. Faizunnessa herself, however, realized that there could be no hope for her society without modern education. Born in an aristocratic zamindar family, she spent her childhood behind strict purdah and was educated at home. Though the family spoke in Urdu like most *sharif* families of the time, Faizunnessa through her own efforts and love of knowledge acquired mastery over Bengali, Sanskrit, Urdu and Persian.

At a time when even the liberal reformers, Sir Syed Ahmed Khan in north India and Abdul Lateef in Bengal, hardly thought it necessary for women to acquire education beyond the most rudimentary stage,[9] Faizunnessa foresaw the importance of both Muslim men and women acquiring Western education. With this in view, she took various measures for the spread of education. She established a free Madrassah at her residence in Paschimgaon which today functions as Faizunnessa Degree College. In 1901 she founded an English middle school named after her daughter, Badrunnessa. She also set up primary schools at each of her administrative centres (*kacharis*) in her estate. Perhaps her single greatest achievement was the establishment of an English-medium school for girls in 1873, several decades before Rokeya founded the Sakhawat Memorial in Calcutta in 1911. The Faizunnessa Girls' Pilot High School was designed for *pardanashin* girls. Faizunnessa was assisted in her efforts by Kalicharan De, the famous Brahmo leader of Comilla. A hostel was subsequently added to the school. Many women who later became eminent studied in this school, though the initial response from the Muslim community was lukewarm. It was later taken up by the government and converted into a high school.[10] The school was founded a few years prior to the establishment of the Eden Female School in Dhaka. Faizunnessa

---

[9] Gail Minault, 'Sayyid Mumtaz Ali and Huquq-i-Niswan', *Modern Asian Studies* (Cambridge, April 1990).

[10] For more details about Faizunnessa, see Abdul Quddus, Preface to *Rupjalal* (Dhaka, 1984), and Moniruzzaman, *Faizunnessa Chaudhurani* (Dhaka, 1988).

may therefore be regarded as the pioneer in Muslim women's education in Bengal.

In 1889 this unusual lady received the title of Nawab from Queen Victoria for the administration of her estates, and her philanthropy. Douglas, the Magistrate of Comilla, impressed by Faizunnessa, recommended her to the Queen for a title. The award of the title Nawab to a Muslim Lady in those times created quite a stir and was flashed in contemporary newspapers.[11]

We do not know many details about Faizunnessa's life, although she has added a short autobiographical note to her book, *Rupjalal*. In addition there is a diary, which gives us an idea of her daily routine, her business affairs and household chores. She describes a happy childhood, divided between play and study. When she had reached adolescence, Mahamud Ghazi Chaudhuri, a distant relative who was already married, caught a glimpse of her and fell in love with her. After Faizunnessa's father died, her mother finally yielded to Mahamud Ghazi's entreaties for marriage. Faizunnessa describes the first few years of her marriage as being happy and her husband as being extremely devoted.[12] She believed that, subsequently, her husband's first wife used black magic to win back Mahamud Ghazi's heart and to make him hate her. In any case, Faizunnessa vowed never to set eyes on her husband again, returned to her paternal home to assume responsibility of the estates and devoted her life to philanthropy, social work, piety and study. She was an efficient administrator, though her public dealings were always conducted behind a curtain, observing purdah in its strictest and literal sense.

The Age of Rokeya

The first woman to launch a systematic and uncompromising campaign for women's education was Rokeya Sakhawat Hossein (1880–1932). She was born into a zamindar's family in Payrabad, Rangpur. A pioneer of the women's movement in Bengal, she was a writer, educationist, social worker, and a visionary who worked unceasingly for female education which she considered the first

---

[11] Abdul Quddus, *Rupjalal* (Preface), pp. 15–16.
[12] Faizunnessa Chaudhurani, *Rupjalal* (Preface, Dhaka, 1984).

pre-requisite for emancipation. Said Abdul Mannan in a glowing tribute: 'She was the forerunner of our modern sensibility and contemporary awareness, of our emancipated intellect, not just the pioneer of the women's movement alone . . . a finest bloom of the Awakening in Bengal.[13]

Rokeya's abiding contribution was in the sphere of education:

> She was too well-read and observant to overlook the fact that women in patriarchal societies are exploited and oppressed but her immediate deep concern was for the group to which she belonged and which she knew best, Bengali Muslim women.[14]

The separation between the public world of men (the *bahir*), and the private world of women (the *ghar*) was particularly sharp in the Muslim community and maintained by the ideology and practice of purdah or *abarodh* (strict seclusion). Rokeya was put in purdah from the age of five:

> From the age of five I had to observe purdah and had to conceal myself even from women. Men were in any case not allowed free entry into the *antahpur* (inner house). I was too young to understand what all the fuss was about, yet I would have to conceal myself and observe strict purdah.[15]

The idea of going to school was out of the question. Rokeya reminisces:

> I never entered the precincts of a girls' school or college in my childhood. What little I have learnt was due to my older brother's love and care for my education . . . . Other relatives taunted us, but neither my brother nor I paid any heed to this.[16]

Shamsunnahar Mahmud, Rokeya's first biographer, paints a graphic picture of the scene:

---

[13] Abdul Mannan Syed, *Begum Rokeya* (Foreword, Dhaka, 1983).

[14] Roushan Jahan, *Inside Seclusion*, p. 6.

[15] Rokeya S. Hossein, *Abarodhbasini* (Episode no. 23), *Rokeya Rachanabali* (The Collected Works of Rokeya, Dhaka, 1967).

[16] Rokeya S. Hossein, cited by Shamsunnahar Mahmud in *Rokeya Jibani* (The Life of Rokeya, Dhaka, 1987), p. 39.

Their father disapproved highly of Rokeya's learning English or Bengali. Brother and sister would wait for nightfall . . . The two would gather their books, and as darkness engulfed the world, a dim light would be lit in the youngsters' rooms. By candlelight the brother taught while the sister drank deep at the fountain of knowledge.[17]

Rokeya learnt Bengali from her older sister, Karimunnessa, and English from her husband, Sakhawat Hossein. Rokeya dedicated volume II of her book *Motichoor* to Karimunnessa, who was herself a poet though her poetry never saw the light of day.

Rokeya's workplace was Calcutta where she founded the Sakhawat Memorial Girls' School in 1911. This was considered to be her signal achievement because the school was an integral part of her ceaseless campaign for the education of Muslim girls and their journey out of *abarodh*. No one before or after her has worked so tirelessly for the cause. At first, the medium of instruction was Urdu. (Rokeya lamented the fact that she could not start a Bengali section even fourteen years after the founding of her school.) This reflects the pro-Urdu culture of the *sharif* (upper or aristocratic) families of Bengal at the time. The scholars, a handful in number, sat on the floor huddled together in one classroom.[18] Their first formal lessons under the syllabus of the school were conducted in Urdu. Given that Bengali was not part of the syllabus, one is confronted here with the problematic of the Bengali Muslim identity. Several of the women writers themselves were acutely aware of it and discussed it at length, sometimes as part of the contemporary debate on the matter. At other times, the question was tangentially touched upon.

The most engrossing aspect of the discourse was the question of the Bengali language. The question had vexed Bengali Muslims from the medieval period since the sixteenth century. In 1800, the British founded a college at Fort William for the purpose of imparting training to British civilians. In the first fifty years of the

---

[17] Shamsunnahar Mahmud, ibid., p. 38.
[18] Interview taken in Dhaka (1991), of Mrs Aktarunnessa (b. 1905), one among the first batch of students at Sakhawat Memorial School.

College, 177 local teachers and other staff were employed and, of these, 117 happened to be Muslim. Yet all of them cultivated Urdu, Arabic or Persian and wrote in these languages. Bengali was looked upon as the language of the 'others' — the Hindus. The upper-class Persianized *'Shurafa'* used Urdu or Persian in north India, the centre of Muslim culture in India. The *sharif* (or *ashraf*) of Bengal emulated them and looked down on the bulk of the Muslims, lower-class in origin and status, who spoke and wrote in Bengali.

But, as the nineteenth century unfolded, and the socio-economic, educational and cultural world of Bengal responded to the forces of modernization, the Bengali Muslims' attitude regarding the language question changed. The new educated middle class came forward to advocate the use of Bengali. The elite retreated into residual pockets of Persianized culture, dreaming of vanished glory. So it was that Mir Mosharraf Hossain, Kaikobad, Nausher Ali Khan Yusufzai, Ismail Hussain Shirazi, Nojibur Rahman, Kazi Emdadul Huq, and others started their literary careers in chaste Bengali, reminiscent of Bankim and Vidyasagar.

The women writing in this period followed in their footsteps. Nawab Faizunnessa Chaudhurani furnishes a clear example of this dualism in the Bengal Muslim psyche. Although she was born into a *'sharif'* landed family which cultivated Urdu, this remarkable woman taught herself Bengali and her two books were written in that language. What urged Faizunnessa to learn and express herself in the language of the common people, a language that had been shunned by her community even in her own generation? Faizunnessa provides no clue; she does not describe her transition to Bengali, or the circumstances which attended this, as Rokeya briefly did, some decades later.

Rokeya, whose circumstances were somewhat similar to those of Faizunnessa, addressed the issue of learning Bengali more directly and poignantly. In her preface to *Motichoor*, she narrates how shocked her father was when he discovered his elder daughter, Karimunnessa, reading a Bengali book. Such things were forbidden in the Saber household. Later, however, Rokeya's father's attitude relaxed considerably. Rokeya returned to this problem in her writings, time and again. In *Niriha Bangali* (The Docile Bengalee), written in 1903 she chose the national character of the Bengalee as the target of her sarcasm and wit. In a note added to this essay in 1908 Rokeya paid a tribute to Bengali youth, lauding their courage. This note was written in the wake of the Swadeshi Movement which followed the partition of Bengal in 1905. It is significant that Rokeya does not adopt the viewpoint of the Muslim League, which had already been established. Although Rokeya's school was an Urdu-medium one, she lamented the fact in the dedication to her sister at the beginning of *Motichoor* vol. II (1921). She ardently wished to set up a Bengali-medium section at Sakhawat, but as late as 1927, of the 114 girls at the school, only two were Bengali-speaking. What does this indicate? The Muslim elite of Calcutta still favoured a pan-Islamic, pro-Urdu culture. Those who had acquired progressive ideas regarding the education of girls, whether they belonged to the old landed gentry or to the new professional middle-class, were still wary of stressing their Bengali identity. Perhaps the mofussil elite was quicker to imbibe the spirit of the emergent middle-class Bengali Muslim culture.

Rokeya's situation perhaps best illustrates the ambivalence in cultural identity that plagues Bengal Muslims down to this day. Shaista Ikramullah (b. 1915) lived in the same city and era as Rokeya. Her autobiography, *From Purdah to Parliament*, describes her life from her upbringing in a conservative elite family of Calcutta to her entry in public life after the benefit of a higher education. Yet she does not once mention Rokeya, who ran her school, the Anjuman-i-Khawmateen-i-Islam, just around the corner from Mrs Ikramullah's home. The latter was a true representative of the Persianized Calcutta Muslim elite.

Other Bengali Muslim literary women of Rokeya's generation and those of a few decades later testify to some element of Urdu culture in their background. They all knew how to read the Koran in Arabic and were able to speak Urdu, but they wrote in Bengali — from Nurunnessa to Mahmuda Khatun or Sufia Kamal. There was no question of writing in Urdu, even if their mothers had used it. For Faizunnessa it was almost revolutionary to use Bengali; for Mahmuda Khatun or Sufia Kamal it was only natural. They discovered that a world of transformed cultural ethos was awaiting them and they themselves helped to mould it. The women's decision to write in Bengali reflected a historically inevitable as well as a conscious process of cultural change.

Rokeya had to go from door to door, entreating guardians to send their wards to school, guaranteeing security and purdah by offering covered transport for the girls. Students recall the phaeton (horse-drawn carriage) and motor-bus which took them to school. The school went a long way in legitimizing formal education for girls. At the Bengal Women's Education Conference in 1926 Rokeya delivered the presidential address:

> The opponents of female education say that women will become wanton and unruly. Fie! They call themselves Muslims and yet go against the basic tenet of Islam which gives women an equal right to education. If men are not led astray once educated, why should women?[19]

Rokeya's bold formulation of women's emancipation as laid down in her numerous writings, specially in *'Stree Jatir Abanati'* (The Degraded Condition of Women) and *'Ardhangi'* (His Other Half)[20] is as relevant now, sixty years after her death. To her, women's emancipation meant the establishment of equal rights for women in the educational, economic and political spheres. That alone would ensure a just society where men and women could work side by side in harmony, like 'the two wheels of a cart'. 'Rokeya is hailed as the pioneer of Muslim women's awakening because no one before her raised the issue of gender exploitation and women's rights in such clear terms'.[21]

It was difficult at first to get Muslim girls to break the barriers of *abarodh* and attend their school, and just as difficult to get teachers. Initially most teachers were non-Muslims. Later Rokeya found able co-workers in Shamsunnahar Mahmud (1908–64), Sara Taifur (1888–1971), Mamlukul Fatema Khanam (1894–1957), Kaniz Sabzewari and Anwara Bahar (1919–87). They all worked

---

[19] Cited in Maleka Begum, *Banglar Nari*, p. 83.
[20] *Rokeya Rachanabali*, pp. 17–31 and 35–44.
[21] Maleka Begum, *Banglar Nari*, p. 85.

untiringly to help the Sakhawat School stand on its feet during the first phase of the Muslim *nari jagaran*.

The school had a host of well-wishers, male and female, though orthodox opinion did its best to discredit Rokeya's efforts and throw aspersions on the women who attended the school. However, men and women from the Brahmo, Hindu and Muslim communities from all over India congratulated Rokeya and lent her support. Liberal dailies and periodicals such as the *Mussulman*, and *Amrita Bazar Patrika*, *Mohammadi*, *Saugat*, and even *Al-Eslam* supported the cause of women's education.

Rokeya can be said to follow in the tradition of the great Bengali reformers, Rammohan Roy and Ishwar Chandra Vidyasagar. In the words of Abdul Mannan Syed:

> Pragmatism and secularism in place of spiritualism, individualism in place of emotionalism, a spirit of critical enquiry in place of unquestioning acceptance of tradition and authority—Rokeya was an epitome of these renaissance traits.[22]

Following in Rokeya's footsteps, in a manner of speaking, was Shamsunnahar Mahmud, a writer, educationist, teacher, social worker and, later, a parliamentarian in East Pakistan. She was born in an enlightened family of Noakhali, being related on her father's side to Fazlul Karim, one of the first Muslim graduates of Bengal. Her maternal grandfather, Maulana Abdul Aziz, was one of the founding members of the Muslim Suhrid Sammelani. Nonetheless, her childhood was spent in the strictest purdah in Chittagong and like Rokeya she was an *abarodhbasini*. The difference was that she persevered with her formal education and successfully acquired a number of degrees. At the age of nine she was taken out of Dr Khastagir's Girls' School in Chittagong in order to observe purdah. Nahar never forgot the uprooting. In her reminiscences of her schooldays she says:

> What a vast institution, and how large the number of students. And of these only three or four were Muslims, no more.... The daughters of many illustrious families—Amiyamakha, the elder

[22] Abdul Mannan Syed, *Begum Rokeya*, p. 52.

sister of the revolutionary Kalpana Dutta, and the sister of Deshpriya Jotindramohan Sen, studied there.... I had gone up to class VI when the issue of purdah was brought up. At the age of nine ... I was taken out of school so that purdah would not be violated.[23]

Nahar started her studies under a male Hindu tutor at home. She describes the thick curtain that separated her from her tutor, a measure taken by the family to seclude her. Shamsunnahar passed her Matriculation Examination with excellent marks and steeled herself for the next phase of her personal struggle — permission to join college. The poet, Nazrul Islam, wrote Shamsunnahar a letter of consolation:

> I do not know what is to become of you.... I suspect that whoever your guardian may be, he cannot be touched by the light of the twentieth century enlightenment. Perhaps that is why you have to plead and weep to procure permission to go to college.[24]

Shamsunnahar finally did get admitted to the Diocesan College in Calcutta. The figure of the *burqa*-clad Muslim housewife-student (she had been married in the meantime) was often a source of amusement for the relatively more emancipated Brahmo and Hindu women in that exclusive institution. However, Shamsunnahar surprised everybody by securing the twentieth place among all the students who had appeared for the Intermediate of Arts examination under Calcutta University in 1928. She obtained her Bachelor's degree with distinction in 1932 and was accorded a civic reception by Rokeya's Anjuman-i-Khawmateen-i-Islam the same year. In her address Rokeya said:

> We are assembled here on the occasion of Nahar's passing her

---

[23] Shamsunnahar Mahmud, *'Ami Jakhan Chhatri Chhilam'* (When I was a Student), *Smriti Barshabani*, Calcutta, 10th year, 1357 BS, cited in Shahida Parveen, *Begum Shamsun Nahar Mahmud o Samakalin Nari Samajer Agragati* (Begum Shamsun Nahar Mahmud and the Progress of Contemporary Muslim Women), unpublished M. Phil thesis, Rajshahi University, 1986.
[24] Shamsunnahar Mahmud, *Nazrulke Jemon Dekhechi* (Nazrul As I Saw Him, Calcutta, 1958), p. 80, cited by Shahida Parveen, ibid., p. 22.

B.A. .... This is an honour for all of us women .... I pray that more women follow Nahar's footsteps.[25]

At the initiative of A.K. Fazlul Huq, the Chief Minister of Bengal at the time, Lady Brabourne College was set up in Calcutta in 1939 for the education of Muslim girls. Shamsunnahar accepted the post of teacher in Bengali at the College in the same year. In 1942, even as World War II raged and Bengal was in the throes of the Quit India Movement, Shamsunnahar appeared for the Masters' examination as a Private candidate: 'I was writing away — while the activists were engaged in confrontation with the police downstairs. Tremors went through the University building intermittently as the activists chanted their slogans'.[26]

Shamsunnahar acknowledges her deep debt to Kazi Nazrul Islam as a source of inspiration. In her reminiscences she quotes from a letter he wrote to her on the condition of women in Bengal:

> The fate of our countrywomen is indeed lamentable. I have seen so many women of great promise wasted under the cares heaped on them by society and by the household. They are imprisoned by the demands of the household as if by an impregnable wall. That wall will never crumble unless women themselves revolt. Where is that brave woman who will launch the attack? Her destiny beckons.[27]

Dhaka: Eden Girls' School and College

Meanwhile, Dhaka had been following its own course of modernization and reform. The first formal English-medium school was the Eden Female School named after Bengal's Lieutenant-Governor. Dates for the school's founding vary. The school was later merged with Kamrunnessa, and has no independent existence now. According to one source, the Brahmo leader Brajasundar Mitra (who founded girls' schools in his village Shimuliya in 1864, and

---

[25] Cited by Anwara Bahar Chowdhury, *Shamsunnahar Mahmud* (Dhaka, 1987), p. 20.
[26] Shamsunnahar Mahmud, *'Ami Jakhan Chhatri Chhilam'*.
[27] Kazi Nazrul Islam, cited by Anwara Bahar Chowdhury, *Shamsunnahar Mahmud*, p. 28.

another in Comilla) set up the Eden Female School in 1875.[28] Hashmat Ara in one article, cites 1878 as the year in which Ashley Eden established a Middle Vernacular school for girls in Dhaka.[29] She says in another article: 'In 1880 a girls' school was founded in Lakshmibazar (in old Dhaka) and named after the then Lt. Governor, Sir Ashley Eden. This was the first 'female' school for girls in the region'.[30]

She also observes that on her visits to the schools of old Dhaka she found no documents had been preserved.

The *Bamabodhini Patrika* of March 1880 (no. 182), in a discussion on female education, stated that out of 153 students at Eden in 1880, only one was a Muslim. In 1911 the number of Muslim girls rose to 25, while there were 209 Hindus, eight Christians, one Parsee, one Eurasian.[31]

Akhtar Imam (b. 1919), an eminent student of Eden Girls' School and College, in her memoirs *Eden Theke Bethune* (From Eden to Bethune), gives a vivid picture of the Eden School of her times. She traces the story of Eden School, which was drawn along much the same lines as Bethune School in Calcutta, from the 1920s to the close of the 1940s. The school was located at Sadarghat in 'Old Dacca'. Although the British Government thought the Eden School 'miserably housed' and the teaching 'below the proper

---

[28] Mohammad Shamsul Alam, *Rokeya Sakhawat Hossein: Jiban o Sahitya Karma* (The Life and Works of Rokeya Sakhawat Hossein, Dhaka, 1989), p. 61.

[29] Hashmat Ara, 'Itihaser Bandhur Path Periye Dipali Holo Kamrunnessa' (Dipali became Kamrunnessa in History), *Dainik Desh*, June 21, 1989. The year 1878 is also cited by S.M. Ali in 'Education and Culture in Dacca during the last Hundred Years' in Enamul Haq, ed., *Muhammad Shahidullah Felicitation Volume* (Dhaka, 1966).

[30] Hashmat Ara, 'Dipali Bidyalay Je Pradeep Jaliyechhilo' (The Lamp Lighted by the Dipali School), *Dainik Desh*, Jan. 7, 1989. Bengal Education Consultations 1154, September 1878, 135–6, cited in Sharifuddin Ahmed, *Dhaka: A Study in Urban History and Development* (London, 1989), p. 72.

[31] *Report of the Progress of Education, Eastern Bengal and Assam, 1907–1908 to 1911–1912*, vol. 1, p. 95, cited in M.K.U. Molla, 'Women's Education in Early Twentieth Century Bengal', *Bengal Studies*, University of Michigan, East Lansing.

mark', the townspeople certainly looked up to it.[32] Akhtar Imam reminisces:

> There was a rule at Eden which boys' schools did not have. The *Ramayana* and *Mahabharata* were read as texts from the very lower classes. No one minded. We, the Muslim girls, would enjoy the stories of Ram and Ravana, Sita's exile, the battle of Kurukshetra . . . . In writing of those days in Eden, lost forever, the names of so many former Muslim students come to my mind.[33]

Akhtar Imam provides a sizable list (but no dates) of women who studied at Eden in the early part of this century. Many of these women became eminent later and contributed to the women's educational movement in Bengal. They include Altafunnessa, Akhtar Imam's older sister, who did her B.A. from Bethune and worked variously as School Inspectress, Headmistress of Calcutta Female Training School, etc., and Jahanara Haider who passed the Matriculation examination with distinction from Comilla Faizunnessa Girls' High School in 1933 and came to study at Eden College. Jahanara, who observed strict purdah and never forsook the *burqa* (which many other Muslim women had done at that time), later studied English at Bethune. Akhtar Imam refers to herself and Jahanara Haider as the first two Muslim women to graduate with Honours. Rabeya Khatun came from Rajshahi to study at Eden; she later studied at Bethune. She worked as Headmistress at several schools and was the first Principal of the Female Training College at Mymensingh. Khodeja Khatun came from Bogura and made her career as an educationist, retiring as principal of Eden College. Maleka Akhtar Bano studied with Akhtar Imam in school. She was one of the pioneers among Muslim women studying science and later obtained a Ph.D. from the U.K. She worked as professor of Chemistry at Eden Girls' College for many years. The list is long and includes Afsarunnessa, Sitara Begum, Nur Jahan Begum (editor of the weekly *Begum*, the most popular women's journal of the region), Jamshedunnessa, Lutfunnessa Zoha, Zobaida Khatun,

---

[32] M.K.U. Molla, ibid., p. 42.
[33] Akhtar Imam, *Eden theke Bethune* (From Eden to Bethune, Dhaka, 1990), p. 17.

Lulu Bilquis Bano, Laila Arjamand Bano — all of them later built up careers as writers or educationists.

About the role of Eden Girls' school and college, Akhtar Imam comments: 'It would not be wrong to say that many of the Bengali women, who subsequently crossed the barriers of superstition and ignorance were emboldened by the trail-blazing examples of the Muslim women whom I have mentioned.[34]

Akhtar Imam regards Fazilatunnessa Zoha (1905–76) as a model for the women of the time. She made history in 1925 as the first Muslim woman to receive a Bachelor's degree and, subsequently, a Master's degree in mathematics. Fazilatunnessa came from an ordinary family in Tangail, and was self-made. She passed the Matriculation examination from Eden School with flying colours in 1921. After completing her Bachelor's from Bethune College in Calcutta, she came to study Mathematics at Dhaka University which had been founded in 1921. The founding of Dhaka University was a milestone in the educational history of East Bengal. Lila Nag, the revolutionary and pioneer of the women's movement in Dhaka, was the first female student at Dhaka University. Fazilatunnessa was the first Muslim woman to study there. Her result in the M.A. examination in 1927 created a stir in all circles and Nazrul Islam himself wrote a poem in her honour. Nasiruddin, the editor of the progressive periodical *Saugat* (which upheld the cause of women's emancipation and awakening), arranged a reception for Fazilatunnessa in Calcutta, disregarding the opposition put up by the orthodox quarters which did not want a woman to be accorded a 'public' reception. The event described by Nasiruddin in his book *Bangla Sahitye Saugat Jug* (The Saugat Era in Bengali Literature) (Dhaka, 1985) illustrates the difference between the progressive-liberal and conservative-orthodox discourse that had developed in the Muslim community. Fazilatunnessa also chose education for a career. She was the head of the Department of Mathematics at Bethune College in Calcutta, and later its Vice-Principal till 1947. 'It was a rare honour for a Muslim woman to become a vice-principal in a premier educational institution in those

---

[34] Akhtar Imam, ibid., p. 23.

days.'³⁵ In 1947, her family opted for Pakistan and Fazilatunnessa came to Dhaka and took charge of Eden College as its principal.

Daulatunnessa Khatun (1918–?) had a career somewhat different from all the other women mentioned. Married at a very early age, she went to Eden Girls' School till 1930 at which point she had to join her husband's family in Gaibandha. Daulatunnessa, however, pursued her studies in private and ultimately obtained the B.A. degree. She was one of the few Muslim women to take part in the national movement against the British. Few Muslim women were able to do so. Daulatunnessa organized women's *samitis* (associations) in Gaibandha and these carried on the work of Gandhi and the Civil Disobedience Movement in remote villages of Bengal. Just at age fourteen, she had decided it was her mission to work among the women of rural Bengal. Her oratorical skills drew crowds. Her achievement was that she carried the message of nationalism and political issues into the Muslim *andarmahal.*

Lila Nag and Fazilatunnessa paved the way for women entrants to Dhaka University. Koru Kona Gupta who joined the Department of History in 1935 was the first woman to be appointed as teacher at Dhaka University. By the close of the 1930s middle class Muslim families were sending their female wards to educational institutions. The *bhadramahila* was coming into her own. The obstacles in her way had not vanished, although they were not the same as in the days of Rokeya. At least some of the women had come a long way from the time when a thick curtain separated Shamsunnahar from her male tutor in the precincts of her own home!

Dipali Sangha becomes Kamrunnessa

The story of Dhaka's educational history will not be complete without a recapitulation of Lila Nag's activities through the Dipali Sangha.³⁶ Eden School was an 'elite' institution where the medium

---

³⁵ Akhtar Imam, ibid., p. 37.
³⁶ For an account of Lila Nag's contribution, see Maleka Begum, 'Dhaka Women in Political Struggle', paper read at Seminar on 'Dhaka: Past, Present, Future', at the Asiatic Society (Dhaka, 1989), and Maleka Begum, *Banglar Nari Andolan.*

of instruction was English, and the principals British. By the second decade of the twentieth century, India had a moderate nationalist as well as a more clandestine 'terrorist' movement aimed at the overthrow of the British Raj. The Hindu/Brahmo section of Bengal took the lead in these movements while the majority of Muslims, lagging behind in the race for education and government jobs, kept a cautious distance, participating but occasionally. However, the national movement had co-opted the women's movement in Bengal, and this had created a new set of attitudes which sought to establish more nationalistic modes of education.

In 1905 the Swadeshi movement was launched to protest against the partition of Bengal. Secret revolutionary societies were formed. By the 1920s they were extremely active. In Dhaka, members of revolutionary societies, such as the Anusilan Samiti and Jugantar Samiti, turned their attention to the state of female education. There was practically no school for girls during the period, save Eden which, they felt, adhered to British ideals and interests. 'Nationalist Hindu/Brahmo and middle class families did not get much opportunity to send their girls to these schools.'[37]

Under these circumstances, Lila Nag, with the help of her co-activists, established four girls' schools during the years 1920–8. They were Dipali 1, renamed Kamrunnessa Girls' High School; Dipali 2, the present day Banglabazar Girls' High School; Nari Shiksha Mandir, the present day Sher-e-Bangla Girls' School; and Purana Paltan Girls' School.

Dipali School 1 was originally founded some time before 1924. Lila Nag realized the urgent need for a Muslim girls' school and she helped to transform it into Kamrunnessa Girls' High School, named after one of the wives of Khwaja Ahsanulla, Nawab of Dhaka. Kamrunnessa's daughter, Aktar Bano, separated from her husband, lived independently, looking after her own estates. A Hindu lawyer (probably called Jogesh Chandra) was her trusted adviser and friend. On his untimely death in an accident, Aktar Bano donated some land to the Ramakrishna Mission for a temple and also some land to the Dipali Sangha for a school to be named

[37] Hashmat Ara, 'Itihaser Bandhur'.

after her mother. Thus the Kamrunnessa Girls' High School came into being in 1924. This was, however, over fifty years after Nawab Faizunnessa had founded her girls' school in Comilla, in 1873.

Educational Statistics

Census figures for the year 1881 reveal that the number of female students at the primary level during 1881-2 was around 17,000 in Bengal, of whom 8.9 per cent were Muslim.[38] The figure rose to almost 58,000 in 1901-2 of whom 10.9 per cent were Muslim. In 1931-2 the number increased to 5,35,000 of whom an amazing 56.5 per cent were again Muslim. The attendance of Muslim girls was greater at the primary level but declined steadily at the middle and higher levels. During the period under review, Muslim girls in some areas had access to traditional educational institutions such as *maktabs*. These mainly imparted religious education. From the late nineteenth century onwards there was a move towards growing secularization of the curricula at these schools, initiated by the government. But the whole process of modernization seemed to favour the growth of secular, government-patronized or assisted schools drawn along western lines which often imparted education in English.[39]

Before 1906 there were three high schools for girls in East Bengal: Eden in Dhaka, Khastagir in Chittagong and Alexander in Mymensingh. Official records, however, declared that the state of education in this region was deplorable.[40]

Bethune School did not admit Muslim girls as late as 1895.[41] The traditional obstacles to female education still persisted —

---

[38] Shamsunnahar Mahmud in 'Muslim Bange Stree Shiksha' (Women's Education in Muslim Bengal), *Monthly Mohammadi*, 14th year, 1st issue, 1347 BS.

[39] See Kazi Shahidullah, *Patshalas into Schools* (Calcutta, 1987).

[40] For details on female education in Bengal in the early 20th century, see M.K.U. Molla, 'Women's Education', and Shila Bose, *'Rajnaitik Patabhumikay Banglay Muslim Narishikshar Bikas* (The Progress of the Education of Muslim Women in the Context of Bengal Politics), 1905-1917', *Aitihasik*, no. 2 (April 1988).

[41] Maleka Begum, *Banglar Nari Andolan*, p. 47.

purdah, early marriage, lack of material facilities and government patronage, the rigid orthodoxy of the Muslims compared to the Hindu and Brahmo communities, and the lack of trained female teachers.

Educational schemes for Muslim women received fresh impetus after the partition of Bengal in 1905, due both to increased government patronage and to a heightened awareness within the community.[42] 'The new provincial government wanted to do all in its power to encourage female education by affording guidance and assistance on practical lines.'[43]

Distinguished persons such as Nawab Salimullah, Nawab Ali Chowdhury and Rai Dulal Chandra Dev, were invited to participate in committees on female education. Whereas in 1901–2 the number of female students in East Bengal was 5,564, in 1906–7 the figure rose to 16,468.[44] The enrolment at Eden increased from 125 in 1904 to 244 in 1911, and at Alexander from 100 to 170. In 1905 there were three English middle schools in the province, none aided by the government. By 1911 the province had five English middle schools, one being the Faizunnessa Girls' School in Comilla.

Shamsunnahar writing in 1940 thought that the future was not bleak and she refers to the early decades as a 'moment of Muslim women's awakening.'[45]

II Creativity

The Early Period

Most of the Muslim *bhadramahilas* mentioned above took up the pen at some point of time. They composed poems with romantic themes, such as moonlight in a garden, the summer breeze, or a mother's tenderness. Most wrote stories of romance and betrayal

---
[42] For the effects of partition on female education, see M.K.U. Molla, 'Women's Education', and Shila Bose, *'Rajnaitik Patabhumikay'*.
[43] M.K.U. Molla, 'Women's Education', p. 42.
[44] Shila Bose, *'Rajnaitik Patabhumikay'*, p. 58.
[45] Shamsunnahar Mahmud, *'Muslim Bange'*, p. 55.

or of domestic strife and joy, turned out the occasional novel, and narrated the life stories of great men and women. They also expressed their views on the burning issues of their day and analysed social problems, especially purdah and *abarodh*, women's education, and occasionally, the problem of the Bengali Muslim identity. Like that of the Brahmo and Hindu women who preceded them, the literature left behind by Bengali Muslim women of the early twentieth century provides a wealth of fascinating material for scholars attempting a historical reconstruction of the period under review.

There have been a few studies of the writings of Bengali Muslim women but they are restricted to the field of literary criticism. To date there has not been any attempt at analysing their creative work in the context of the emergence of the Muslim *bhadramahila*.[46] I have selected, in this paper, an overview of representative literary works which reveal the changing emphases in women's issues. The *bhadramahilas* often wrote in more than one genre. Rokeya was an essayist as well as a writer of stories, just as Razia was both a poet and an essayist. It is difficult for anyone at the end of the twentieth century who studies the lives of the *bhadramahilas* of eighty years ago to appreciate the courage required to give public expression to their thoughts and feelings. Yet the story of the emergence of the *bhadramahilas* can come alive only if this is borne in mind.

The first woman to write in modern prose was Bibi Taherunnessa. Her essay in the form of a long letter, *Bamaganer Rachana*, appeared in the *Bamabodhini Patrika* (February-March, 1864). In her essay, Taherunnessa pleads for women's education. Not much is known about her except that she was a student of the Boda Girls' School in Calcutta. In its June issue of 1897, the *Bamabodhini Patrika* published a poem by a Muslim lady, Latifunnessa, who had passed the examination of the Campbell Medical School. The poem

---

[46] Prof. Mujeer Uddin, *Bangla Sahitye Muslim Mahila* (Muslim Women in Bengali Literature, Dhaka, 1967); Begum Jahan Ara, *Bangla Sahitye Lekhikader Abadan* (The Contribution of Women Writers to Bengali Literature, Dhaka, 1987); Anisuzzaman, *Muslim Manosh o Bangla Sahitya* (The Muslim Mind and Bengali Literature, Dhaka, 1964).

was titled *Bangiya Muslim Mahilader Prati* (To the Muslim Ladies of Bengal).

However, the credit for being the first Bengali Muslim woman in modern times to write a full-length book goes to Nawab Faizunnessa Chaudhurani, the author of *Rupjalal*. The dilemma of Urdu and Bengali as the medium of expression, one perceived to be more attuned to 'Islamic' culture than the other, was the source of the problem: of Bengali Muslim identity. It is relevant that Urdu was considered the more appropriate vehicle of expression for the *sharif* families but the women of those very families chose to articulate their thoughts in Bengali.

Faizunnessa's *Rupjalal*, her only extant literary work, was published from Dhaka in 1876. The work which one may call a proto-novel of sorts is beginning to receive attention from scholars of Bengali literature, but is yet to be appraised by social scientists. *Rupjalal* is a remarkable, hybrid picture of an age in transition; of a sensibility poised between the medieval *punthi* mentality and the modern prose one. Most scholars refer to it as a *kabya* or long poem. The greater part of it is written in sing-song *punthi* style; this is interspersed by passages written in chaste prose reminiscent of Bankimchandra Chatterjee. The book revolves around the romantic yearning of Prince Jalal for Princess Rupbano. A host of characters are invoked — djinns, fairies, ogres, saints, gods, satan, and ordinary mortals. The sweep is epic and has the flavour of the Islamic-Hindu syncretic ethos of rural Bengal. The book is considered semi-autobiographical. Its tone and temper differs distinctly from the literary tradition of the future *bhadramahilas* who, fed on Bankimchandra Chatterjee, Sarat Chandra Chatterjee, Tagore, Mir and other 'modern' writers, would not have allowed themselves the frankly sexual imagery and allusions in *Rupjalal*.[47]

Azizunnessa was probably the first woman whose writing was published in a periodical, *Islam Pracharak*, edited by a Muslim. In its seventh or eighth issue of 1902, *Pracharak* published Azizunnessa's poem, *Hamd-Ishwar prashasti* (Hymn in Praise of God). She

---

[47] Cf. Rokeya's *Padmarag*, Akhtar Mahal's *Niyantrita* or Fatema Khanam's *Dor*. The women depicted are very chaste and although gender oppression is often discussed, sexuality is rarely mentioned.

also translated Oliver Goldsmith's *The Hermit* into Bengali in 1884.[48]

Khairunnessa (1870?–1912) wrote around the same time as Azizunnessa. Her essays appeared in *Nobonoor*. In 1904 she published an essay *'Amader Shikshar Antarai'* (The Impediments to Our Education), and in 1905 a piece entitled *'Swadesh Anurag'* (Love for the Homeland). In *Swadesh*, she appealed to women to boycott foreign goods in support of the Swadeshi Movement. Her *Satir Patibhakti* (The Devotion of a Chaste Wife) was a manual for women, listing the duties of a good wife. Statistics on its popularity are not readily available; further research might indicate the importance of the book in the didactic discourse aimed at women in the early part of the twentieth century. Khairunnessa was probably the first of the early women writers to formulate her ideas on social and political issues at some length.

Although all the women writers we discuss came from prosperous homes, not all of them lived in the urban centres of liberal influence. Mossamat Sohifa Bano (1850?–1926) of Sylhet pursued a quiet literary career in a semi-rural moffussil atmosphere, far from the din and clamour of Dhaka and Calcutta.

Social Critics: Rokeya, Shamsunnahar, Razia

Before Faizunnessa's works were discovered, Rokeya Sakhawat Hossein was usually hailed as the first Muslim female writer of modern times. Rokeya started her literary career in 1901 when her essay *'Pipasha'* (The Thirst) appeared in *Nabaprabha*. Her next piece *'Alankar na Badge of Slavery'* (Jewellery or Badge of Slavery) created a stir. It was published in the journal *Mahila* (1310 B.S./1903) edited by Girish Chandra Sen from Calcutta. There was almost no arena of literature where Rokeya's pen did not venture — poetry, short story, satire, essay, novel or fantasy. Writing in the age of Tagore, if her work lacked in creativity, it was compensated by wit, clarity and an ever present dedication to the cause of women. I shall discuss in detail a few selected passages from a cross-section of her

---

[48] Anisuzzaman, *Muslim Banglar Samayik Patra* (Periodicals in Muslim Bengal, Dhaka, 1969), p. 39.

work — relating, for instance, to the *bhadralok*, to the formulation of Rokeya's feminist theory, to domestic ideology, and to the birth of the 'new woman'.[49]

To begin with, let us consider Rokeya's satirical poem 'Appeal' (published in 1922), written at a moment when the *bhadralok* were alarmed by the prospect of the British government recalling their titles (such as, Khan Bahadur, Rai Bahadur etc.) in the wake of the anti-government nationalist activities. Here Rokeya was at her witty, sarcastic best. In the poem, the Bengali *bhadraloks* gather to draw up an appeal to the government not to cancel their titles by decree:

> Some enjoy vast estates most
> And some weighty titles boast
> O' let us all gather round
> And appeal to the exalted Crown—
> Better the pain of death by far
> Better by many times we vouch
> But 'titles' alas, we cannot live without . . .
> Some British paper has decreed
> Cut the titles, off with the tails
> Of all the stupefied 'bhadro' males of Bengal
> That is what they deserve, no doubt.[50]

This was a much discussed poem at the time of its publication and was written at a particular political moment. Rokeya satirizes the 'moderate' stand taken by '*bhadralok* politicians' at a critical juncture in the history of Bengal.

Though Rokeya's feminism is woven into most of her writings, there are some pieces which are exclusively concerned with the problems of women. Into this category fall '*Stree Jatir Abanati*' (1905), '*Ardhangi*' (1905) and '*Narir Adhikar*' (Women's Rights), her last work, published posthumously.[51] In the remarkable fantasy,

---

[49] For an analysis of Rokeya's literary works see: Motaher Hossain, *Sufi Begum Rokeya: Jiban o Sahitya* (Life and Literature, Dhaka, 1986); Abdul Mannan Syed, *Begum Rokeya*, and M. Shamsul Alam, *Rokeya Sakhawat Hossein: Jiban o Sahitya*.
[50] Abdul Mannan Syed, *Begum Rokeya*, p. 63.
[51] Abdul Mannan Syed, ibid., p. 85.

Sultana's Dream, her only work in English, Rokeya gave full rein to her imagination by depicting 'Ladyland', a realm where women assumed the public role and men stayed indoors. It is hailed as a radical piece of feminist writing though Rokeya herself was not a radical. Rokeya's only novel *'Padmarag'* (1924) is a narration of life in Tarini Bhavan, a sanctuary where women of all creeds have found refuge and live a life of dignity. The contemporary periodical *Samyabadi* in its *Falgun* 1331 B.S. (1925) issue reviewed *Padmarag* and recommended it to 'every man and woman'.

One of the most interesting features of the novel is the moment of renunciation by Ayesha Siddika. When Latif, her husband, asks her to return to him Siddika declines the offer even though this was the moment she had been waiting for. She chooses a life of independence over the longed for but perhaps illusory prospect of domestic bliss with Latif. The scene as described in *Padmarag*:

> Siddika: I had set my goal in life long ago . . . . I understood God did not decree the life of a householder for me.
> Latif: I cannot take this as your last word. Do you have anything against me?
> Siddika: No.
> Latif: Then will you be my wife? Guardian of my home and hearth?
> Siddika: No. You must go your way and I mine.[52]

Latif was quite the Renaissance man — educated, enlightened, romantic — drawn in the image of the Muslim *bhadralok* who was making his appearance on the scene at the turn of the century. Was Siddika quite the 'new woman', the *bhadramahila* reflected in literature? Siddika was indeed partly the new woman, educated, independent, romantic and hard-working, but feminine. Yet her renunciation of domestic bliss went much beyond (perhaps even against) the creed of the *bhadramahila*.

To the *bhadramahila* in fiction and in reality the conjugal home was a cherished goal and its preservation one of her sacred duties. This duty was now no longer to be an oppressive burden imposed

---

[52] Rokeya S. Hossein, *Rokeya Rachonaboli*, p. 459.

by patriarchy, but an integral part of a partnership (matrimony) willingly entered into. This was, at any rate, what the new ideology of the domestic proclaimed. Predictably enough, Siddika, a few pages later, broods over recent events and tells herself that a husband is a wife's most precious asset. But though she refuses to divorce Latif she perseveres in her decision to remain alone. Why did Rokeya resort to this ambivalence in her only novel? Perhaps Siddika's was a rare and lonely choice — a comment on the domestic bliss the *bhadramahila* was offered.

Several of Rokeya's works are concerned with the role of women in the domestic sphere — the family with woman as its guardian. In *Sugrihini* (The Good Housewife), Rokeya emphasizes the domestic role women have to play in society and the need to be equipped for this through proper education which included cooking, nutrition, nursing, chemistry, mathematics, and horticulture. Rokeya often used the 'perfect householder' argument to promote female education and induce parents to send their daughters to her school. In *Griha* (The Home), Rokeya illustrates how though a woman may live in a household and contribute most of the labour required for its upkeep, the home does not belong to her. She has no property rights nor any effective power other than that which is bestowed on her by a considerate male. As such, Rokeya concludes, a majority of women only inhabit their homes; they are in fact 'homeless'.

Shamsunnahar Mahmud grew up in a family which had taken to Western liberal education and government employment very early and had crusaded for women's rights. Her first work, *Punyamayee* (The Virtuous Woman) was published in 1925, when she was only seventeen, and written when she was ten. In a brief introduction to the book, she pays homage to her grandparents who had founded the Muslim Suhrid Sammelani almost forty-five years ago.[53]

Punyamayee contains short biographies of eight great women of the Muslim world who served as role models. Among them were the mystic, Rabeya, the Prophet's daughter, Fatema, and his wives,

---

[53] Shamsunnahar Mahmud, Foreword in *Punyamayee*, cited by Anwara Bahar Chowdhury in *Shamsunnahar Mahmud*, p. 46.

Ayesha and Khadija. *Begum Mahal* (The Queens' Quarters) is another biographical work by Shamsunnahar — it records the lives of great Pathan and Mughal women of medieval India. But Shamsunnahar's most well-known book is her biography of Rokeya Sakhawat Hossein, her mentor and comrade in the crusade for women's education. *Rokeya Jibani* (The Life of Rokeya), the first biography of Rokeya, was published from Calcutta in 1937. In an eloquent passage Shamsunnahar says:

> The name we remember in this dawn of women's awakening is none other than that of Rokeya Sakhawat Hossein . . . . From the late nineteenth century onwards, progressive youths had embarked on a programme for women's education, but the nation truly rose when the call came from within — the call given by Rokeya whose torch burned so bright . . . . Our journey has not crossed its zenith . . . as we advance, our triumphant banner will tip for a moment in her honour.[54]

Shamsunnahar was primarily an educationist and much of her writing is concerned with various aspects of education in Bengal (primary education, Bengali Muslim women's education, etc.). In 1933, Nahar and her brother Habibullah Bahar jointly brought out the progressive periodical *'Bulbul'* from Calcutta.

Razia Khatun Chaudhurani (1907–34), during her brief life, made a name as an essayist, poet and short-story writer. Being married to a politician, Ashrafuddin Ahmed Chowdhury, Razia was perhaps one of the few female writers who had an opportunity to come very close to the politics of the time — the Swadeshi Movement, Khilafat Movement, etc. Razia's political views are reflected in her short story *Sramik*.

All the essays save one, in the slim collected works of Razia Khatun, bear the word 'women' in the title. They deal with the education of Muslim women, women's role in the home and outside, purdah and its perversion *abarodh*, the status of women in Islam, and motherhood. In *Samaje o Grihe Narir Sthan* (Women's Place at Home and in Society), Razia says:

---

[54] Shamsunnahar Mahmud in *Rokeya Jibani*, cited by Anwara B. Chowdhury, ibid., pp. 52–3.

For so long Muslim women suffered all oppression in silence. Today a few are getting education and their eyes have opened .... Ah! It is a wonder that we have managed to survive so far at all! There are societies for prevention of cruelty to animals, the government has laws to hang murderers, and though millions of women like us, are dying slow deaths in the dungeon of *abarodh*, no one turns a glance in this direction.[55]

Like many writers of the time, Razia distinguishes between purdah (modesty in dress and behaviour) and *abarodh*, a patriarchal distortion of purdah which makes women invisible behind the *andarmahal*. This is a 'leitmotif' in the writings of the first half of the twentieth century and recurs often enough to suggest that the purdah-*abarodh* formulation was an intrinsic part of the mental makeup of the typical *bhadramahila*. Rokeya in *Stree Jatir Abanati* and *Ardhangi*, Shamsunnahar in her Preface to *Punyamayee*, Razia Khatun in *Samaje o Grihe Islame Narir Sthan, Purdah o Abarodh*, M. Fatema in *Taruner Dayittwa* (The Responsibility of the Youth), all construct a golden age of Islam in the past when women enjoyed all the rights granted them in their religion. Most of these women glorified women's status in Islam and Razia Khatun goes to the extent of stating that it is the only religion that grants women rights and hence is superior to Christianity or Hinduism. Here she falls short of the secularism Rokeya displayed in her famous attack on religious books. By not going into specifications, she avoided the pitfall of ethnocentricism.[56] The matter is further confounded when one reads a passage such as the one cited below from her short story *Narir Dharma* (Women's Duties). Here Razia depicts the harmful effects of 'modernization' whereby women of the *andarmahal* are forcibly brought out of purdah into the social world of clubs and parties. Mahbub, a government employee with 'misplaced' Western notions of modernity forces his beautiful wife Rowshan to leave

---

[55] Razia Khatun Chaudhurani, *Rachana Sankalan* (Compilation of Essays, Comilla, 1982), pp. 10–14.

[56] Rokeya's frequently quoted passages on famous religious texts, originally printed in '*Amader Abanati*' (Our Degradation), *Nabanoor*, 1904, were expurgated when the essay appeared in book form the next year.

her purdah and mix with his colleagues and their wives. At a party, a senior colleague tries to assault Rowshan. The events that follow are tragic. Rowshan's bitter lament as she replies to Mahbub's letter of divorce:

> I have one thing to say: woman's modesty is above everything. Therefore, sentence her to a dismal death behind *abarodh*, even that is preferable — but do not drag her into a world of animal lust![57]

A similar puritanism may be seen in other women's writings of the period, for instance in Akhtar Mahal's *Niyantrita* (The Controlled One) and Mamlukul Fatema's *Dor* (The Door). Sexuality as a subject was taboo for the *bhadramahilas*. Their writing suggests that most of them felt it was 'liberated' enough to talk of husbands and wives enjoying a full relationship in the sense of participating in household events together, eating together, talking to each other, expecting mutual love and respect, and a wife accompanying her husband wherever his job took him rather than spending years with her mother-in-law. These were measures of great change at that period and had been inconceivable some decades earlier. (A similar process operated in the case of Brahmo *bhadramahilas*, according to Murshid and Borthwick.) Thus, the women who wrote and who were themselves both catalysts and objects of the transformation, were painfully sensitive and alert to the continuously lurking accusation of sexual lapse that might be brought against them. Often, one may infer, the only self-defence available was to take refuge behind an exaggerated puritanism. It was almost as though the price to be paid for stepping into the *bahir* (public space) from the *ghar* (the home) was a deliberate desexualization on the part of the women concerned. We cannot, of course, rule out the use of purdah as a strategy. Rokeya herself wore a *burqa*, and when asked why, she is said to have replied that she would resort to any measure to preserve the school for girls she had founded. I quote a passage from Razia Khatun's *Samaje o Grihe* (Society and Home):

---

[57] Razia K. Chaudhurani, *'Narir Dharmapy'* (Women's Virtues), *Mashik Mohammadi*, 3rd year, no. 1, 1336 BS.

This word *sati* is an illusion. It is applied at random to women, but there is no equivalent word for men, in Bengali, or even in English — the language of that 'highly civilized' race. *Satittva* or chastity and similar expressions have been invented solely for women it seems. Fie on men . . . . Why is it that a man never loses his chastity in the same manner as a woman is said to lose it?[58]

Thus, the *bhadramahilas* expressed a variety of opinions and it is hard to reduce them to a stereotype.

Fiction: Nurunnessa, Akhtar Mahal, Fatema Khanam

Among the women in this generation of writers, Nurunnessa Khatun Bidyabinodini (1892–1975) was probably the most purely literary. She was born into a *sharif* family in Murshidabad district; her father was in government service. Her family placed no obstacles in the path of her quiet pursuit of education within the *andarmahal*. In the preface to her novel *Swapnadrishta* (One Seen in a Dream) she says:

I have never had the experience of sitting on a school bench. Neither have I ever sat in front of a tutor with an open book. To quench my own thirst and curiosity I taught myself some letters of the alphabet and tinkered with a few books on my own.[59]

Nurunnessa must have taught herself well, for her works were widely known. She was married in 1912 to a lawyer from Serampore (in Hooghly), who encouraged her literary activities. Nurunnessa's works include two 'domestic' novels, one historical novel, three novellas and several essays. She was awarded the titles of Bidyabinodini and Sahitya Saraswati (dates not available) by either the Nikhil Bharat Sahitya Sangha, or the Bangiya Sahitya Sammelan it is not known exactly which, for her contribution in the field of literature.[60]

[58] Razia K. Chaudhurani, *Rachana Sankalan*, p. 11.
[59] Nurunnessa Khatun, Foreword, '*Swapnadrishta*', in *Collected Works* (Dhaka, 1970).
[60] The controversy over this is referred to by Rashid al Faruqi, *Nurunnessa Khatun Bidyabinodini* (Dhaka, 1987), p. 85. According to him, *Saugat* in its

Nurunnessa's novels *Swapnadrishta* and *Atmadan* (Self-Sacrifice) were published in 1923 and 1925 respectively. She referred to the first as a 'domestic novel' and to the second as a 'domestic conversation based on real events'. Both novels are set among the emergent middle-class *bhadralok* in Muslim society. Both contain supernatural events that are indispensable to the plot. In *Swapnadrishta*, it is a dream. In *Atmadan*, it is the substitution or sacrifice of one life for another through prayer. Significantly, it is a woman who wins back her brother's life from the grip of death, by giving her own. Did Nurunnessa's work point to some extreme notion of female sacrifice in the ethos around her? The three novellas, *Bhagyachakra* (The Wheel of Destiny), *Bidhilipi* (The Destiny), and *Niyoti* (The Fate), are unusual in that they portray *purbarag* (the first stage of romantic feeling and attraction, according to the ancient Indian taxonomy of the various stages of love and sexual attraction). Also interesting is the fact that the author narrates her stories in a Brahmo, Christian and Muslim setting. This has led her biographer to comment:

> The distinguishing feature of the triad is the depiction of romantic love. This may appear natural in the case of Hindu and Christian communities, but must be deemed unnatural in the case of Muslim society. The reason may well be that Muslim society had not yet been able to shake off the nightmarish shackles of the strict seclusion (*abarodh*) with which their womenfolk were encircled.[61]

In contemporary fiction, there was description of romantic attraction but not of *interaction* between the sexes before marriage. This was a time when romantic love between married couples was a bold idea. Thus fiction made much of indirect contact, through glances, or single words, or a book left behind. In Akhtar Mahal's *Niyantrita*, for example, the story unfolds around the heroine's intense, lifelong love for a distant male relative based on a few

---

Bhadro 1385 BS issue stated that Nurunnessa received the titles from the Nikhil Bharat Sahitya Sangha. Possibly the titles were awarded to her sometime in the 1930s.

[61] Rashid al Faruqi, ibid., p. 38.

The Early Muslim Bhadramahila

glimpses caught of him during childhood. In this context, Nurunnessa's portrayal of pre-marital romantic feelings in her novellas represents a major change in the treatment of male-female interaction.

The concept of courtship and romantic attachment before marriage had filtered down from Victorian England into the culture of Bengal *bhadraloks* towards the end of the nineteenth century.[62] It had found its way into the *weltanschauung* of a segment of the emergent Muslim *bhadralok* and some among them accepted the idea of romantic love, which was reflected in their fiction. The works of Nazrul Islam, for example, reflect the new shift. It was relatively rare in the work of female writers. A passage in Nurunnessa's *Niyoti* is almost a liturgy for the feudal traditional order and a celebration of the new one in which the concept of romantic love is legitimized:

> Alas, proud lady, mistress of such vast estates, come and see this pitiful sight! Litigation, jealousy and hostility may create barriers but nothing can separate the pure and heavenly union of two hearts. Nothing can stand in the way of true love — it is like the swiftest, strongest stream, taking everything in its sweep — divine and limitless.[63]

In the first half of this century 'arranged marriages' were the dominant and, perhaps, the only mode of matrimony. Excepting Fazilatunnessa, it seems that all the women mentioned had marriages arranged for them by their guardians. And yet the idea of romantic love and the happy household was gaining ground. The concept of love rather than duty as a basic ingredient in marriage and home life was new, a part of the emergent ideology of the domestic — manifest in the perfect companion-mother-householder role that the *bhadramahila* set herself.

Nurunnessa was also an essayist though not a prolific one. Like those of her peers, her essays are also devoted to topical issues:

---

[62] Sombuddho Chakravarty, *Unabingsha Shatabdite Bangali Bhadramahila* (The Bengali Gentlewomen of the Nineteenth Century), unpublished Ph.D. thesis, Calcutta University, 1989.

[63] Nurunnessa Khatun, *Niyoti*, cited by Rashid al Faruqi, *Nurunnessa*, p. 47.

women's education, Hindu-Muslim unity, the evils of *abarodh*, and the matter of Bengali Muslim identity. Though never an activist like Rokeya or Shamsunnahar, Nurunnessa always upheld the cause of women's rights in the presidential addresses she had to deliver in various literary conferences and her own writings.

Akhtar Mahal Syeda Khatun (1901–29) was born into a wealthy and enlightened family of Faridpur district in East Bengal. Her brother Mujibur Rahman was one of the first Bengali Muslims to enter the Indian Civil Service. In the short biographical note attached to her book *Niyantrita* it is stated:

> Though she was born into a well-educated family, Akhtar Mahal never had the opportunity to go to school or college. She was taught some Urdu, Arabic and Bengali by a house-tutor.... But her thirst for knowledge was unbounded.... Her extreme passion for books *was considered a sort of madness by the people around her*.[64]

Akhtar Mahal was married in 1913 to the son of a respectable family in Noakhali. Though the education of girls was not uncommon among her in-laws, the prospect of a daughter-in-law deeply immersed in poetry and writing was not looked upon with favour. She continued to write secretly.[65]

At a time when merely reading a novel depicting romance and love was deemed immoral by many, Akhtar Mahal tried to grapple with the issue of love and attraction. Her first novel *Niyantrita* (1927–8) describes Ayesha's secret love for a married man. Although no exchange between the two ever takes place Ayesha pronounces the harshest judgement on herself. In the words of the introduction to this work by a male author:

> 'For an unmarried girl to fall in love with a married man — this Ayesha considers an abominable sin, which could result only in suffering and tragedy'.[66]

[64] Afsarunnessa, Biographic note to Akhtar Mahal Syeda Khatun's *Niyantrita* (Dhaka, 1979). Italics are mine.
[65] Afsarunnessa, ibid.
[66] Abdul Kader, Introduction to *Niyantrita*.

In *Maran-Baran*, the heroine realizes that the husband she adored was actually in love with another and had married her only for convenience. The description of a forbidden encounter between him and the other woman is vivid and sensuous, one of the rare passages of this kind found in the *bhadramahilas'* writings in this period. Later, at the sight of a repentant husband, the forgiving heroine is convinced her husband was innocent. 'The temptress Laili had led her angelic husband into a moment of folly.'[67] The writer of the introduction to the book commends the faith, trust and dependence displayed by women towards their husbands in the story.[68]

Mamlukul Fatema Khanam (1894–1957) was born two years after Nurunnessa. Her father was an employee in the Railway Department. She too was educated at home; but unlike many others of her time, Fatema Khanam worked to support herself as a teacher in Calcutta (Sakhawat Memorial) and Dhaka (Posta Girls' School). Married into an orthodox family, she felt compelled to leave her husband in Manikganj and moved to Dhaka with her children where she eked out an existence. Only seven of her short stories survive today in the form of a slim reprint *Saptarshi* (Seven Sages) (1964), and several letters written to Abul Fazal, a young writer and editor of the short-lived literary journal *Tarun-Patra*. Abul Fazal records his great regard for this enlightened and affectionate lady whose house had often served as a meeting-place for the literary sessions of Dhaka's up-and-coming, younger, liberal, Western-educated generation. Abul Fazal considers Fatema Khanam as one of Rokeya's lesser known co-workers.

The theme of romantic love before and during marriage runs through several of Fatema Khanam's short stories, for example, *'Ashray'* (Shelter, 1926), *'Sagar-Sangyog'* (The Meeting of Oceans, 1926), and *Dor* (Bond, 1930). The most finely drawn portrait of *purbarag* occurs in *Ashray*. Both Azad and Hena are drawn in the romantic tradition of the time — pledged to each other for eternity, surmounting all odds till destiny binds them together in the sacred

---

[67] Akhtar Mahal, *Maran-Baran*, in *Niyantrita*, p. 82.
[68] Abdul Kader, Introduction to *Niyantrita*.

bond of marriage. This, from the pen of a woman who had to spend a lifetime of loneliness away from a husband, whom she could not accept as her true companion for life because he was not enlightened enough.

Poetry: Mahmuda Khatun, Sufia Kamal

Mahmuda Khatun Siddiqua (1906–77) and Sufia Kamal (b. 1911) lived in the age of Tagore and Nazrul. Both were poets, and their poetry was influenced by the romantic tradition of that age.

Mahmuda Khatun's early education started at home but she did attend a school up to the sixth class. Her father Khan Bahadur Muhammad Suleiman was a Divisional School Inspector, and had studied at Presidency College, Calcutta. She had the good fortune of being tutored at home by Nojibur Rahman, author of the popular novel *Anwara*. Mahmuda has a slightly unusual account of her life in purdah:

> Muslim society observed strict purdah — my aunts wore *burqas* (veil) and had to be covered with a mosquito net in the rare event of ever having to travel. Even I was put in purdah at the age of twelve and taken out of school. But the world outside was so irresistible for me that *I disregarded grandma's instructions and would ramble in the garden whenever I could* [69] (emphasis added).

Mahmuda Khatun published three volumes of poetry *Posharini* (The Saleswoman) in 1931, *Man o Mrittika* (Man and His Land) in 1960, and *Aranyer Shoor* (The Melody of the Woods) in 1963. Her life was devoted entirely to literature for though married once, she never had to raise a family. She graced many literary conventions and often delivered the presidential addresses at these without a *burqa*, a rare feat for a Muslim woman of the time.[70] Mahmuda had the good fortune to come into contact with two of the greatest literary figures of Bengal: Sarat Chandra Chatterjee and Rabindranath Tagore. The most memorable public occasion for Mahmuda

---

[69] Unpublished memoirs of M.K. Siddiqua, cited by biographer Begum Akhtar Kamal in *Mahmuda Khatun Siddiqua* (Dhaka, 1987), p. 20.

[70] Begum Akhtar Kamal, ibid., p. 21.

must have been the civic reception accorded to novelist Sarat Chandra Chatterjee at Albert Hall, Calcutta, in 1936, where she read a paper. A secular outlook and emphasis on communal harmony were intrinsic traits of Mahmuda's character and literary work throughout her life.

She reminisces about her meeting with Rabindranath Tagore at his home in Jorasanko:

> I watched with wonder . . . he seemed to radiate light . . . . He chatted with us for a while and then said: 'I am struck with wonder that you have been able to cross the barrier of purdah. See . . . just as plants cannot grow without sun and air, human beings cannot bloom without air and light. The Lotus has to grow out of the mud towards light in order to reach full bloom.[71]

Sufia Kamal, the youngest of the generation of writers discussed here, was born into a zamindar's family in Barisal. As a child she probably never dreamed that she would one day be a renowned poet and social worker. She started her literary career in the 1930s, and her role may be compared to that of Mahmuda Khatun. After a full life as wife and mother, poet and head of the major women's organization in Bangladesh, Sufia Kamal is revered today as a conscientious voice of society, ever vigilant in upholding human rights in general and women's rights in particular.

Conclusion

When Nawab Faizunnessa founded her school for girls in 1873, the response from the Muslim community was discouraging. Only a handful sent their daughters to study there. By the time Lady Brabourne College was established in 1939, the situation was very different. In fact the College had been set up in response to a demand from the Muslim community. Muslim political separatism had intensified by now and Brabourne was established just a year before the Lahore Resolution which took the campaign for Pakistan to a new phase.

[71] M.K. Siddiqua, unpublished memoirs, ibid., p. 26.

Muslim girls continued studying at Bethune, but a sizable chunk of the new generation of *bhadramahilas* graduated from Brabourne. In the 1930s the labours of Faizunnessa, Rokeya, Lila Nag, and Shamsunnahar seemed to bear fruit. This was a decade which saw a quickening of the pulse in many middle-class Muslim families all over Bengal. The old order finally made peace with the new — many apprehensions were laid to rest and many tensions resolved. New ones took their place. Women in many instances physically discarded the *burqa*, the symbol of the *andarmahal* and stepped out into the world equipped with a new creed of puritan morality. They embarked on literary and, later, other careers, and their desire for education intensified. In the words of an ex-student of Brabourne:

> As I crossed the portal of the college that first day, I felt suddenly charged with energy and hope, for life seemed to promise so much. I had wanted to be a doctor, but my family did not like the idea of the long hours of work involved and the late hours I might have to keep. Never mind, a B.A. in English was just as attractive. For a moment I remembered grandma — so talented, so intellectually curious and so quick — withering away in the *andarmahal*, and felt a pang. But I told myself she would have been happy to see me today standing here with the whole world before me.[72]

(Note: All translations from the Bengali texts cited here are by the author.)

---

[72] Interview (1990) taken in Dhaka of Mrs Farrukh Mahal (born 1928) who studied at Lady Brabourne in 1946 and B.M. College in Barisal. Mrs Mahal later joined Bidyamoyee Girls' School in Mymensingh as Assistant Teacher in 1948.

5

Conformity and Rebellion: Girls' Schools in Calcutta

Raka Ray

Theorizing resistance and rebellion has been one of the hallmarks of recent work done by historians and social scientists in India. Increased attention has been paid to the 'subaltern' consciousness, and to the everyday acts of rebellion engaged in by oppressed groups. While much of the discussion has focussed on colonial India and on the actions of peasantry (though there are exceptions), resistance by actors within other institutions has not been examined as closely.[1] Yet the school is a perfect site for the examination of the tensions between hegemonic forces and counter-hegemonic impulses since as a state apparatus the school attempts to perform both accumulation and legitimation functions.[2] As a cultural and economic institution then, the school is a contested site where students, male and female, rich and poor, try to sort out the multiple messages they receive. While excellent work has been done in the macro-processes that schools are embedded in, intra-school processes are largely unexamined. We have increasing evidence about how schools reproduce social and economic inequalities in society and how they are structured so that the social division of labour is reproduced. But students, like workers, do not

---

[1] See for example various articles in the volumes of *Subaltern Studies* edited by Ranajit Guha (New Delhi, Oxford University Press).

[2] See Henry Giroux. 'Theories of Reproduction and Resistance in the New Sociology of Education: A Critical Analysis', *Harvard Educational Review*, vol. 53, no. 2 (1983) and Michael Apple, *Cultural and Economic Reproduction in Education* (London, 1982).

passively receive messages.[3] They actively construct their own cultures of resistance.

Writers such as Paul Willis, R.W. Connell, Jean Anyon, Christine Griffin and Angela McRobbie have made the contradictions, conflicts and resistances of students their starting point and have highlighted the importance of looking at the ways in which students struggle to 'make sense' of their experiences in schools — given that their own experiences at home and in their communities may teach them to see the world differently from the way the school teaches them to.[4] Trouble making has come to be seen as a rational form of resistance to conventional schooling.

If the problem with theories of social change in the seventies was that the ruling classes appeared too much in control, too systematically powerful — thus leaving no room for change and struggle initiated by the subordinate classes, the problem with many recent formulations of resistance is that meaningful struggle and change are seen everywhere.[5] If every contrary act as well as every act of resignation and submission is seen as resistance and is celebrated as such, the concept loses all significance. Thus while it is true, as Michael Apple puts it 'no set of social and institutional

---

[3] Michael Apple, *Education and Power* (London, 1982).

[4] See Jean Anyon, 'Social Class and School Knowledge', *Curriculum Inquiry*, vol. 11, no. 1 (1981); R.W. Connell, Dowsett et al., 'The Experience of Patriarchal Schooling', *Interchange*, vol. 2, no. 3, 1982; Christine Griffin, *Typical Girls* (London, 1985); Angela McRobbie, 'Working Class Girls and the Culture of Femininity', Women's Studies Group, ed., *Women Take Issue* (London, 1978) and Paul Willis, *Learning to Labour* (New York, 1977).

[5] For structuralist theories of social change in the seventies see Louis Althusser, 'Ideology and Ideological State Apparatuses' in *Lenin and Philosophy and Other Essays* (London, 1971); Pierre Bourdieu and Jean Claude Passeron, *Reproduction in Education, Society and Culture* (London, 1977) and Samuel Bowles and Herbert Gintis, *Schooling in Capitalist America* (New York, 1975).

For some interesting critiques of the Subaltern School's analysis of resistance, see Tom Brass, 'Moral Economists, Subalterns, New Social Movements and the (Re-)Emergence of a (Post-)Modernised Middle Peasant', *Journal of Peasant Studies* (1991); K. Balagopal, 'Drought and TADA in Adilabad', *Economic and Political Weekly* (Nov. 25, 1989) and Rosalind O'Hanlon, 'Recovering the Subject', *Modern Asian Studies*, vol. 22, no. 1 (1988).

arrangements can be totally monolithic',[6] the actions of those who live within these institutional arrangements are bounded by them. The type of resistant behaviour adopted by students within the school system depends both on their subjective evaluation of their interests and the limiting social constraints within which they find themselves — and not all behaviours have transformational capacities.

The distinction between interest in resisting and capacity to resist is a crucial distinction not often made. If the ultimate objective of resistance is collective action or some other transformational practice, we must consider *capacity* to act. Thus within the school, the construction of time, space, of the curriculum itself and pedagogic practices that actually inhibit or enhance the capacity to create a counter-culture must be understood.

In this paper, I will examine the creation of and implications of the counter-school resistances among both elite and non-elite girls in India — the different ways in which, given the structure of their schooling experience, the girls fight against elements which oppress them, or adapt to them. I assume in my analysis that responses to situations in a given society depend greatly on its cultural, social and economic organization, and that individual options are limited by one's position within the particular configuration of class and patriarchal structures at each point in history. I chose to focus on girls' education because of a continuing interest in the different ways in which men and women engage in collective behaviour and learn to express their acceptance of and resistance to the system.[7] Thus the questions addressed here are: given the capitalist and patriarchal structure of the school's bias in India, how do girls (both elite and non-elite) react to what the school teaches

---

[6] Michael Apple, *Education and Power*, p. 93.

[7] See for example Temma Kaplan, 'Female Consciousness and Collective Action', *Signs*, 7 (1982), pp. 545–66; Deniz Kandiyoti, 'Bargaining with Patriarchy', *Gender and Society*, vol. 2, no. 3 (1988), pp. 274–90; Maxine Molyneux, 'Mobilization Without Emancipation: Women's Interests, the State and Revolution in Nicaragua, *Feminist Studies*, vol. 11, no. 2 (1985), pp. 227–53 and Ilina Sen, ed., *A Space Within the Struggle: Women's Participation in People's Movements* (New Delhi, 1990).

them? What is it about the structure and content of education that elite and non-elite girls try to resist, and what limits their capacity to do so?

I will answer these questions using data from ethnographic investigations carried out in Calcutta in the summer of 1986, when I attended eighth grade classrooms in St. Mary's Convent (henceforth SMC), an elite private school for girls, and in Tripti Girls' High School (henceforth TGHS),[8] a government aided school for mostly working class and lower middle class girls. There were 30 students in the TGHS class and 40 in the SMC class. I attended all their classes with the students as well as several of their extra-curricular activities. During the breaks or in between classes I talked to the students informally both in groups and individually. We spoke about a wide range of topics — their school and home lives, their interests, and their hopes and fears for the future. Before I left each school, I handed out informal questionnaires to the students and asked them to write down the things they had been talking to me about for the past few months. Most of the girls took the task very seriously and added more information to what they had already told me about their feelings for the school and their concerns for the future. I also spoke at length to the two school principals and class teachers. The bulk of my data, however, come from my observations as I sat at the back of the classrooms, watching and listening to classroom interactions.

For the remainder of the paper then I will briefly describe women's education in India, and the specific practices of schooling in SMC and TGHS and then discuss the conflicts and resistances I observed in the two schools.

Capitalism, Patriarchy and Schooling in India

The majority of Indian women live under what Kandiyoti calls Classic Patriarchy[9] — if not actually, then normatively. The patrilocally extended household represents a powerful cultural ideal.

---

[8] The names of the schools have been changed to guarantee anonymity.
[9] Deniz Kandiyoti, 'Bargaining with Patriarchy'.

Women within this system marry fairly young into households headed by their husband's fathers and their dowries are transferred directly to their husbands' families. As the material base for Classic Patriarchy crumbles, women act to protect themselves either by pushing outward or by trying to prop up the old system. It is in this era of rapid social change that new forms of struggle and resistance emerge as women start to work outside the home in increasing numbers while either trying to adapt to pre-existing cultural ideals or trying to create new ones. In such a situation, the school system becomes a perfect site for the playing out of the tensions between old and new forces and of the contradictions that arise between the conflicting roles allotted to women.

> In Calcutta, the forerunners of the present-day girls' schools were started in the 1800s by missionaries who felt that the existence of intelligently educated mothers . . . is essential to the training of a race of intelligent and high-sprited sons and brothers and husbands.[10]

Schools received a boost by the mid 1800s. Women's education became one of the most hotly debated topics throughout the nineteenth century, as a new breed of western educated young men who were influenced by liberal nineteenth century ideas found that the condition of their women did not fit in with their new-found values. Should women be educated? How much education was sufficient? Would education override a woman's primary duty to her husband? Would daughters-in-law no longer obey their mothers-in-law? What were appropriate subjects for women to study?[11] As Karlekar puts it, the most workable solution to the obvious conflict between the ideals of education — the creation of a spirit of enquiry and independence of thought — and the appropriate norms for women, was to educate women, but to construct separate syllabi and subjects for them.[12] Special textbooks were therefore written geared towards

---

[10] As quoted in Meredith Borthwick, *The Changing Role of Women in Bengal 1849–1905* (Princeton, 1984), p. 65.

[11] Widely read and influential journals of the time which carried the debates include *Bamabodhini Patrika, Jnanankur,* and *Review of Education in India.*

[12] Malavika Karlekar, 'Women's Nature and Access to Education' in Karuna

making women more 'rational' beings by teaching them mathematics and grammar, while at the same time holding out the ideal of good and industrious wives.

The foundations of the education system laid by the British remained relatively unchanged in post Independence India. The educational state apparatus is governed and directed by either central or state governments and given an important place in each Five Year Plan. Both utilitarian and social justice goals ostensibly guide the educational system. Thus the National Commission on Education observes: 'the education of girls should receive emphasis not only on grounds of social justice but also because it accelerates social transformation'.[13] Yet the same group also justifies the education of women in terms of its importance for population control. The 1964 Kothari Commission clearly continued the dual view of education for women when it stated that the need for educating women was greater than for men because women were responsible for the 'full development of our human resources, the improvement of homes and for the moulding of the character of children during the most impressionable years of infancy'.[14] The basic assumption still is that boys and girls should be given separate but equal opportunities for education since they will have separate roles in life. As I shall soon show, girls from different class backgrounds are also to have separate goals in preparation for their later lives. The underlying principle of girls' education has traditionally been and remains double edged. On the one hand the education system must be responsive to changes in the labour process and be ready to teach new skills to 'fit' the needs of the economy. On the other, it must continue to teach a set of relatively unchanging skills, that is, the management or performance of housework, since regardless of class background, housework remains in women's domain. The assumptions of a continuing sexual division of labour are rarely challenged in theory or in practice.

Chanana, ed., *Socialization, Education and Women: Explorations in Gender Identity* (New Delhi, 1988), p. 133.

[13] Ministry of Human Resource Development, Government of India, *National Policy on Education* (New Delhi, 1986).

[14] Quoted in Karlekar, 'Women's Nature and Access to Education', p. 153.

Schooling in Practice

As the educational system stands today, the schools with the highest prestige are those established during the colonial era, and which still adhere to the patriarchal, hierarchical standards and elite values of an Eton or Harrow, where command over the English language and proper deportment are of supreme importance. These are the British style public schools which charge exorbitant fees, are residential and almost exclusively male. There are also quasi-public schools run by religious foundations, business concerns and by the Inter-State Board for Anglo-Indian Education. Under this rubric fall the most elite schools for girls, as well as other less exclusive private nonresidential schools. Within the government's own school system are special school for 'gifted' children of government employees, children of civil servants and soldiers, 'model' or pace setting schools. The mass of children go to general government or government aided schools which are either free or require nominal fees. Of the two schools discussed here, SMC is a quasi-public exclusive girls' school and TGHS is a general government aided school.

SMC was founded in the 1850s for children of the newly created, westernized Indian elite. Over the years it has maintained its elite status and is the school Calcutta elites wish to send their daughters to. The fees are fairly high (about Rs 100 a month in 1986), and because of the fees and other expenses (two separate uniforms, required charities etc.), most children are prevented from seeking admission to the school. The girls' fathers are the city's top professionals and businessmen and many of their mothers have careers. Many of the girls have travelled abroad or intend to do so in the future. They have complete financial security and are fully aware of it.

Teachers at SMC aim to teach the girls how to think and how to become ladies — not to become the brightest students, but the most well-rounded. Their students tend to go less to the most highly academic colleges and more to colleges which are in many ways extensions of SMC. Thus their approach is far more to produce a certain kind of person in the tradition of the liberal western elites, than to teach specific marketable skills.

TGHS was founded in 1945. It is a government-aided school (i.e. the government pays the faculty and staff salaries monthly) that does not require fees from its students, but requires them to pay school maintenance costs (Rs 46 a year). Its students wear uniforms, but are not required to buy textbooks, and lunch is provided free for those who cannot afford it. Girls who come to TGHS are children of clerical workers, low-grade management and factory workers — children who are sometimes too poor to bring lunch and whose parents might be illiterate. The majority of mothers do not earn, and those who do have clerical or school teaching jobs. The mothers have complete responsibility for the house and do not have any hired help, which is representative of the Indian lower-middle class. The girls usually have to carry considerable domestic responsibilities and often many brothers and sisters to look after at home. It follows that academic expectations from them are low.

Let us consider the differences between the two schools in terms of their different charters.[15] The social charter determines to a great extent the values, subjects and characteristics that the school attempts to teach its students, and therefore also determines the aspects of schooling and culture that its students react to.

SMC's charter is easier to define than that of TGHS because its clientele is so limited and homogeneous. Most of SMC's students possess the same 'habitus', and are assured of high status either before or from the moment they enter the school. Before entering SMC they have elite status because of whose children they are. SMC provides a clear means to retain their status, and indeed can significantly enhance the status of those on the margins, or for those new middle-class parents who are seeking ways to ensure social and cultural capital for their children. It is not easy to get into SMC.

---

[15] The charter is defined as an attribute of an organization's—in this case the school's—relation to its environment, that is, its relation to and its position within the social structure, according to Allen Barton in *Organizational Measurement* as quoted in John Meyer, 'The Charter: Conditions of Diffuse Socialization in Schools' in Richard Scott, ed., *Social Processes and Social Structures: An Introduction to Sociology* (New York, 1970).

Parents and children have to go through a series of interviews, and a long wait (perhaps as long as two years) before the child is accepted. Just the fact of acceptance automatically confers prestige. This then is SMC's charter. It is chartered to produce elite women. This involves two things. First, it must produce women who will be the wives of elite men and must therefore have the appropriate domestic and social graces. Secondly, as wives of elite men and as elite women themselves, they must have leadership capacities, for they will be the 'leaders' of society. If any women are admitted to the male dominated professional spheres, it will be these — female managers and lawyers will come out of this group.

TGHS is chartered to develop necessary domestic skills in their students so that they are able to perform household chores most efficiently, and if need be to discharge clerical duties. They are groomed to develop dispositions suitable for these tasks. These women need to be able to function in the economy as low-paid white-collar workers, and their likelihood of achieving this increases, but is not assured, on successful completion of their schooling. The aim of the school, according to the very realistic expectations of the principal, is to help as many students as might be possible to pass the School Board Examination at the end of twelfth grade to do so.[16] Clearly, not everyone will pass these examinations. Those who will, will have the chance of going to college, and a greater chance of contracting a better marriage. The meritocratic ideology finds its home in institutions such as these. As far as the students are concerned, therefore, the school has considerable power over them. Unlike in SMC, just getting in is not sufficient. It is the staying power that counts, and the successful completion of the final examination that will make the biggest status difference to their lives.

Basil Bernstein offers a useful way to look at the complex of behaviours and skills a school attempts to transmit. The *Instrumental Order* consists of the specific skills the school seeks to instil in

---

[16] These examinations are statewide, and the degree of success in these examinations determines whether you go to college or not, and indeed which college you go to.

its students. The *Expressive Order* relates to the 'conduct, character and manner' the school wishes to transmit to its students — a moral order which is intended to bind the whole school together as a distinct moral collectivity.[17]

The Instrumental and Expressive Orders

The Instrumental Order can be examined in terms of its curriculum, its pedagogic practices and its evaluation techniques. The curriculum reveals what counts as valid knowledge and whose knowledge is considered valid. Thus is the sphere of what Raymond Williams calls 'selective tradition', where highly selective knowledge from the past is presented to students as 'the tradition'. The textbook epitomizes the strong classification of knowledge, that is, it clearly demarcates knowledge from what is not knowledge. In India, the textbook *is* the curriculum. The teacher's role is usually that of an interpreter of the textbook and students are expected to learn both the content and the style of their textbooks.[18] In both SMC and TGHS the curriculum is well defined, with a sharp boundary between the commonsense knowledge of the pupil and the un-commonsense knowledge of the school. However since the educational system is primarily a middle class one, it is more responsive to the knowledge brought to school by the girls of SMC rather than the girls of TGHS. Both schools have similar core curricula, and both teach physical education. The TGHS girls learn in addition sewing (twice a week), work education and social work (which here means hygiene and first aid and similar skills), while the SMC girls learn General Knowledge, Moral Science, dancing and sewing or cooking (once a week).

In both schools the teacher is the only one who can transmit knowledge, and is the one who provides answers and solutions rather than the students, though this principle holds more strongly for TGHS than for SMC. Typically SMC classes consist of the

[17] Basil Bernstein, *Class, Codes and Control: Towards a Theory of Educational Transmission* (London, 1975), vol. 3.
[18] Krishna Kumar has a fascinating article in *Economic and Political Weekly* 30 (1986), on how the textbook functions in India.

teacher explaining certain chapters of the text and asking students questions to test their understanding of the material. Often a student is asked to explain the text in her own words. Questions are often phrased to engage the student's imagination.

'If you were Shakespeare . . . '

'How do you think the author felt . . . '

In TGHS on the other hand, the teacher often reads the textbook in class, stopping here and there to give explanations when she feels they are needed. In general, she does not ask many questions, and when she does, contrary to the practice in SMC, insists that answers be given in the same words as hers. In TGHS, rote learning is the most encouraged form of learning. Little attempt is made to make classes exciting and teachers are usually in a hurry to get through their material. The pedagogic practices in both schools fairly accurately reflect the stated aims of the principals — to get the girls of SMC to think for themselves and to get the TGHS girls to pass their examinations. Bright students are made much of in TGHS. Since they do not expect everybody to pass their School Final Examinations, they are very careful with those they expect to do well. The principal told me that often, just before the final examinations, she takes her best student home, and sees that she gets undisturbed rest, food and study time so that nothing can stand in the way of her success. It is this student who might end up in college with the highest chance of success. In class, the teachers pick out the potential successes and address themselves to the chosen few, often directing questions at them. In SMC on the other hand, teachers are extremely careful not to appear selective. Very often, once a girl has answered a question, the teacher is careful not to call on her again unless nobody else can respond to the next question. As one teacher explained to me, the objective is to give everybody a chance to speak and not to encourage too much competition amongst the girls. Those who are in SMC are already assured of their future, whereas TGHS cannot assure everyone a successful future and thus must tailor its pedagogic and evaluative practices accordingly.

The Expressive Order concerns itself with the transmission of the values and norms of the dominant moral order, and may or may not be as important as the instrumental order, depending upon the social location of the school. TGHS for example is far more concerned with the instrumental order and SMC with the expressive order, as can be seen by the comments made by both principals and teachers:

> Principal of TGHS: My girls need economic independence above all, but I also want to teach them to be womanly and caring.
>
> Class teacher in SMC: I want to teach the girls how to think for themselves, yet to be disciplined and well mannered.

In SMC, for example, students are graded not only for their academic performance, but also for their revealed personality traits. Every quarterly grade report contains grades for traits such as courtesy, responsibility, leadership and punctuality. No such parallel grading scheme exists in TGHS.

Although SMC and TGHS girls spend approximately equal hours in school, SMC is a far more 'total' institution in Goffmanesque terms. Whereas the TGHS girls go home after school (to help their mothers or to do their homework), SMC girls often stay back or come back later to play or to participate in extra-curricular activities. Thus far more of their lives actually revolve around their school than do the lives of the TGHS girls.

Rituals are a major means of transmission of the expressive order. While both schools have daily assemblies where the students congregate to pray, sing and to hear words of advice from the principals, the most elaborate rituals in SMC are the House rituals.[19] Students are expected to participate in debates, dramas and sports not for self glory but for the glory of the House. Each week, a

---

[19] The house system is a British import which involves 'fictional communities within the school . . . each community has its own set of consensual and differentiating rituals, together with their inductive subsets' Bernstein, *Class, Codes and Control,* p. 57. Each student bears allegiance to her House and many of the extra-curricular activities focus on inter-house competitions.

House is placed in charge of the cleanliness of the school or discipline, and students develop a collective vested interest in carrying out the duties allotted to them. The House is penalized if a student comes late to the school assembly or is untidily dressed. The ultimate ignominy is to be punished by being deprived of one's House badge. House pride and consciousness thus go a long way in SMC to keep the girls in line, in the name of a greater cause. Though a House system exists in TGHS, little symbolic importance is attached to it.

TGHS attempts to transmit a fairly straightforward instrumental and expressive order to its students, and stresses the instrumental over the expressive. In terms of curriculum, pedagogy and evaluation, the actual content of material through knowledge of textbook is emphasised and there is a sharp delineation between the teacher and the taught. The students are evaluated primarily on the basis of their academic ability and the aspirations of the few are developed rather than the aspirations of all. Hierarchy and dominance are clear in the expressive order and there is little leadership training. The school wants of the student that she pass the examination rather than become a particular type of woman. It therefore controls fewer facets of the person than does SMC.

SMC on the other hand treads a delicate balance between open and closed orders. Whereas knowledge boundaries and boundaries between the teacher and the taught are sharply delineated, the teachers do draw the students into discussions, and do not selectively pay attention to the brightest students. The ritual order celebrates both hierarchy and dominance and participation and co-operation. While some students are given prestigious positions within the school, and prefectship is glorified, so too are co-operation, sacrifice and service. This delicate line needs to be followed, I would claim, because of SMC's particular social location. It must produce women who are the future elite of society and therefore must have both 'feminine' and leadership qualities. The SMC award is given every year to the graduating senior who is seen to best embody both sets of virtues. TGHS's social location does not require it, indeed does not make it useful, to attempt to transmit such a combination of qualities to its students.

Resistance and Conformity at SMC and TGHS

Given the structure of the schools and the particular configuration of social forces in Calcutta within which these students live their lives, what are the contradictions and conflicts that the girls face and how do they react to them? In this section, I lay out information from the interviews as well as from observation and identify the range of behaviours (both resistant and non-resistant) which was present to varying degrees in each school, but before we examine them, a word of caution is in order. It is easy to slip into two kinds of errors in this case — the error of the romantic and the error of the skeptic. I do not wish to romanticize the reactions of the students, nor to predict that the seeds of tomorrow's revolution have been planted in them. Yet, I am unwilling to dismiss their resistances as irrelevant or meaningless. It is important to understand how from a fairly young age, girls try to sort out the mixed messages they receive. It is important also to understand why they act the way they do and under what circumstances they accept or reject strictures on their behaviour. Thus in the typology which follows, I describe behaviours which have transformational capacities as well as those that do not, for some strategies are indeed successful and others are not. As all typologies must be, this too is ideal-typical, and while it cannot capture all of the variations in response, it does throw into relief the basic differences between the responses of the girls in SMC and TGHS.

'When we marry we become our husbands'

Less than half the girls from TGHS and over half the girls from SMC said they would work after marriage, even though all the girls wanted to go to college.[20] The girls answered various questions about marriage, equality and their worries about their future. Perhaps the most fascinating answers I received was to the question 'are women in India oppressed?'. Every single TGHS girl said that

[20] In actual fact, the TGHS principal informed me, very few TGHS students are expected to go to a three year college, and of those who do go, the majority would do the pass course.

they were, and many described with considerable perceptiveness the lack of freedom women face and the unfairness of their treatment.

'We aren't free. When we marry we become our husbands'

'We aren't cared for, and are insulted and neglected in our society'

'We live in a male dominated society and women are deprived of freedom and their rights, and can't move about openly in the streets'

On the other hand, though 12 SMC girls said that women were oppressed, 7 said they were not, 9 said 'perhaps' and 'somewhat' and 4 said 'not in civilized India'.

'Yes, I guess [they are oppressed] in rural areas'

'No. I think that if a woman tries, she can make her life successful.'

Stemming from their differing perspectives of women in Indian society are their fears about their future. The girls of TGHS thus worry primarily about their lack of control over their lives. They are afraid they will not be allowed to complete their studies, or do what they really want after marriage. They worry about educational success and about not 'shaming' their parents by their actions. In contrast, one quarter of the SMC girls said they had no worries about the future, and about half said their fears focused on not being an academic or financial success.

The oppression of women appears very remote from the girls of SMC, even though statistics show that problems with dowry, for example, should affect the SMC girls equally, if not more than the TGHS girls. Yet both at home and at school, SMC girls are repeatedly told or shown that they are very privileged and thus seem to have internalized the message. Convinced of their good fortunes and pitying of those who have less than them, they cannot see their gender oppression because of their overwhelming class privileges. The girls of TGHS do not have easily available domestic help, and help their mothers cook and clean and look after the younger children in the family. They are thus acutely aware of the responsibilities of adult women. When asked what their mothers did in the house, they were able to describe in great detail their mothers' activities from the time they woke up to the time, after cooking, cleaning, sewing, taking the children to school and back and saying evening prayers, they fell asleep. In answer to the same question SMC girls responded:

> 'She supervises the general housekeeping'
>
> 'She *only* cooks the food (emphasis mine)'
>
> 'She doesn't do anything much. She goes to kitty parties sometimes and sometimes tidies the house. The rest of the work is done by the ayahs.'

Students in both schools receive messages about how to be a woman. Thus when asked about the ideal attributes women should have, TGHS students mentioned most frequently such attributes as compassion, softness, gentleness, charity and generosity, sacrifice and endurance, purity and adeptness at housework. Compassion was also mentioned most often in SMC (but nineteen times as opposed to forty times in TGHS), followed by femininity, sophistication, dignity and politeness and then independence. Their responses indicate in many ways the success of the two schools in creating different classes of women who are going to lead very different lives. The answers to the questionnaires give us some indication of the conflicting norms the girls face, but their reactions when faced with conflict were revealed to a far greater extent when I sat at the back of the class and observed them as they went about their daily activities.

Accommodation and Resistance

One of the most common behaviours I observed was what Merton would call Conformity, an acceptance and genuine belief in both the goals and the methods of the school (representing, as it does, the dominant cultures).[21] Willis calls this integration.[22] This is

[21] Robert Merton, *Social Theory and Social Structure* (New York, 1957).
[22] Paul Willis, *Learning to Labour.*

typified in the SMC belief that it is good to be ladylike, and good to be disciplined because 'it is important for a woman to have good manners and get on in society.' Also representative of this kind of behaviour is the anxiety on the part of some TGHS girls because of their faith in the school as the means to a 'respectable' job. As one of the girls complained:

> I feel like crying because I do my work with so much care and (the teachers) don't bother to examine it minutely. How can I improve?

Here she had so accepted the importance of education for the future (and of the instrumental order of the school), that she was frustrated because she thought the teachers were not taking their duties seriously enough.

Both SMC and TGHS girls considered discipline to be very important, and there was a considerable amount of self-monitoring going on at any point. If the teacher was not in class, several girls would take it upon themselves to remind the class to be quiet. On one occasion, one of the students in SMC actually took down the names of those who were talking and presented the list to the teacher.

However, very often, what appeared to be conformity at first glance, could be resistance in various forms. The girls had an incredible capacity to appear to be conforming, and this was not surprising given the emphasis on form in all aspects of their school life.

The modal response of the TGHS girls was one of 'pragmatic acceptance' or 'strategic compliance'. This occurs when one settles for something because one feels one has no choice. One may or may not personally believe in the values the school tries to instil in one, or in the educational process, but may realise that one would be worse off without it. Many of the girls are in school simply because the alternative is so much worse — not being in school, being forced to work as somebody's maid, or having to do household chores all day. This is why so many of them are constantly scared that their education will be interrupted, not because they really believe that education is the best thing for them. They know that they cannot afford to be too disruptive and noisy for fear of being thrown out. In the words of the principal, 'our girls never behave very badly with their teachers . . . they are too poor to fool around.' So they come to school everyday, going through the motions of each class sometimes participating, sometimes not, looking forward to free periods when they can be with their friends. Putting up with irrelevant material and teachers' caustic comments, is preferable because school is a more comfortable place to be in than home. The fact that they do not often complete their homework and are more often than not ill-prepared for class contradicts the supposed values of the educational system. They do not experience joy in learning, but a profound sense of helplessness and incapacity to act.

The situation appears very clear to them. They, as women, must get married. They have no choice. As married women they might get a husband or mother-in-law who treats them badly. Again, since they do not choose their husbands themselves, they have no choice. Therefore, what they need to do is to find ways to deal with the situations they might face and to find ways to be happy under difficult circumstances. In school, for example, certain rules cannot be broken — rules of discipline, for one. So the TGHS girls do not break discipline rules, but they do find ways to resist being forced in class to listen to things they are not interested in. They specialise in what I call 'withdrawal' techniques.

A typical withdrawal technique is a blank stare. As the teacher teaches them about the physical geography of North America, the girls sit at their desks, looking at her blankly. She asks questions. No one answers. She loses her temper and speaks sharply to them, and no one responds. She gives up and continues teaching. To all intents and purposes, these are perfect little school girls, well behaved and attentive, but what they are really doing is resisting being fed material totally irrelevant to their lives. They accommodate outwardly the expressive order and resist inwardly the instrumental order.

What are they thinking about when they stare ahead blankly? They often daydream and live out fantasy lives of chivalrous men and romance, of being with tender and caring husbands, of getting married dressed in beautiful clothes and jewellery. In rejecting the official ideology of schooling, these girls replace it with an ideology of marriage, family and romance. Thus there are at the same moment elements of good and bad sense in their actions — a partial comprehension of reality which then gets turned against them as they succumb to the patriarchal myths that pervade the culture.

The two most common behaviours I observed at SMC, though they were also present (to a far lesser extent) in TGHS, were negotiation and 'quiet resistance.' The SMC girls constantly negotiated with their teachers for less work, different work or more interesting work. For example, they tried to bargain with a very demanding physics teacher to give them fewer problems to solve. When they failed to get their way, the whole class simply copied the problems very slowly so that the teacher could not get beyond the fourth problem with them. The girls knew they had that power and used it as far as they could. And when one student suggested a reduction in work or a change in topic, it was usually followed by a barrage of pleas from the rest of the class. This class unity was conspicuously absent from TGHS possibly as a result of both TGHS policy of encouraging competition among students and the relative lack of confidence on the part of its students.

An amusing and fairly representative example of negotiation was an incident with the Physical Training (PT) master, well known for his insistence on discipline, who would never allow the girls to rest if they were tired, but would insist that they run around for the entire period. One of the girls declared to me that she was not in the mood to play for 45 minutes and would try to figure out a way to get out of it. She went up to the teacher and told him she could not play that day because 'Sir, it's my time of the month (here she blushed delicately), you know . . . my family is very strict about not letting me run around at this time.' The PT instructor had no choice but to agree. He could not discuss it with her, and she knew it. When she went back to her friends, she was applauded enthusiastically for her performance.

Quiet resistance is clear resistance, but done covertly so that one will not be caught. It is unlike withdrawal to the extent that here, girls are actually engaged in illegal activities, but covertly so that nobody sees them. Withdrawal technique means saying to the teacher, 'I don't have to listen to you really, as long as I pretend I do'. It does not require any overt or covert action. Resistance is purely in the head. Quiet resistance on the other hand amounts to saying to the teacher, 'I can get away with disobeying you right under your nose. Your control over me is not complete'. The most typical example of this, and one that is rampant, is doing homework during boring classes or during classes taught by teachers known for not being able to maintain discipline. This is not only a clear indication about not being interested in the subject, but also a direct violation of classroom norms.

During one moral science class, the students were divided into five sections, each of which had to discuss such topics as the Gift of Love, the Gift of Beauty (subtopics of Life is a Wonderful Gift). The group I was in talked briefly about the topic and then began to discuss the Wimbledon tennis tournaments which were being played then (with special emphasis on the 'cute' players). Yet when the teacher asked them if they were done, they clamoured for more time. The message was clear. They would play the teacher's game and give the answer she was looking for, but did not necessarily value it themselves, and would not suppress for long things that were of real interest to them.

The behaviours I noticed at SMC and the withdrawal behaviours I noticed at TGHS were distinctly female ways of resisting aspects of the education system which they did not like, or which they felt was imposed on them. There were some cases of outright and open rebellion in SMC, but absolutely none at TGHS. There were two extremes at SMC: the tomboy, who refused to accept the ideology of femininity and who deliberately mocked those who did try to live up to it; and the extremely coy and flirtatious, who did no work and talked openly about her experiences with boys — a taboo subject. Needless to say, the flirtatious girls actually held positions of high prestige amongst their fellow students. These types were relatively rare (I saw only a few in the SMC class I observed) and are thus the exception rather than the rule found in each classroom (Table I).

Table I
A typology of resistant behaviours and their environments

Type of behaviour	Visible alternative to present system	Type of subversion
Conformity	Immaterial	None
Pragmatic acceptance	None seen	Internal. Not externalised. Outward form maintained. 'You cannot control my mind.' Alternative values unofficially maintained.
Negotiation	Glimpsed	Bargaining for more autonomy. Use of 'common sense' and 'partial penetration' as bargaining weapons.
Quiet resistance	Glimpsed	Discovery that control is not total. Formulation of grievances and of actions based on them. Assertion of alternate values. Requires more communal action than withdrawal. More direct disobedience, but no desire to be caught by authorities.
Open rebellion	Found	Deliberate flouting of rules and conventions with intention of being discovered. Usually found only where there is support, e.g. in the case of tight subcultures

We need to be very clear about the differences in the resistances observed at the schools, for not only are the forms of resistance distinctive, but so too are their causes. Resistance has different meanings and implications in the two schools. Without minimizing the costs of resistance for the SMC girls, we must recognize that the stakes are higher for the girls of TGHS, which does not automatically confer status on the students at their entrance as SMC does.

What are the TGHS girls resisting so silently and yet so persistently? What realizations have they come to that impel them to do so? And what does an act of resistance which is not outwardly manifested mean in such a context?

One of the major realizations is that the school is in fact not the great equaliser of opportunity. As one girl said to me of the wealthier girls. 'There is nothing to stand in the way of their success'; and of the boys, 'we aren't ever encouraged and given the same opportunities as them.' They know that the girls in SMC and boys in general receive qualitatively different education from them. They know the value of spoken English in Indian society today and resent the fact that while they are repeatedly admonished to work hard and learn their lessons well, a better knowledge of spoken English which would actually get them further, is denied to them.

Both sets of girls are subjected to a great extent to the same Hindu patriarchal myths, novels and songs — to the traditions transmitted and celebrated from generation to generation. Both are taught the virtues of selflessness and sacrifice for the family and the ultimate value of family over individual. But the TGHS girls are simultaneously far more aware of the oppressive aspects of patriarchy and less openly resistant to them. While they articulate their fears and resentments quite openly:

> What if I am not able to establish myself in this male-run society?
>
> What if I can't stand the tortures after marriage?

Their concerns centre around how best to adapt themselves and how to protect themselves, not on how to get out of the oppressive situation. We have here a situation where, economically, individual action is not really feasible. A female clerical worker or even a primary school teacher would find it nearly impossible to live solely on her salary. Increasingly, in the lower-middle class, it has become necessary for both husband and wife to work in order to ensure a standard of life they aspire to. As rents soar in the cities and consumer prices continue to increase, the constraints on individual action become tighter still. Since these girls are intimately involved in material production centred in the home, they are far more acutely aware of the financial constraints of households than are the SMC girls, and are therefore more aware of the near impossibility of breaking out of old support structures, however oppressive they might be. While they romanticise marriage and the wedding ceremony itself, and often talk about it with their friends, they are simultaneously aware of the problems associated with it, especially if they have older sisters. Family demands certainly are oppressive to them, and to some extent they know how difficult it will be in the future for them, but they feel they have no choice but to carry on within the present situation and try to carve out spaces of autonomy inside it.[23]

Structurally then, the best strategy for resistance is in fact the one they have chosen — withdrawal. These girls, when faced with the harsh reality of their future, and with the difficult living conditions of the present, find a mental escape route for themselves in the world of romance and day-dreaming. Thoughts about other lives and adventures deliver them from the deadly drudgery of their present and future lives. Their highly structured school experience and the tight control over their overt behaviour and physical movements in fact create the perfect situation for withdrawal. TGHS's closed school system demands that students learn in great detail a narrow range of subjects that they will be tested on. Other aspects of their lives are rarely delved into, unlike in SMC. In other words, the instrumental order is stressed to a great extent over the expressive. The rituals they go through are neither as central nor as glorified as the SMC rituals, and the symbolic order is not as tightly woven. The girls are able to retain a greater degree of distance from and a more critical attitude toward their school experience. They

---

[23] It must be remembered that these girls are only fourteen and fifteen years old. They have not as yet experienced directly many of the hardships associated with being a woman in India. Some of their resentments against the patriarchal system are therefore vague and diffuse, and it is not clear exactly which aspects of marriage and the family they oppose.

are not as immersed in the school and its values. True, they are unable openly to show their resentment, but it exists.

The girls in SMC appear to be far more forthcoming and rebellious than the TGHS girls. They are quick to criticise and quick to defend. Their resistance is mainly to the particular combination of patriarchal and capitalist culture that they are faced with. On the one hand, SMC is chartered to produce ladies — women who are graceful and giving and are successful wives and mothers — thus it stresses the importance of quietness, gentleness and good manners. On the other hand, it must stress leadership since these girls are groomed to have the qualities of leadership both culturally and morally. They are also the only women who will be able to break into primarily male occupations, thus supposedly dispelling the myth of exclusion of women from these occupations. To this effect the girls learn that creativity and assertiveness and responsibility are also valued. The fact is that values of leadership and womanhood as they are usually articulated are in direct contradiction to each other. The difficulty of believing in and trying to live out this combination of contradictory expectations creates anxiety and confusion in the girls.

When the SMC girls resist, they often resist the restrictions that are imposed on their newly found creativity and energy by the requirements of discipline. Discipline is the most loved and hated word amongst the girls. They resent the amount of discipline imposed on them, yet look down on schools that do not have the same reputation for producing 'well disciplined' students. They find it difficult to switch roles on and off — to be rewarded for leadership at one point and to be admonished for being too 'pushy' and 'not giving others a chance' the next; to be encouraged to write creative answers but to have points deducted because they did not draw a line at the end of an answer. The promise of openness so swiftly followed by closure is not easy to deal with. Yet the girls of SMC are bound up with a powerful status order built around the values of their school and are integrated into a peer structure that reinforces the values of the school. Their interests are in a very real way tied to the interests of the school, and to that extent, hegemony is more successful at SMC than at TGHS.

1. Girijasundari Debi (b. 1894), the editor's aunt. Widowed at the age of 15—not remarried —photograph taken at the age of fifty.

2. Kamala Debi (b. 1895). Daughter of Sir Ashutosh Mukherjee, Chief Justice of Calcutta High Court and Vice-Chancellor of Calcutta University. Married at the age of eight in 1904, widowed in 1905, remarried in 1908. This widow-remarriage gave rise to considerable debate at that time.
(Courtesy Justice Chittotosh Mukherjee).

3. Batakrishna Ghosh, Bar-at-Law and his wife Binapani Ghosh. Married in 1905, when the bride was 12 and the groom 18 years old.
(Courtesy Ms Sita Ghosh).

4. Bhakti Roy Chowdhury (b. 1904).
Wife of Sachindranath Roy Chowdhury of Santosh.
(Courtesy Ms Sita Ghosh).

5. Rajarani Debi (b. 1880). Wife of Haricharan Gupta, who was a teacher of Bengali, Fort William College, Calcutta. (Courtesy Mr Ajit Gupta. This is a photograph of a painting).

6. Swarnakumari Debi (b. 1855).
Daughter of Debendranath Tagore, sister of Rabindranath Tagore; achieved fame as a writer; was editor of the reputed journal *Bharati* for over fifteen years.
(Courtesy Badal Basu, Ananda Publishers, Calcutta).

7. Gyanadanandini Debi (b. 1852).
Wife of Satyendranath, son of Debendranath Tagore; went to England alone for a visit; an innovator in dress reform for women.
(Courtesy Badal Basu, Ananda Publishers, Calcutta).

8. Begum Rokeya Sakhawat Hossein (b. 1880).
Married to Sakhawat Hossein; author, educationist,
pioneer of the women's movement in Bengal.
(Courtesy Headmistress, Sakhawat Memorial Girls' High School, Calcutta).

9. Inner Quarters. A Muslim home in old Dhaka. Date on the gateway once read '1822'. (Courtesy Dr Sonia Amin).

10. Nurunnessa Khatun Bidyabinodini (b. 1892). Author; upheld the cause of women in writings and lectures. (Courtesy Dr Sonia Amin).

11. Sufia Kamal
Poet, social worker and activist in women's organization.
(Courtesy Dr Sonia Amin).

12. Saraladebi Chaudhurani (b. 1872). Daughter of Swarnakumari Debi, wife of Rambhuja Datta-Chaudhury; writer; activist in nationalist movement; a pioneer of women's movement in Bengal.
(Courtesy Badal Basu, Ananda Publishers, Calcutta).

13. Basanti Debi (b. 1880).
Married to Deshabandhu Chittaranjan Das; activist in the freedom movement; became President of the Bengal Provincial Congress in 1921. (Courtesy Ms Swarupa Das).

Conclusion

The girls at SMC and TGHS, when faced with the ideologies taught to them and embedded in the structures of the school, do not meekly accept what they are taught. They do challenge and resist the school's assumptions both consciously and unconsciously since often the ideology of the school is in direct contradiction to their lived experiences — to their culture. Their perceptions of these conflicts are shaped both by their schooling experience and their socio-economic background. The girls of TGHS thus have a greater *interest* in resisting. But since the forms of resistance depend on *capacity* to resist, which is in turn shaped by material conditions as well as by cultural norms, the most common form of resistance for the girls of TGHS is that of maintaining form and subverting content, for there are severe negative sanctions for violation of form. The importance of form transcends specific institutions and though TGHS and SMC girls operate under very different conditions, this constraint is applicable, in varying degrees, to both of them.

However as we have seen, most of the students' behaviours do not in fact threaten the system, but assist in their survival within it. To that extent, they are survival strategies rather than revolutionary strategies. Women neither unconsciously absorb nor consciously reject the strictures placed on them. Rather, they engage from, as we have seen, an early age, with the form and substance of the gendered and class-specific norms and carve a space for themselves within it. That space, while defined by their market and domestic options,[24] is creatively moulded by the girls' skills and imagination. It is through ethnographic investigations of specific institutions that we can understand better both the contexts for and consequences of the development of women's survival and coping mechanisms.

(An earlier version of this paper was published in the *British Journal of Sociology and Education*, vol. 9, no. 4, 1988).

[24] Deniz Kandiyoti, 'Bargaining with Patriarchy'.

6

The Freedom Movement and Feminist Consciousness in Bengal, 1905–1929

Bharati Ray

A sitting of the Women's Congress was just over, and the local air was still charged with the excitement of this conference.

'Did you go?' asked Amiya.

'Of course I did', Hena said with much pride.

Bibhuti knew that Hena was an ardent participant at the Conference.

So he asked, with some curiosity, 'And what did you do there?'

Hena feigned surprise. 'Have you not seen the press reports?'

'Yes indeed I have, but a first hand report is always more interesting', Bibhuti said with a smile on his lips.

Hena was not too pleased with Bibhuti's remark and retorted rather heatedly, 'If you think so, why did you not go there yourself? You could have had a ring side view'.

Bibhuti said mollifyingly, 'No, I am interested, honestly, I am really curious to know why you need a separate Congress for women'.

'The Chairperson made that quite clear at the start of the session', said Hena.

Bibhuti had carefully watched and studied the proceedings of the Women's Congress and its programmes, and did not find the movement worthy of acclaim. The whole affair, he thought, was unnatural. He could not comprehend the great effort that was going on to create a separate entity for women. He was equally puzzled as to how the establishment of equal rights for women would prove to be a blessing for the world. So he asked in a calm voice, 'Would a confrontation between men and women lead to any benefit to the society at large?'

'At least there will be no harm done', Hena retorted. 'Women need some relief from the injustice they have been subjected to all these years'.

Devjani was sitting quietly but was getting heated up, while Bibhuti continued, 'Injustice! This hostile attitude of yours to men, this suspicion that men have unceasingly conspired to put women down, is nothing but imported ideas from Europe. Can't you shake yourself free of these prejudices?'

'I am sorry I cannot accept what you are saying. It is only the sign of a narrow outlook if you consider all imported ideas from Europe as untouchable', said Hena.

Yes, this is all very true, Devjani thought to herself. But surely, she felt, Hena could produce a more powerful argument in support of her remark to quash Bibhuti's observation. She could have said that if every idea from Europe was to be discarded, then why did the Indian Congress subscribe to the theory of democracy? After all, the concept of democracy was not native to India. Devjani wished to speak out but since she did not know these people well enough she was diffident.

Bibhuti spoke up. 'You have all put on tinted western glasses through which you cannot see the light from the east, and this leads you to view anything from the east as narrow and limited.'

'May be', Hena replied, 'But I hope you will come to realize that you cannot suppress women for long through your banter and derision'.

Bibhuti picked up his khadi wrap and said, 'Strange indeed is your thinking which I cannot appreciate, in fact I do not even wish to understand it.' He then turned the direction of the debate and continued, 'When the nation is passing through a severe crisis, when all our energies are deeply enmeshed in our revolt against administrative and economic mismanagement, is it the right time to start a civil war between men and women? We have in front of us a massive struggle for our country's freedom when the need of the hour is for everyone, Hindus and Moslems, men and women, to stand together. Instead of this all you are doing is to create disharmony between men and women. A great mistake'.

Devjani was stunned. How could a person who was so concerned with his country's freedom be so blind to someone else's aspiration for liberty? From the sincerity of his beliefs and the fire in his eyes when he talked about the country's freedom one could not doubt at all the intensity of his feeling on this point. Yet how could the same person be so averse to allowing the same advantages to women? Bibhuti protested when the British vaunted that under their rule Indians lacked nothing and lived in great peace and harmony. But when it came to women the same person accepted without any hesitation that the authority of men over women was right and proper. If we found an Indian who supported British domination, we would condemn him as a coward, a weakling, a bootlicker. And when the issue of women's emancipation was raised, Devjani thought, how could one accept opposite views? Self interest did make one so blind.

Hena quietly riposted, 'Of course. The point is you cannot think outside the success of your own mission. But please do not forget that besides the interest of the country, women have their own interest as a separate entity from men. For us the liberation of the country makes little sense if we, women, are to be kept shackled inside our homes. This we must declare unequivocally'.[1]

Women in India participated in large numbers in the freedom struggle against the British colonial rulers. While their involvement has been an object of historical concern,[2] its linkage with the women's movement and its implications for the shaping of a feminist consciousness have not received the same attention. The

---

[1] Translated by Sukhendu Ray from the original Bengali, Shantisudha Ghosh, 'Pather Ingit' (The Signpost) *Jayasree*, vol. 1, no. 3, 1338 BS/1931 AD. Shantisudha Ghosh used to teach Mathematics in a college in Barishal and later became Principal of Hooghly Women's College. She was an active member of the Jugantar Party, a revolutionary group in colonial Bengal, and later joined the non-co-operation movement led by Gandhi.

[2] See, for instance, Manmohan Kaur, *Role of Women in the Freedom Movement, 1857–1947* (New Delhi, 1968).

objective of this paper is to look briefly at the role of women in the anti-colonial struggle and explore the concurrent process of the emergence of a 'consciousness' among women about the realities of a patriarchal culture. The paper, however, looks at only Hindu urban middle class[3] women of Bengal and focuses on the period from 1905 to 1929. The year 1905 witnessed the beginning of the *swadeshi* movement in Bengal,[4] while 1929 marked the end of one phase of the political crusade, a new phase opening with the Civil Disobedience movement in 1930.[5]

I argue that the twentieth-century women's movement in India was inextricably bound with the freedom movement. This is not to say that the women's movement in India is unconnected with the growth of other movements like the workers' or peasants' movements, but, rather to state that the crucial juncture or the historical point from which feminist consciousness began to be fashioned, arrived with the freedom struggle. In colonial Bengal, socio-cultural and political responses to colonialism were not unrelated but were facets of the same phenomenon, i.e. the growth of nationalism. Political awareness was intimately connected with social awareness. Women's entry into the public 'male' world of politics undermined

---

[3] Ashok Sen, *Iswar Chandra Vidyasagar and His Elusive Milestones* (Calcutta, 1977) gives a good analysis of this class in the context of Bengal. Joanna Liddle and Rama Joshi, *Daughters of Independence* (New Delhi, 1986), emphasize that 'the middle class in India came to consist primarily of the educated professional groups, with the merchants and industrialists in the minority' (p. 7). See also B.B. Misra, *The Indian Middle Classes* (Oxford, 1961), esp. pp. 12–13. Ali Muhammad Idris, *Bangladesher Upanyas Sahitye Maddhyabitta Shreni* (The Middle Class in the Novels of Bangladesh, Dacca, 1985), pp. 1–4 & 30–1, gives a succinct description of this class in the context of Bangladesh. What constituted Bengal during the period of our study was partitioned in 1947, when India became independent, into West Bengal and East Pakistan (now Bangladesh).

[4] Sumit Sarkar, *The Swadeshi Movement in Bengal, 1903–1908* (New Delhi, 1973) gives a good account of the *Swadeshi* movement.

[5] On 31 December, the last day of the year 1929, the Indian National Congress declared *Purna Swaraj* (full independence) as its goal. For those present on the occasion, the pledge was 'an unforgettable experience, almost spiritual in content'. Vijayalakshmi Pandit, *The Scope of Happiness: A Personal Memoir* (New Delhi, 1979), p. 92.

the socially constructed artificial dichotomization of the 'male' sphere of the public and the 'female' sphere of the domestic domains. This inevitably meant that alterations at many levels would follow. It made women aware of the existing gender inequalities in Indian society[6] and generated an urge for freedom from the grip of prescribed belief-systems and roles which had historically operated against their interests. Once women 'crossed the *Lakshmanrekha*[7] (forbidden boundary), their consciousness underwent a metamorphosis. While all middle class women were not equally transformed, nor able to reconstitute new roles for themselves, a considerable number of them evinced a desire for equal socio-political rights along with men, questioned the culture of patriarchy, and strove to build up an organizational network of their own. This paper demonstrates the various channels through which their political and social awareness was both formulated and articulated.

Background

At the beginning of the nineteenth century, Bengali women existed in a deplorable state of ignorance, illiteracy, superstition and physi-

---

[6] For detailed description, see A.S. Altekar, *The Position of Women in Hindu Civilisation* (Banaras, 1956); *Report of the Committee on the Status of Women in India* (Govt. of India, New Delhi, 1974); Neera Desai and Maithreyi Krishnaraj, *Women and Society in India* (Delhi, 1987), especially Chapter I; Bharati Ray, 'Beyond the Domestic/Public Dichotomy: Women's History in Bengal, 1905–1947' in S.P. Sen and N.R. Ray, eds., *Modern Bengal: A Socio-Economic Survey* (Calcutta, 1988), pp. 240–56; M. Allen, 'The Hindu View of Women' in M. Allen & S.N. Mukherjee, ed., *Women in India and Nepal* (Australian University Press, 1982). A relevant article based on autobiographies is Srabasi Ghosh, 'Birds in a Cage', *Economic and Political Weekly*, Oct. 1986, pp. 88–96.

[7] I have borrowed the words from Alturi Murali's article 'Perspectives on Women's Liberation: Andhra in the Nineteenth and Early Twentieth Centuries', in *Studies in History*, vol. 3, no. 1 (January–June '87), p. 117. Murali argues in the context of Andhra, that because of the male political elite's inability to comprehend the culturally-structured life of women, men left them behind. But women's participation in politics acted as a catalyst for a wider change in their perspective and socio-cultural outlook. If changes in women's consciousness in Andhra 'can be seen from the 1920's', in Bengal it can be traced from the Swadeshi movement.

cal seclusion. Kailasbasini Debi (b. 1837) said that women were like 'beasts', unable to voice their feelings. Men thought that 'they could establish ascendancy over women as over beasts.'[8] *'Meye, meye, meye, tush karle kheye'* (A daughter burns like slow fire). This simple local proverb both reveals and encapsulates the social devaluation of girls and women and the dominant male-biased social ethos. It is well known that the movement for the improvement of women's condition was started in the mid-nineteenth century and that its leadership was provided by men. Various aspects of the socio-religious movement have been discussed in several studies.[9] Briefly, *sati* was abolished, widow remarriage permitted and women's education introduced. The process, however, did not emerge out of a political and social vacuum. Placed in its historical context, it had two important components. First, there was the emergence of an urban culture as distinguished from the rural one and the growth of an English-educated professional generation at odds with traditional zamindars. This new elite, the *bhadralok*, constituted the junior partners of the colonial rulers. The objective of the reform movement, supported by them, was not to attack the prevalent patriarchal system in any way, or to challenge the power and position enjoyed by men, nor even to make women equal partners of men in the societal or economic roles outside the family. Its purpose was to improve the position of women within the patriarchal framework and to make them more capable of fulfilling their roles as wives and mothers within the family. In short, they were to be better equipped to lend the *bhadralok* social support in the colonial world and to produce 'enlightened' sons for them. That is why the paradigm of a model woman was imported from Victorian England with the 'traditional' qualities of Indian women added to it.

The reform movement was historically the upshot of the tussle

---

[8] Kailasbasini Debi, *Hindu Mahilabaner Hinabastha* (The Degraded Condition of Hindu Women, Calcutta, 1863), p. 61. Kailasbasini Debi was taught to read by her husband. She published another book which gives a graphic description of women's social and educational status in the late nineteenth century.

[9] See, for instance, N.S. Bose, *Indian Awakening in Bengal* (Calcutta, 1960) and David Kopf, *The Brahmo Samaj and the Shaping of the Modern Mind* (Princeton, 1977).

between two ideologies, the colonial and the indigenous. The changes envisaged and made were attempts to challenge 'the pretended supremacy of the culture of the colonizer' as well as 'to reassert the cultural identity of the colonized'. The Christian missionaries as well as the Utilitarians had severely attacked the Indian civilization, specifically on the issues of gender relations. Because of the low status of Indian women, the 'woman question' provided a convenient tool to establish and assert the moral superiority of the colonial rulers over the colonized. The cornered colonized elite, sought to defend their culture by projecting a 'glorious' Hindu past when the position of women had been high. The medieval period, in terms of this new reconstruction, merely meant a decline from an early greatness. There followed a strategic reconstruction of the 'glorious' women of the 'glorious' ancient period.[10] In effect, as a result of the double pull in two opposite directions — the Western model and the Indian ideal — Indian women were expected to combine in themselves the womanly qualities prized both in the 'modern' West and in the 'ancient' East. The models of both the

[10] This issue has been competently dealt with in Meredith Borthwick, *The Changing Role of Women in Bengal*, 1849–1905 (Princeton, 1984), pp. 26–108. See also K.N. Panikkar, 'The Intellectual History of Colonial India: Some Historiographical and Conceptual Questions' in S. Bhattacharya and Romila Thapar, ed., *Situating Indian History* (Delhi, 1986), esp. p. 428. Amales Tripathi 'The Role of Traditional Modernisers: Bengal's Experience in the Nineteenth Century', *Calcutta Historical Journal*, 1983–84, crisply comments that the western challengers were distinctly at an advantage in the given situation of Bengal. Politically dominated, economically exploited, staggering under a severe famine, Bengal was almost bankrupt culturally. The Sanskrit tradition had long lost its creative power; the Vedic studies were almost forgotten; Nadia, the classic centre of Sanskrit education in Bengal, was in a pitiable state. Vina Mazumdar, 'The Social Reform Movement from Ranade to Nehru' in B.R. Nanda, ed., *Indian Women from Purdah to Modernity* (New Delhi, 1977), pinpoints the urban middle class character of the movement. For a recent analysis, see Uma Chakravarti, 'Whatever Happened to the Vedic Dasi? Orientalism, Nationalism and a Script for the Past' in Kumkum Sangari and Sudesh Vaid, eds., *Recasting Women* (New Delhi, 1989). Lata Mani goes further and claims that the debates on the *sati* were argued almost exclusively in terms of scriptures and that 'what was at stake was not women, but tradition.' See Lata Mani, 'Contentions Traditions', in *Recasting Women*, esp. p. 118.

women of the 'glorious past' as well as the Victorian English women were, of course, idealized. The image of the perfect Victorian lady did not correspond to the realities of the life-situations of the middle class women of Victorian England.[11] Even so, the created stereotype continued to be projected. While women were to be educated and 'modernized', they were to bear all the traditional responsibilities of a respectable home and depend totally on the male head of the family. Not unnaturally, the educated women at the receiving end of male patronage, internalized male concepts of the new womanhood. They declared that women should be able to read and write Bengali, and preferably some English (presumably to communicate with the ruling class), learn household skills and aspire to become *sumata* (good mother) and *sugrihini* (good housewife).[12] Their writings reveal their keenness to cultivate the tastes which their husbands appreciated and to become their 'worthy' companions. In practice, the age-old Indian norms were not rejected, while all the time examples of Western women were cited.

While nineteenth-century contradictions were not resolved in the twentieth century, new forces and influences were released to shape the contours of women's consciousness. To be sure, British feminists like Annie Besant and Margaret Cousins brought Indian women under the influence of Western feminist ideologies,[13] and

---

[11] For confirmation of this point, see Mary Wollstonecraft's classic work, *A Vindication of the Rights of Women* (London, 1875) and P. Branca, *Silent Sisterhood: Middle Class Women in the Victorian Home* (London, 1977).

[12] *Bamabodhini Patrika* (The Journal for the Enlightenment of Women), the premier women's journal of the nineteenth century, is replete with such essays. One often notices an ambivalence in educated women's writings as well as in their behaviour-pattern. An interesting example is that of Dr Kadambini Ganguly (b. 1861), the first lady doctor in Bengal, who used to knit laces sitting in the carriage while on her rounds to visit her patients. She seems to have been a shade too anxious to please her husband's relations by his first marriage. Punyalata Chakravarty, *Chhelebelar Dinguli* (My Childhood Days, Calcutta 1381 BS/1974 AD), p. 12.

[13] Annie Besant had been active in England as a suffragist. She later came to India and settled down in Madras. She gained wide reputation as a Theosophist and was the President of the Theosophical Society for many years. She became involved in the women's movement in India and also in Indian politics, played

the spread of women's education generated new ideas.[14] But the crucial difference in the shift in women's images, ideas as well as life-situations was made during the freedom movement. By the end of the nineteenth century, the educated elite, who had earlier collaborated with the Raj — chiefly in their own interests, but also because they had hoped that British rule would transform India on the pattern of Britain — had become disillusioned with their allies. They realized that far from developing India, the British were actually hindering its development and 'touching the pockets of the Indian bourgeoisie'.[15]

Women's Political Participation: The first phase 1905–10

If the intelligentsia in other parts of India were experiencing disillusionment gradually, in Bengal they were woken up with a rude jolt by the partition of Bengal brought about by Lord Curzon. The anti-partition or Swadeshi movement, although initiated as a protest against a political move, was motivated by the urge of the aspiring

---

a key role in forming the Women's Indian Association (1917) and was elected the President of the Indian National Congress in the following year (1918). Margaret Cousins was a Theosophist and a suffragist from Ireland. She helped in the formation of the WIA and later, the All India Women's Conference (1927). It may be mentioned in this connection that Dorothy Jinarajadesa was also associated, like Cousins and Besant, with the foundation of the WIA.

[14] For a brief analysis, see Bharati Ray, 'Women of Bengal: Transformations in Ideas and Ideals', *Social Scientist*, vol. 19, numbers 5–6, May-June 1991.

[15] They had admired the British, applauded British principles of government, which they wanted India to emulate, and expected the British to help them in their task. But soon they realized that real improvement in India was 'incompatible with foreign domination'. After all, the driving force behind capitalistic expansion was not 'abstract missions of civilisation, but the very concrete hunger for super profits.' Hiren Mukherjee, *India's Struggle for Freedom* (Calcutta, 1986), pp. 21 & 91. Bipan Chandra, *The Rise and Growth of Economic Nationalism in India* (New Delhi, 1966) gives a good analysis of the conflict between the economic aspirations of the Indian bourgeoisie and colonial interests. See also his essay, 'The Indian Capitalist Class and Imperialism before 1974' in Bipan Chandra, ed., *Nationalism and Colonialism in Modern India* (New Delhi, 1979), esp. pp. 146–7.

Bengali elite to break the system of British monopoly capitalism and to create new opportunities for their own participation in the commercial and industrial fields. This drive explains the widespread propaganda against the use of British goods and the promotion of indigenous products. Bengali men sought women's help in the movement in order to strengthen it. In bringing women into the movement, they took care not to conjure up a foreign model of womanhood. Nationalism required sustenance from the past, from the traditions, customs and institutions of one's own country. And, therefore, the nationalist appeal was to the indigenous Indian concept of women as the embodiment and transmitter of tradition. Moreover, the nationalist leaders subtly converted the socio-economic struggle against the British into a worship of the motherland, which was in its turn transformed into a mother-goddess.[16] The major limitation of this stance was that it infused the movement with Hindu religious colour and thus restricted Muslim participation in the cause. In its favour, the invocation of the mother-goddess, the *shakti* (primal power), was an appeal to an extremely powerful, pre-Aryan concept in Bengal, and the appeal was, in the ultimate analysis, to time-honoured woman-power.[17] The transformation of nationalism into religion made women's entry into politics easy. Religion being a culturally decreed female domain, the technique reached Hindu women's hearts because they could

---

[16] The intellectuals helped the politicians to achieve this transformation in the domain of culture. Rabindranath Tagore in a song written during this period portrayed Bengal as Goddess Durga who had appeared from within the heart of the land. Abanindranath Tagore represented India as *Bharatamata* (Mother Goddess India) in one of his famous contemporary paintings. Ramendrasundar Trivedi created almost a text of rituals, *Bangalakshmir Bratakatha* (Calcutta, 1905).

[17] Kali is the premier deity in Bengal. The image of Kali 'suggests, as clearly as any symbolism can ever do, the dominance of the Female Principle over the Male Principle', Ashok Rudra, 'Cultural and Religious Influences', in Devaki Jain, ed., *Indian Women* (Delhi, 1978), p. 49. For a recent analysis of Kali, see David Kinsley, *Hindu Goddess* (Delhi, 1987), pp. 2–3 & 95–131. In Bengal, the chief festival, *Durgapuja* represents the story of Goddess Durga destroying Mahishasur, the symbol of evil.

effortlessly identify themselves as parts, however small, of the same *shakti*. Women in Calcutta as well as in mofussil towns responded to men's call in large numbers and joined the movement.

(i) Direct Participation

Of the direct participants in the movement, Saraladebi Choudhurani (b. 1872) was the first Bengali woman leader in the Indian national movement. A daughter of Swarnakumari Debi (b. 1855),[18] this remarkable woman made her debut in the political arena through the medium of music. The song composed by her and sung by over fifty girls assembled from various provinces evoked great response and enthusiasm at the Congress session in Calcutta (1901). Her signal contribution, however, lay in the formation of youth groups. Saraladebi believed that the improvement of health and physique of youths was an essential first step to the success of the national movement. She, therefore, formed her *akhra* (a physical fitness club) and *Byayam samiti* (gymnasium) which also provided links with *biplabis* (revolutionaries). In 1902 she introduced Birashtami Utsav which was followed by Udayaditya Utsav (named after the Hindu zamindar of Jessore) — festivals to celebrate physical prowess and valour. On these occasions young Bengali men displayed their skill with the sword and the *lathi* (stick), and paid homage to Bengali heroes. Sarala argued that people in Bengal were impressed by the heroic tales of Rajput leaders, but tended to forget their own heroes.[19] After her marriage with Rambhuj Datta Chaudhuri of Lahore, she worked to spread the gospel of nationalism in the Punjab, edit the Bengali journal *Bharati*, and maintain her close

---

[18] Swarnakumari Debi was the elder sister of Rabindranath Tagore. She was an author, edited the journal *Bharati* for several years, was associated with the Theosophical Society and became the President of the ladies' section of its Bengal branch. She founded the *Sakhi Samiti* (Women's Friendly Association, 1886) the first women's society in Bengal initiated by a woman. Along with Kadambini Ganguly, she attended the Congress session of Bombay in 1889 as a delegate.

[19] Saraladebi Choudhurani, *Jibaner Jharapata* (Memoirs, Calcutta 1382 BS/1975 AD), pp. 33–48, 128–43 & 153. This is an excellent autobiography but deals only with her life before her marriage.

links with the Suhrid Samiti of Mymensingh, a secret revolutionary society founded in 1900.[20]

Apart from Saraladebi, there were a number of women in Calcutta as well as in mofussil towns who were drawn into the political struggle, although we are familiar with only a few names. Hemantakumari Choudhury (b. 1868), who edited the well-known women's journal *Antahpur* from 1901 to 1904 and later became an active Gandhian nationalist, participated in the movement, delivering fiery speeches and organizing meetings. Lilabati Mitra (b. 1864) along with her husband Krishnakumar Mitra, the noted editor of *Sanjivani*, actively helped the *swadeshi* cause. Labanyaprabha Datta (b. 1888), who later courted imprisonment during the Civil Disobedience movement in the 1930s, joined the Swadeshi movement and persuaded her husband and family to give up the use of foreign goods. Snehashila Choudhury (b. 1886), the latter-day woman leader at Khulna in rural Bengal, organized ladies' meetings where she delivered inspiring speeches to persuade women to give up imported bangles and wear *sankha* (locally made bangles) instead.[21]

Throughout Bengal women observed 16 October 1905 — the actual day of the partition — as a day of protest.[22] Five hundred women gathered in Calcutta to watch the foundation of the Federation Hall: a fair number assembled at Ramendrasundar Trivedi's house at Murshidabad to listen to the patriotic composition, *Bangalakshmir Bratakatha*, read out to them by his daughter, Girija Debi. In Dacca, Ashalata Sen (b. 1894), a girl of eleven, under the inspiration of her grandmother Nabashashi Debi, went from house to house persuading women to join the *swadeshi* cause. In Barisal,

---

[20] 'Samitis and Associations of Mymensingh', Freedom Papers, No. 58 (West Bengal State Archives, Calcutta).

[21] Kamala Das Gupta, *Swadhinata Sangrame Banglar Nari* (Women of Bengal in the Freedom Struggle, Calcutta, 1963), pp. 63 and 212. This work gives biographical sketches of a good number of women freedom fighters of Bengal.

[22] Swarnakumari Debi gives a vivid description of the day, *Bharati*, vol. 32, no. 2, June 1908. Interestingly, on that day many Bengali Christian women teachers went to missionary schools without wearing shoes as a mark of protest. 'An account of the Swadeshi Movement', Freedom Papers, No. 66.

Manorama Basu, a young housewife, led a procession of women on the streets, defying all traditional norms of womanly behaviour. Later, at Barisal (April 1906) two hundred women attended the Provincial Conference.[23] In Khulna, a number of women attended the meeting addressed by Kaliprasanna Kavya-bisarad, one of the key-figures in the movement, where they broke their glass bangles in a gesture symbolic of the boycott of foreign goods; women came to listen to Bipin Pal in Bhola and Suren Banerjee at Tangail. Meetings exclusively of women in support of *swadeshi* in Calcutta, Dacca, Barisal, Chittagong, Mymensingh and Khulna were reported in the *Sanjivani* and other local papers.[24] The *Sanjivani* also published a report that the boycott was enthusiastically supported by Bengali women (i) Srimati Dinamani Choudhury, zamindar of Santosh of Mymensingh, was trying to persuade her subordinates to use only country-made articles; (ii) the widow of Lakshman Chandra Aush Choudhury, the zamindar of Mauganganj, was attempting to do the same; and (iii) Srimati Ambuja Sundari Das Gupta of Jalpaiguri was successfully persuading local women not to use foreign articles.[25] The *Bamabodhini Patrika* reported, 'Women like men are organising meetings in towns as well as villages to express sorrow at the partition of Bengal, and are taking the *swadeshi* vows. At several meetings women are coming forward to inspire men, while at home they are initiating their sons, brothers and husbands to the worship of the motherland'.[26] Many

[23] *Sanjivani*, 19 April, *Sandhya*, 18 and 23 April 1906, RNNB (Report on the Native Newspapers in Bengal, West Bengal State Archives, Calcutta). See also Chhabi Ray, *Banglar Nari Andolan* (Women's Movement in Bengal, Calcutta, n.d.), p. 80 and *Sahitya Sadhak Charitamala* (Biographies of Litterateurs), vol. 6, no. 70, p. 72.

[24] S. Sarkar, *Swadeshi Movement*, p. 288. It is of special interest to note that at Mymensingh, a major centre of the movement, public women gave up the use of imported liquor, and the police were reported to have committed outrages on them in order to 'terrify them into giving up their sympathy for *swadeshi*'. *Bangavasi*, 11 Jan. and *Sonar Bharat*, 18 Jan. 1908, RNNB.

[25] *Sanjivani*, 24 and 31 Aug. and 28 Sep. 1905. Similar reports of women's activism were published in *Jyoti*, 28 Sept. 1905, Daily *Hitavadi*, 22 April 1906, RNNB.

[26] *Bamabodhini Patrika*, vol. 43, Nov. 1905. *The Indian Mirror*, 28 Jan. 1906

women stopped wearing foreign clothes even on festive occasions. Many took up weaving to make clothes for their families. The use of hand-spun cloth had become an important national symbol.

Women's journals, especially *Suprabhat*, edited by Kumudini Mitra (b. 1882) and *Antahpur*, founded by Banalata Debi (b. 1880),[27] gave publicity to *swadeshi* brands, such as 'Bengal Chemicals' 'New Floral Hair Oil' and 'Oriental Soap', manufactured by the Oriental Soap Factory. These advertisements, one must note, did not exploit feminine figures or images. The entire emphasis was on the indigenous character of the goods, for example, 'manufactured entirely with Bengal's capital and Bengal's labour'.

(ii) Indirect Participation

Direct participation was not feasible for women in the *biplabi* (revolutionary) movement that broke out during the last phase of the *swadeshi* movement. Women were not included initially in the *samitis* or revolutionary associations; the prevailing ideology of the time was too conservative and the risks too formidable to allow women to participate on an equal basis with men. Nevertheless, many women helped the *biplabis* silently from the background. Sarala Debi Choudhurani and Sister Nivedita[28] maintained close links with the *biplabis*. Kumudini Mitra organized a group of dedicated Brahmin women to serve as messengers between different *biplabis*; these women were kept under watch by the police.[29] Mataji Tapaswini, a Marathi lady and the founder of Mahakali Pathshala, a girls' school in Calcutta, allowed her school building to become the office of a secret society — Banga Dharma Sammilan — and

---

echoed the same sentiments and noted 'a general awakening among Indian women as a result of the partition agitation'

[27] Kumudini Mitra (later Bose) was the daughter of Lilabati and Krishnakumar Mitra. For a short biographical sketch, see Prabasi, 1350 BS/1943 AD. Banalata Debi was the daughter of Brahmo reformer Sasipada Banerjee. She edited *Antahpur* from its inception till her death in 1900.

[28] Sister Nivedita was not a Bengali by birth, but an Irish woman. She came under the influence of Swami Vivekananda and dedicated herself to the service of India, especially in the field of education.

[29] Manmohan Kaur, *Women in India's Freedom Movement*, pp. 91–3.

a 'rendezvous for political extremists'.[30] In many a middle class family, women as mothers, sisters and sisters-in-law helped the cause of the revolutionaries. Women used to give shelter to absconding *biplabis*, hide or transport firearms and functioned as couriers.[31] Saudamini Debi of Faridpur, Sarojini Debi, Priyabala Debi and Mrinalini Debi of Barisal, Brahmomoyee and Chinmoyee Sen of Dacca are but a few names of the women (about whom not much is known) who rendered such help to the *biplabis*.[32]

The overwhelming regard women exhibited for Kanailal Datta who was hanged to death for killing Naren Goswami (who had turned an approver) inside the Alipore Jail (1908) was particularly impressive. They assembled in large numbers to have a last look at his body which was carried in a procession for his funeral. They chanted, 'Blessed is Kanai, and blessed is Kanai's mother'.[33] This kind of spontaneous demonstration by women took many of the

---

[30] Mahakali Pathshala, Home Political (Confidential) Proceedings, no. 111 (1–3), (West Bengal State Archives, Calcutta).

[31] Satish Pakrashi, *Agnidiner Katha* (Memoirs: Tales of Those Revolutionary Days, Calcutta, 1947), p. 93.

[32] Examples may be multiplied. Of the more well-known women, Labanyaprabha Dutta regularly used to hide revolvers and proscribed books to assist her *biplabi* brother. Sarojini, the sister of Aurobindo Ghosh, stood solidly by him and collected funds for his defence when he was being tried for the Alipore Bomb conspiracy. Lilabati Mitra welcomed him to her home on his release from imprisonment despite warnings that it might impede the release of her own husband, Krishnakumar Mitra. Charushila Debi of Midnapur gave Khudiram Bose shelter for a few days after his attempted assassination of Kingsford at Muzaffarpur. She had to go underground during Khudiram's trial. See Kamala Das Gupta, *Swadhinata Sangrame*, pp. 63, 286 and 67–8. Also *Sanjivani*, 2 July and 26 Nov. 1908, RNNB. Haridas and Uma Mukherjee, *Swadeshi Andolan O Banglar Nabayug* (The Swadeshi Movement and the New Era in Bengal, Calcutta, 1961), pp. 171–3, describes a case of open support shown by a group of women to *biplabi* Bhupendranath Datta's mother when he was imprisoned for the publication of two 'seditious' articles in *Jugantar* (1907) which he edited.

[33] The *Sandhya* reported that the women showed as much grief for him as they would if their own child had died. The crowd of women was so large that not even on occasions of great magnificence were so many ever known to have assembled. *Sandhya*, 11, 12 and 13 Nov. 1908, RNNB.

British observers by surprise. The *Daily Telegraph* of London commented that women of the type of Russian nihilists and English suffragists had appeared in Bengal, and that the Bengali ladies were 'the most obstinate and most dangerous antagonists of the English'.[34] The colonial rulers decided that in order to curb the growth of sedition among women, the recording of *swadeshi* songs on gramophone discs should be proscribed and the plays performed in theatre halls, which were frequented by ladies, be censored. Consequently, the boat of Mukunda Das, the noted folk singer, was thoroughly searched. Orders were passed prohibiting the sale of gramophone records of the songs 'Bandemataram' and 'Amar Desh'. The play 'Jiban Sandhya' (then being staged at the Star Theatre) was allowed to be performed only after 'objectionable' passages and songs had been omitted.[35] Despite these precautionary measures, the increasing political awareness of Bengali women caused a contemporary Japanese historian, Shumei Okawa, to observe, 'As the time has come when politics is discussed in the *zenana*, it can be safely said that no longer can the British sleep without anxiety'.[36]

Women's Political Participation: The second phase 1910–29

The Swadeshi movement petered out and the freedom movement, led by the Indian National Congress, remained somewhat dormant during the early years of the First World War. But the activities of individual Indian revolutionaries like Rashbehari Bose, Raja Mahendra Pratap, V.D. Savarkar, M.N. Roy, Abani Mukherjee and Jatin Mukherjee continued to inspire men and women alike in India.[37] Meanwhile, economic antagonism between the colonial power and the educated Bengali *bhadralok* grew deeper and the

---

[34] *Dainik Chandrika*, 18 and 20 Nov. 1908, RNNB.
[35] *Sandhya*, 9 Dec. and Basumati, 5 Dec. 1908, RNNB.
[36] Cited in Masayuki Usada, 'Aswini Kumar Dutta's Role in the Political, Social and Cultural Life of Bengal' (Unpublished thesis, Calcutta University, 1977), p. 223.
[37] Ashalata Sen, 'One Woman's Saga' (Mimeograph), p. 4. This is one of the rare autobiographies of a woman leader from a district town of Bengal.

economic discontent of the indigenous merchants was on the increase.[38] This discontent surfaced through Gandhi's call for the Non-Co-operation movement of the 1920s and later in the 1930s.[39]

Women's interest in politics, once roused during the Swadeshi period, continued (although on a lower key) during the next decade, until the emergence of the Home Rule agitation under a woman, Annie Besant. Besant began to agitate for India's cause for freedom by founding the Home Rule League (1916). Her involvement inspired many an Indian woman (for example, Kamaladevi Chattopadhyaya) and, in a sense, smoothed the way for the immense contribution that women made under Gandhi.[40] The election of Annie Besant as President of the Indian National Congress — the first woman to occupy this post — and the holding of the Congress session under her leadership in Calcutta contained a special message for women. Women's political activities during the next phase proceeded in two directions: first, an agitation for 'vote for women' (undoubtedly inspired by the Western suffrage movement and fostered by Margaret Cousins), which was specifically a woman's issue and, second, participation in the freedom movement along with men.

[38] This issue has been competently dealt with in Rajat Kanta Ray, *Social Conflict and Political Unrest in Bengal, 1875–1927* (Delhi, 1984), pp. 150–85 and 225–30. One may also cite, as an example, a letter written by the Secretary, Bengal Piecegoods Merchants' Association to Gandhi on 31 May 1928, in which he bitterly complained that the Bengali mercantile community was in dire stress because of the 'jute impasse' in Bengal and because of the crisis in tea, coal and other industries. Nothing was being done, he mentioned, to redress the growing burden of economic depression under which the people suffered. AICC papers (Nehru Memorial Museum and Library), file No. G-48 and G-48 K.W. 1927–31.

[39] The support of the merchants and traders for this movement has been noted by several historians. See Sabyasachi Bhattacharya, 'Cotton Mills and Spinning Wheels: Swadeshi and the Indian Capitalist Class, 1920–22', in K.N. Panikkar, ed., *National and Left Movements in India* (New Delhi, 1980). This testifies to the eminently middle class character of the movement in which women of this class were also largely involved.

[40] Interview with Kamaladevi Chattopadhyaya, Oral History Project (Nehru Memorial Museum and Library), p. 6. The interview gives a good insight into this remarkable woman's life and works.

(i) The Struggle for Votes for Women

Contrary to the earlier belief that women encountered 'very little opposition' to their demand to vote,[41] it has now been established that the right to vote was not granted to women without pressure from organized women. In one sense, the demand for franchise was an attempt by the women of the elite classes to find a room for themselves in the established power structure, thereby strengthening the monopolistic hold of the same groups on the political system. Even so, there is little doubt that to those who voiced the demand, it represented protest against a socio-political structure which excluded women from access to political power.[42]

The organized political move by women in this sphere was formally initiated when a franchise delegation led by Sarojini Naidu and including Margaret Cousins, Annie Besant, Dorothy Jinarajadasa, Uma Nehru, Ramabai Ranade and Abala Bose,[43] met the Secretary of State, Edwin Montague, and demanded equal franchise for women. Their main argument was that the advent of women would transform the vitiated political world and would be especially conducive to the healthy development of children. Although the Montague-Chelmsford scheme sidetracked the issue, the Southborough Franchise Committee was set up to look into it. Sarojini Naidu, Annie Besant, Herabai Tata and Mithan Tata went to

---

[41] See, for instance, Hannah Sen, 'Our Own Times', in Tara Ali Baig, ed., *Women of India* (Delhi, 1958), p. 35.

[42] Vina Mazumdar, ed., *Symbols of Power: Studies on the Political Status of Women in India* (New Delhi, 1979), p. ix. Mazumdar also argues that some women might have exercised considerable power through informal channels and their hold on some men, but there was no opportunity of wielding power by 'women as a group'.

[43] For a biography of Sarojini Naidu, poet and freedom fighter, see V.S. Navarane, *Sarojini Naidu, An Introduction to Her Life, Work and Poetry* (New Delhi, 1988). Vijayalakshmi Pandit, *Scope of Happiness*, gives a succinct account of Uma Nehru's character and activities. For a contemporary account of Ramabai Ranade, see S. Sorabji, 'Ramabai Ranade', in E.C. Gedge and M. Choksi, eds., *Women in Modern India* (Bombay, 1929). Abala Bose (b. 1865) daughter of the social reformer Durga Mohan Das and wife of the famous scientist Jagadish Bose, was one of the pioneering women educationists in Bengal.

London in 1919 to give evidence before the Joint Parliamentary Committee (appointed to refine the Montague-Chelmsford reforms) in favour of women's franchise. The Joint Committee left the responsibility of the final decision to the future Legislative Councils of India for each province.[44] The centre of gravity of the women's franchise was shifted from the all-India theatre to the individual provincial arena. Among the provinces, Madras took the lead in removing the sex disqualification for legislative franchise and also in receiving a woman, Dr Muthulakshmi Reddy, as a member of the Legislative Council.[45]

In Bengal, the chief women's organization to fight for the franchise was the Bangiya Nari Samaj (Bengali Women's Association, 1921) guided by Kumudini Bose, Kamini Roy (b. 1864), Mrinalini Sen (b. 1879) and Jyotirmoyee Ganguly (b. 1889).[46] This body attempted to mobilize support for their cause from the male intellectual elite and political leaders, such as Ramananda Chatterjee, Surendranath Banerjea and Bipin Chandra Pal. Despite this, the resolution to permit women to vote was defeated in the Bengal Legislative Council in 1921.[47] Notwithstanding their disappointment, women persevered in their struggle. They organized protest meetings and continued to lobby for their cause. The Bangiya Nari Samaj also affiliated itself to the Madras-based Women's Indian Association in order to learn from the latter's organizing experience. It simultaneously concentrated on gaining the right for women to vote in the Calcutta Municipal election, which it succeeded in doing

---

[44] Aruna Asaf Ali, 'Women's Suffrage in India', in S.K. Nehru, ed., *Our Cause* (Allahabad, n.d.), pp. 351–7; Geraldine H. Forbes, 'Votes for Women: The Demand for Women's Franchise in India, 1917–1937', in Vina Mazumdar, *Symbols of Power*, pp. 4–8; see also J.M. Everett, *Women and Social Change in India* (New Delhi, 1979).

[45] See Muthulakshmi Reddy, *My Experiences as a Legislator* (Madras, 1930).

[46] The life of Kamini Roy, poet, teacher and social worker, has been described in *Sahitya Sadhak Charitamala*. For a short biographical sketch of Jyotirmoyee Ganguly, educationalist and freedom fighter, and daughter of Kadambini Ganguly, see *Prabasi*, Paush 1352 BS/1945 AD. Mrinalini Sen, *Knocking at the Door* (Calcutta, 1945) is an excellent autobiography.

[47] *Bengal Legislative Council Proceedings*, vol. IV (5 Sept. 1921).

in 1923.[48] Encouraged by this victory, a women's delegation led by Kamini Roy and two Muslim women, Begum Rokeya Sakhawat Hossein and Begum Sultan Muwajidzada, met the Viceroy, Lord Lytton, to seek his support for their cause. Support also came from a number of small organized *mahila samitis* (women's societies) in the district towns of Dacca, Mymensingh and Chittagong. In 1925 the Bengal Legislature approved a limited female suffrage and in 1926 Bengali women exercised this right for the first time. It symbolized for them formal entry into the hitherto exclusive male public world of political decision-making.[49]

(ii) The Freedom Struggle

Simultaneously with the women's battle for their constitutional right of franchise was their struggle for freedom from colonial rule. There were dramatic changes in the Indian political scenario in 1919–20. As a response to the passing of the Rowlatt Bill and the Jallianwala Bagh Massacre (1919), and strengthened by the upsurge of the Khilafat movement, Gandhi launched the Non-Co-operation movement formally in 1920. The special Congress session in Calcutta gave its approval to the proposed agitation.

In the context of Bengali women's participation in the Gandhian movement, three distinct features are worth noting. First, the identification of the freedom struggle with *deshpuja* and the invocation of *shakti* continued, making women's entry into politics smooth. To quote a leading daily, 'In the Hindu *Shastras* (scriptures), it is stated that when the might of the gods could not put down oppression, it was the might of women which succeeded'.[50] Women responded as before to the appeal. Second, while Gandhi's

---

[48] *Bengal Legislative Council Proceedings*, vol. XI (29 January 1923).

[49] Initially, however, only a handful of women could vote because the right was based on property and educational qualifications. Barbara Southard, 'Plunge into Politics: The Development of Political Consciousness among Bengali Women Reformers in the Dyarchy Era', paper presented at the Annual Conference of the Association for Asian Studies, 1985, is a detailed study of this issue.

[50] *The Dainik Basumati*, 8 Dec. 1921, RNNB. See also *Dainik Bharatamitra*, 8 Dec. 1921. For Women's response, see *The Dhumketu*, 17 Dec. 1922, RNNB.

views were not informed by a feminist perspective, they infused self-confidence into women. His assertion that women were morally better suited than men for the non-violent struggle removed the stigma of their inferiority *vis-à-vis* men.[51] Gandhi's 'stature was high'. Therefore, when women came out in the political field, they encountered no opposition from their family members who knew that 'they were protected'.[52] Third, during the period under survey, Bengal produced political captains of national stature like C.R. Das and Bipin Chandra Pal, and politicized women with leadership abilities, such as Basanti Debi (b. 1880) and Hemaprabha Majumdar (b. 1884).[53] These women leaders had access to the general body of women and helped to promote women's political and social awareness.[54]

As noted earlier, the movement was led in Bengal by C.R. Das. His wife Basanti Debi led women's demonstrations picketing shops selling foreign goods. On 7 December 1921 she was arrested in a public street in Calcutta for hawking *khaddar* along with Urmila Debi (b. 1883) and Suniti Debi. Although they were released after a few hours, their arrest infuriated the public. Urmila Debi put it neatly, 'We also had set an example to the rest of the women; our arrest had produced the desired effect.'[55]

[51] *Young India*, 26 February 1918. M.K. Gandhi, *Women and Social Justice* (Ahmedabad, 1958) provides a general outline of his views on women. He was against women's gainful employment (except through spinning and cottage industries) and preferred women to be a moral rather than an economic force. But his severe condemnation of injustice to women helped them gain some status in society.

[52] Sucheta Kripalani, Oral History Transcript (Nehru Memorial Museum & Library), p. 11. This is confirmed by Kamaladevi Chattopadhyaya, *Inner Recesses, Outer Spaces: Memoirs* (New Delhi, 1986), p. 47. 'To those of my generation the real political history of India begins with the Gandhi era', she says.

[53] Kamala Das Gupta, *Swadhinatar Sangrame* gives good biographical sketches of both the women.

[54] Personal interview with Kalyani Debi, daughter of Basanti Debi, on 19 April 1983.

[55] *Banglar Katha*, 16 December 1921. Urmila Debi's inspiring article, 'Praner Katha' (My Heart Speaks) published in the same weekly on 28 October 1921, argued that since women had always been kept in the background, the nation had not prospered.

During C.R. Das's imprisonment, Basanti Debi became the President of the Bengal Provincial Congress (1921–2) and presided over its session in 1922 in Chittagong. This brought a Bengali woman into the country's frontline political leadership. Her presidential speech emphasized the need to rejuvenate rural India:

> If we have to get back to the simple and best life of India of old days, we have also to revive the dormant villages . . . . We have to reconstruct our villages, to build up our village institutions under the conditions of modern life, but according to the genius of our national life.[56]

The speech testifies to Basanti Debi's concern for grassroot level involvement in the national movement. Like Kasturba in Gujarat, she gave priority to Gandhi's economic doctrines of reviving the village economy and cottage industries which would also restore to women some of their lost economic strength.[57] Her speech was reported to be even more effective than that of Bipin Chandra Pal. The attendance of women at the Conference was impressive. 'Was it due', the press speculated, 'to a lady being the President, or to the political awakening of Bengali women?'[58]

Basanti Debi's close political associate, her sister-in-law Urmila Debi, took active part in the anti-colonial struggle, but chose to dedicate herself primarily to the setting up of the Nari Karma Mandir (Temple for Women's Work, 1921) in order to popularize spinning and weaving among women. Her poor health did not allow her to pursue her mission with the kind of zeal that she would have wished. Hemaprabha Majumdar, one of the five founder-members of the C.R. Das-led Swaraj Party, initially assisted Urmila Debi to run the Nari Karma Mandir. After it finally closed down,

---

[56] *Amrita Bazar Patrika*, 1922, RNNB.

[57] The destruction of cottage industries and the increasing import of mass-produced goods by the colonial rulers had affected adversely women's productive roles in the villages. It may be mentioned in passing that Basanti Debi, too, like the political male leadership was bolstering the image of a glorious India of yesterday. This had proved tactically useful.

[58] *The New Empire*, 17 April 1922 and *Dainik Basumati*, 24 April 1922, RNNB.

Hemaprabha organized the Mahila Karmi Sansad (Forum of Women Workers, 1922). The objective was both political and social, i.e. to give vocational training to women and preach nationalism. It ran a home where destitute women were given shelter. On the political front, Hemaprabha played a crucial role in the steamer strike of Chandpur and Goalanda (1921). She personally went to Goalanda and organized a volunteer force to look after the coolies from the Assam tea gardens. Then, she moved on to Narayanganj to found a women's association. Back in Calcutta, while leading a women's procession, she was injured in a confrontation with the police.[59] When Sarojini Naidu became the Congress President (1926), Hemaprabha proved to be a most valued colleague. These two women along with Kamaladevi Chattopadhyaya became the focal points of contact between the leaders of the freedom struggle and those of the women's movement. Another courageous female leader of the time was Jyotirmoyee Ganguly. She resigned from her teaching job in Ceylon (now Sri Lanka) to join the Non-Co-operation movement. To her belongs the credit of having initiated the first women's volunteer organization during the Calcutta Congress of 1920. Popularly nick-named Debi Choudhurani, she later made impressive contributions to the Civil Disobedience agitation of the 1930s.[60] The entry of women like Naidu, Ganguly and Majumdar into active politics was according to Lakshmi Menon, herself a freedom fighter, 'not only a great asset to the Congress but also a real inspiration to the hesitant womanhood of India.'[61]

The dedication and passion of these women unnerved the colonial bureaucracy. In a report, Clarke, the Commissioner of

---

[59] Kamala Das Gupta, *Swadhinatar Sangrame*, pp. 54–6; *Dainik Basumati*, 9 Feb. 1922, RNNB.

[60] *Prabasi*, 1335 BS/1928 AD: no. 12 and 1352 BS/1945 AD: no. 9. Debi Choudhurani is the central female character in Bankim Chandra Chatterjee's novel, *Debi Choudhurani* (1884). Prafulla, rejected by her husband's family, met Bhabani Thakur while searching for a shelter. She was trained by him to lead a band of armed men who fought for justice and for the defence of the poor. She was renamed Debi Chaudhurani.

[61] Lakshmi Menon, 'Women and the National Movement' in Devaki Jain, ed. *Indian Women*, p. 24.

The Freedom Movement and Feminist Consciousness 197

Police, Calcutta, noted a few names of frontline women agitators such as Basanti Debi, Urmila Debi and Suniti Debi, Hemaprabha Majumdar, Sunitibala Mitra, Uma Debi and Sati Debi of the Nari Karma Mandir, Bagala Som, Mohini Dasgupta, Binapani Debi and Pratima Debi. He observed that the female volunteers were mostly Brahmos. They came out into the streets every day and were joined by male volunteers and other enthusiasts on the way, 'the ladies singing and the male followers exhorting shopkeepers to give up dealing in foreign cloth and stock swadeshi goods'. The procession, as it moved slowly along, grew in strength, until about three or four hundred persons moved in a body, 'traffic being hindered and often entirely blocked'. Clarke warned his superior officers that if no immediate steps were taken, the movement steered by women would grow and inevitably, sooner or later, 'there would be collision between the feminine agitators and the police'.[62] A week later, Clarke again gave an account of increasing political activism of women, in total defiance of the government order prohibiting public processions and meetings. Basanti Debi was at the head of a large crowd in Mirzapur Street; Hemaprabha Majumdar addressed a mammoth meeting at College Square; Binodini Debi and Jagat Mohini Debi arranged a meeting in Hazra Park. The Police Commissioner's cynical comment was that the men in Bengal were taking 'shelter behind the skirts' of women and that 'the Civil Disobedience campaign as it exists in Calcutta is being conducted by women.'[63] The 1928 session of the Congress marked further involvement of Bengali women in political programmes. Subhas Bose decided that female volunteers, like males, should march in military fashion, in uniforms. Latika Ghosh, popularly known as Colonel Latika, was placed in charge of recruiting volunteers. She collected a number of young women from Bethune College and Victoria Institution and the Calcutta Corporation teachers. *The Forward* commented on 28 December 1928 that as the volunteers

---

[62] 'Note on Feminine Agitators' by R. Clarke, CIE, Commissioner of Police, Calcutta, 12 January 1922, Govt. of Bengal, Home Political File No. 48, serial Nos. 1–8, 1922 (West Bengal State Archives, Calcutta).

[63] 'Note on Female Agitation' by R. Clarke, 18 January 1922, ibid.

marched 'there could be traced not a touch of all the frailties that are so commonly attributed in popular minds with the womanhood of Bengal.'

Nor did the mofussil women lag behind. In Midnapur the Union Board boycott was successful due to women's co-operation. In Dacca, Ashalata Sen established the Gandaria Mahila Samiti 'with a view to spreading the spirit of nationalism and the message of Gandhi to local women'. The members of the Samiti carried shoulderloads of Khadi from door to door and organized annual industrial fairs to promote *swadeshi* goods.[64] Not just a few leaders, but masses of women struck at the Raj. Women who would not previously appear before their male relatives now came out on the streets to join processions. A large number of women were arrested in 1922. Of these, particularly sensational was the arrest and conviction of Savitri Debi (who was sentenced to three months' imprisonment), the first woman political participant to be seriously 'punished'.[65] The contemporary press sensed that while women's imprisonment could not bring *swaraj*, if women were sent to jail in large numbers, the effect would be disastrous for the Raj. The nation would be deeply shocked and in the process the anti-colonial struggle would actually acquire 'strength' because of 'the humiliation of women'.[66]

Although the Non-Co-operation movement was abruptly called off by Gandhi after the Chauri Chaura incident, women's political interests in Bengal did not subside. Bengal had been drawn to armed *biplabi* ideology, Gandhi's political influence notwithstanding. While in the Swadeshi era women could provide only indirect help to the *biplabis*, during the 1920s they came out more openly in support of the movement.[67] Leela Roy (b. 1900) organized the Dipali Sangha (1924) in Dacca with the avowed purpose of spreading education among women, but really to initiate them into

---

[64] Ashalata Sen, One Woman's Saga, pp. 5–6.

[65] *Dainik Basumati*, 3 Feb. 1922 and *Swatantra*, 8 Dec. 1922 RNNB.

[66] *Hindusthan*, 8 Dec. 1921 and 9 Feb. 1922 and *Dainik Basumati*, 8 Dec. 1921, RNNB.

[67] For a detailed analysis of women's participation in the *biplabi* movement in the 1920s, see Kamala Das Gupta, *Swadhinata Sangrame*.

revolutionary ideology.[68] In 1927 the Mahila Rashtriya Sangha (National Organization of Women) was established to propagate the ideas of Subhas Chandra Bose. Prabhabati Bose, Subhas Chandra's mother, was the president, Latika Ghosh was the Secretary and Arubala Sengupta the Assistant Secretary of the Sangha. In 1928, Latika Ghosh organized a women's volunteer force during the Congress session in Calcutta. Of the more radically inclined leaders, Santosh Kumari Gupta who organized the Tarakeswar satyagraha of 1923 and made several attempts in the mid-twenties to organize the jute mill workers, became the latter-day women's labour leader.[69] Prabhabati Dasgupta provided the much-needed leadership in the Calcutta and Howrah municipal scavengers' strike of 1928 and the jute mill strike of 1928 and 1929. Many a woman who did not openly uphold the *biplabi* cause rendered indirect help to them by serving as 'post boxes' or carriers of arms and by giving shelter to those who had to go underground.[70]

The 1920s saw the emergence of a movement of great consequence. It was the politicization of students. The custom of early marriage still prevented many Hindu girls from attending high school or college, but those who did were attracted to politics.[71] During the Non-Co-operation movement, many students left educational institutions, and student volunteers led processions to

[68] A number of articles deal with Leela Roy's life and works. See, for instance, Anil Ghosh, ed., *Leela Roy Jayanti Arghya* (Tributes to Leela Roy, Calcutta, 1968).

[69] Manju Chattopadhyaya, 'Santosh Kumari Debi: A Pioneer Labour Leader', *Social Scientist*, vol. 128 (Jan. 1984).

[70] Personal interview with Kalpana Datta (Joshi), a *biplabi* and a freedom fighter (b. 1913), in 1986. See also Bhupendrakumar Datta, 'Pratham Jedin Dhara Pari' (When I was arrested for the first time), *Mandira*, vol. 11, no. 1 (1948). B.K. Rakshit-Ray, *Chalar Pathey* (Calcutta, 1931) is a collection of short stories concerning this theme.

[71] By 1920 many educated Hindu men in urban Bengal had come to believe that some education for daughters was necessary, if only to improve their marital prospects. A Bengali journal published from Dacca noted as early as 1911 the desire of Hindu girls for at least high school education, *Bharatamahila*, vol. 7, no. 5 (1911–12). For a brief description of women's education in Bengal during the period, see Bharati Ray, 'Advances of Education: from Mortar and Pestle to Mortar-board and scroll', in *Naari* (Calcutta, 1990).

College Street, Wellington Square and the Cornwallis Street areas.[72] Women students from several colleges, especially the Diocesan College, went to meetings when Gandhi came to Calcutta;[73] two hundred college students joined the volunteer corps organized by Latika Ghosh in 1928. In a moving piece published in the Bengali weekly, *Banglar Katha*, Urmila Debi described how Bengali girls wearing coarse khadi sarees travelled from place to place in third class compartments in trains (in order to propagate *swadeshi*) and how the porters at the railway stations were eager to assist them. A *bhadralok* in a railway compartment remarked, 'There is little doubt that the country has woken up . . . The sight of unmarried Bengali women coming out of their sheltered home, discarding all old inhibitions, does inspire every person.'[74] Increasingly, women students came forward to hold street corner meetings, travel unaccompanied in trams and buses, collect party funds, and organize strikes and agitations, violating all traditional norms of womanly conduct and derecognizing the domestic/public lines of demarcation.[75]

During the 1920s women students began to evolve their own organizational network. Dipali Sangha of Dacca perhaps deserves the credit for spearheading the first major female students' organized movement in Eastern Bengal, now Bangladesh. Its students' wing energetically promoted primary education. Even more remarkable was their work in the field of women's rights movement. They discussed the question of social rehabilitation of raped women, a bold step at that time.[76] Another student body at the political level was the Chhatri Sangha (Female Students' Organization) of Calcutta, which was started in 1928 with Surama Mitra as President and Kalyani Bhattacharyya (b. 1907) as Secretary. Bina Das (b. 1911), Kalpana Datta (b. 1913) and Kamala Dasgupta, all major actors in the armed movement of the 1930s, were members

---

[72] 'Note on Feminine Agitators' by R. Clarke, Bengal Government Home Political file No. 48, 1922, and *Dainik Basumati*, 10 Dec. 1921, RNNB.
[73] Renuka Ray, *My Reminiscences* (Calcutta, 1922), pp. 16, 28–30.
[74] Urmila Debi, 'Chitra' (A Sketch), *Banglar Katha*, 4 Nov. 1921.
[75] Manikuntala Sen, *Sediner Katha* (Tales of Yesterdays, Calcutta, 1982), p. 46.
[76] Lilabati Nag, 'Dipali', *Bangalakshmi*, vol. 5, no. 7 (1929–30).

of this association. The technique of self-defence (mainly by means of the indigenous style of fighting with sticks and daggers) was taught to the members. Dinesh Majumdar, a dedicated *biplabi* leader, was the trainer.[77] It was not a secret organization and membership could be enlarged. Student members tried to initiate other female students into the movement. Quite a few girls from the Brahmo Girls' School, Victoria Institution, Bethune School and College were enrolled into this organization. A hostel was started by Kalyani Bhattacharyya's mother to provide lodging to some of the members of the *Chhatri Sangha*.[78] The Dipali Sangha and the Chhatri Sangha were closely linked.[79] They were the forerunners of many other female student organizations which were formed later.[80] The historical significance of these student bodies lies in the creation of a female youth power bloc at par with their male counterparts. They trained a body of independent, strong-willed young women who ardently fought for nationalism and initiated other women into the cause. In sum, by the end of the 1920s and the beginning of the 1930s Bengali women, or at least a good section of them, had become political actors.

Emerging Feminist Consciousness

The questions that strike one are: how far were politicized women conscious of the gender asymmetry enforced by the country's traditional framework? While their participation in the anti-colonial struggle may not have stemmed from a desire to transform society, did the involvement widen their horizon and generate a new thought process?

---

[77] Interview with Kamala Das Gupta, Oral History Project (Nehru Memorial Museum and Library).

[78] Interview with Kalyani Battacharya, Oral History Transcript (Nehru Memorial Museum & Library). In the hostel bombs were hidden and were secretly delivered to *biplabis*.

[79] Personal interview with Sunil Das, a freedom fighter, in 1986.

[80] See Renu Chakravarty, *Communists in Indian Women's Movement* (New Delhi, 1980) and Kumari Jayawardane, *Feminism and Nationalism in the Third World* (New Delhi, 1986), pp. 104–5.

It has often been argued that women's political participation was merely an extension of their domestic role. Borthwick suggests in the context of the Swadeshi Movement that the 'struggle against a common oppressor effectively diverted attention from other potential conflicts within the social system'.[81] Tanika Sarkar echoes the same view concerning the movements of the 1920s and 1930s. Since 'patriotism was subsumed within religion', women's politicization fitted into the traditional cultural matrix.[82]

These expositions seem to be borne out by the platform speeches and biographies of contemporary political leaders. The oral interviews with women participants themselves appear to confirm them. Biographies of C.R. Das barely mention Basanti Debi as a political leader;[83] Bipin Chandra Pal's memoir dwells at length on his mother's and grandmother's role as sacrificing housewives;[84] Ashalata Sen unhesitantly stated that she did not approve of women in paid jobs and that when she went to jail she made proper arrangements for her aged father-in-law to be looked after.[85]

Nevertheless, one must not overlook the tremendous changes in women's perceptions that occurred during this period. They *did* step out from the cloisters of their homes into the male preserve of politics and power. Whatever be the rationale explaining this novelty (for example, *deshpuja* or women's special quality of self-sacrifice emphasized by Gandhi), the actual process entailed the blurring of the domestic/public division (although this was intended for a temporary period) and, inevitably, had an immense impact on the lives of not only those who participated, but also on others who sympathized. The ethos of housework as a woman's only work and wifehood/motherhood as the supreme fulfilment of her life under-

---

[81] M. Borthwick, *Changing Role of Women*, p. 361.

[82] Tanika Sarkar, 'Politics and Women in Bengal—the Conditions and Meaning of Participation', *The Indian Economic and Social History Review*, vol. 21, no. 1 (1984), p. 98.

[83] See for instance, P.C. Ray, *Life and Times of C.R. Das: The Story of Bengal's Self-Expression* (London, 1927).

[84] B.C. Pal, 'Samasamayik Katha' (Of Contemporary Time), in *Navyabharat*, vol. 40, no. 1 (1922).

[85] Personal interview with Ashalata Sen in October 1985.

went an alteration, since it was proclaimed that a woman also had important obligations to the motherland, outside the parameter of the home. Moreover, the age-old notion of women's total inferiority to men began to be slowly eroded. Women had proved that they were capable of fighting alongside men.[86] While the political struggle was on, women leaders as well as the rank and file political workers became increasingly aware of their disabilities as women and were eager to be free from them.[87] The protest that was made against British imperialism was also directed at least partially against the unfair patriarchal structure which benefited half the people at the expense of the other half. A significant example is that of Pritilata Waddedar (b. 1912), the young woman who took part in the Chittagong armoury raid and committed suicide on the failure of the mission. She left a suicide note wherein she stated, 'If women still lag behind men, it is because they were deliberately left behind.' They could, however, fight along with men on an equal level at least on the political front.[88]

If, because of the lack of any statistical or archival data, or positive yardsticks, it is not possible to prove a direct corelation between political participation and women's awareness about issues of gender justice, several pieces of indirect evidence point in this direction. One vital clue is that many politicized women fought simultaneously against the Raj and against patriarchal structures. The linkage is so obvious that it may not be too much to claim that women's organizations of the twentieth century were actually

[86] The new social belief in women's power was further strengthened during the 1930s and 1940s. There is little doubt that it was the willing and spontaneous participation of women in the freedom struggle that finally tilted the balance in favour of political equality between the two sexes in the Constituent Assembly. 'It explains the absence of any debate on this question or its implications'. See Vina Mazumdar, 'Introduction', in *Symbols of Power*, p. xvi.

[87] K.N. Panikkar, 'Introduction', *Studies in History*, vol. 3, no. 1, 1987, p. 7 observes that because of women's involvement in social and political areas, 'women did become increasingly conscious of their subordination and attempted to liberate themselves from the patriarchal ideology which they had internalised through the exclusive domestic experience of sexual and nurturing functions.'

[88] Ananta Sinha, *Suryasener Swapna O Sadhana* (The Dream and Struggle of Surya Sen, Calcutta 1384 BS/AD 1977), pp. 95–9.

born out of the struggle against colonialism. Well-known women freedom fighters such as Saraladebi Choudhurani, Urmila Debi, Hemaprabha Majumdar, Leela Roy, Kumudini Mitra, Jyotirmoyee Ganguly, Latika Ghosh and Ashalata Sen, initiated women's organizations to support and train abandoned women and women who had left their homes, revealing their recognition of the need for altering women's life situations.[89] Their speeches and writings articulate both the discontent emerging among women against the institutionalized oppression of their sex and their claim for equal status, rights and power at par with men.

(i) Women's Organizations

As noted earlier, the awareness produced by the anti-colonial struggle was reflected in the world of women. Perception of the need to organize emerged, and this was reflected in the creation of women's associations. In the nineteenth century, men had organized women's associations on their behalf. Only one or two women, like Swarnakumari Debi of Calcutta and Pandita Ramabai of Poona, had initiated women's associations. Sakhi Samiti was established in 1885 and Sharda Sadan in 1892.[90] As the freedom movement progressed, and women participated in it, they thought of organizing their own network. From the early twentieth century, women political leaders determinedly attempted this task. They received an increasing response from other women, who were becoming progressively aware of the devaluation of women in society. Most of these organizations were concerned primarily with issues of gender.

The pioneering women's organization at the all-India level, the Bharat Stri Mahamandal (All India Women's Organization) was

---

[89] This is equally true of women leaders in the rest of India. A few striking examples are: Kamaladevi Chattopadhyaya, Uma Nehru, Sarojini Naidu, Muthulakshmi Reddy, Bai Amman and Hansa Mehta.

[90] Sakhi Samiti aimed at bringing about better understanding among women and educating helpless widows and unmarried girls. See Ghulam Murshid, *Reluctant Debutante* (Rajshahi, 1983), pp. 95–6. Sharda Sadan was established with a view to providing employment and education for women. These two women were closely followed by Ramabai Ranade. She started the Hindu Ladies Social and Literary Club in 1902 and Seva Sadan in 1909 in Pune.

initiated in 1910 by Saraladebi Choudhurani, who may be regarded as the first feminist of modern Bengal as well as the first woman political leader in modern times. It was the first organization run by women to be clearly committed to augmenting woman power. At the opening session, Saraladebi announced that the first requisite was an awakening at the individual level.

> At the very outset, I, a woman, must assume that I am the presiding deity of my house and that I exist. Subsequently, we women must assume that we are the reigning queens of our societies and families, and that we exist.... We must, to start with, look after our personal development and we shall then gradually be in a position to contribute to the social advancement of our country and the world outside.[91]

To achieve this objective, the Bharat Stri Mahamandal attempted to establish links between women intellectuals and activists. It strove to spread education among women and to fight against the institutions of *purdah* and child marriage. The Bengal branch was looked after by Krishnabhabini Das (b. 1864)[92] while Saraladebi was away in Lahore.

Another organization, the Bengal Women's Education League, concerned itself solely with the task of encouraging women's education in Bengal.[93] This body was formed in 1928 consequent upon the Bengal Women's Educational Conference held in Calcutta in 1927, to push for educational reform for women. Saraladebi Choudhurani, Kumudini Bose and Mrinalini Sen, were its enthusiastic members along with the two sisters, Abala Bose (b. 1864) and Sarala Ray (b. 1859).[94] The body suggested the adoption of a reformed syllabus for girls, the introduction of free compulsory primary

---

[91] *Bharati*, vol. 34, no. 12 (1910–11).

[92] For an excellent portrayal of this remarkable woman, see Chitra Deb, *Antahpurer Atmakatha* (An Autobiography of the zenana, Calcutta, 1984).

[93] Barbara Southard, 'Bengal Women's Educational League: Pressure Group and Professional Association', *Modern Asian Studies*, vol. 18, no. 1 (1984), pp. 55–88, gives a good history of the League.

[94] Sarala Ray was a freedom fighter and an educationist. She was the founder of Gokhale Memorial Girls' School and College.

education, and the inclusion of female representation on educational administrative bodies at all levels from the rural to the university stage. Despite their efforts, the Rural Primary Education Act of 1929 made no provision for compulsory primary education for girls and the League, therefore, was not much of a success. None the less, it had made a point, and indicated that educated women were alive to gender-based inequalities in the field of education. More well-known in the same field than the League was the Nari Siksha Samiti (Women's Educational Association, 1919) founded by Abala Bose and helped substantially by Jyotirmoyee Ganguly. It launched several schools in Calcutta, Dacca, Hooghly and Howrah and set up the Vidyasagar Bani Bhawan for vocational training for widows.[95]

The Sarojnalini Dutt Memorial Association, although started by Gurusaday Dutt in memory of his wife Sarojnalini (b. 1887), was taken over by women leaders like Kumudini Bose, Latika Ghosh and Hemalata Tagore (b. 1873) who were associated with it from its inception. The efforts of the Association were directed towards promoting women's welfare not only in terms of adult education and the training of women in some useful crafts and skills, but also hygiene, maternity and child care. It ran a small school of nursing which distributed diplomas to students on their completion of the course after two years.[96] The publication of the Association, *Bangalakshmi*, edited by Kumudini Bose for the first two years, and then by Hemalata Tagore, provides valuable documentation for writing women's history of the period. It pleaded with women in the districts as well as in the villages 'to wake up', form women's organizations to cement woman power and take up paid jobs outside the home, if necessary, instead of starving within it.[97] A major feature of this journal was reporting the activities of

[95] Latika Ghosh, 'Social and Educational Movements For Women and By Women' in K. Nag, ed., *Bethune College Centenary Volume* (Calcutta, 1950).
[96] Personal interview with Arati Dutt, daughter-in-law of Sarojnalini Dutt, and currently the President of the Association. G.S. Dutt, *A Woman of India: Being the Life of Sarojnalini Dutt* (London, 1929) is a biography of Sarojnalini by her husband.
[97] However, in *Bangalakshmi* there was as yet no positive formulation of a

its branches which were organized in several parts of the country. For instance, it reported that the branches in Manikganj (near Dacca) and Kurseong (in Darjeeling district) were training women in self-employment schemes. The *samiti* in Mulghar was doing creditably. Upto this point, women rarely met women from the same area. Now they were meeting regularly, discussing and transmitting ideas, despite the opposition of orthodox sections.[98]

Indeed, an important part of the socio-political scenario in Bengal was that women were organizing themselves at the district level, in tune with the women of the metropolis, both at the political and social/individual fronts. For instance, the Bankura Zilla Mahila Sammelan (Women's Confederation) and the Chittagong Divisional Mahila Sammelan were both playing a double role, promoting *swadeshi* goods at the political level and generating self-reliance among women at the social/individual level. Ashalata Sen founded the Gandaria Mahila Samiti to promote *swadeshi* products and established the Shilpasram (Institute for Teaching Crafts) in Dacca and built it up as a well-knit unit for encouraging self-employment among women.[99]

Of the local-based societies, the most articulate and active was the Dipali Sangha founded by Leela Roy as noted earlier.[100] A semi-political organization, its principal objective was 'to inculcate self-reliance among women and guide them to sort out their own problems'. Its mouthpiece, *Jayasree*, carried on a virtual crusade against the institutionalized oppression of women. It diagnosed

---

demand for women's gainful employment in the public sphere. Most of the suggestions were about how women could earn a little money while working within the home. See, for instance, Indiradebi Choudhurani, 'Meyeder Parivartane Desher Parivartan' (Changes Among Women and Change Within Society) in *Bangalakshmi*, vol. 5, no. 12 (1929).

[98] *Bangalakshmi*, vol. 5, nos. 1 and 2 (1929) and vol. 6, no. 5 (1930).

[99] Ashalata Sen, 'Bikrampurer Nari Andolon' (Women's Movement in Bikrampur), *Jayasree* vol. 1, nos. 2 and 3 (1931). Editorial discussions in *Jayasree* contained information about women's associations in different parts of Bengal.

[100] Leela Ray was ably assisted by Renuka Sen (b. 1909) who established a women's hostel and a branch of the Dipali Sangha in Calcutta. Another equally competent colleague was Shyamamohini Debi (b. 1887), one of the founder members of the Sangha and a freedom fighter.

women's low status in society as rooted in their economic dependence on their male relations, and prescribed economic equality between men and women as the only remedy for the social malady.[101] Its contributors were almost all females; its declared policy was 'to consolidate women's views and inspire them to devote themselves to this task.'[102] The members of Dipali Sangha extended their support to the Sarda Bill (later known as the Prohibition of Child Marriage Act of 1929); some advocated women's right to demand divorce; and some others called for the revision of the *Dayabhaga* school of law prevalent in Bengal, which deprived girls of any share in paternal property, leaving rights of inheritance to male children alone.[103] These were radical claims, viewed from the early twentieth-century standpoint. But then, the Dipali Sangha was perhaps the most feminist political organization among middle class women of the time, and was entirely dedicated to the twin task of arousing women's political and social awareness.

The premier women's organization during the period under survey was, however, the All India Women's Conference (AIWC)[104]

---

[101] *Jayasree*, vol. 1, no. 4 (1931) in its editorial advocated economic equality between men and women. One Kanika Debi also strongly argued for the same cause in her article entitled 'Bangali Meyer Arthik Swadhinata' (Economic independence of Bengali Women), *Jayasree*, vol. 1, no. 5 (1931).

[102] *Jayasree*, vol. 1, no. 2 (1931). The journal preferred contributions by women over those by men. It was argued that there were so few women contributors that they needed encouragement and a forum for building up a women's viewpoint. Every woman reader was requested to become a writer as well.

[103] See *Jayasree*, vol. 1, nos. 4, 7 and 12 (1931). In this context, three points raised by women contributors need to be mentioned. First, it was contended that if a man was free to desert his wife, a woman should have similar rights. Secondly, it was suggested that for a proper discussion on the Sarda Bill, government should invite women representatives for a round table conference. Third, women should enjoy the same rights of succession as men. Ultimately in India, it was only with the passing of the Hindu Succession Act of 1956 that daughters came to have equal shares with sons in the father's property. Further, it is of great import, judged from the contemporary viewpoint, that the members, specially the student members, carried out a crusade against rape.

[104] For a detailed history of the organization, see Aparna Basu and Bharati Ray, *Women's Struggle* (New Delhi, 1990).

formed under the leadership of Margaret Cousins.[105] The first generation of women leaders in India came from the upper classes and was undoubtedly influenced by western concepts and behaviour patterns. Progressively, however, the leadership and membership of the association became more Indian in outlook and more middle class in character. The organization was initially set up as a non-political organization, and its declared concern was only educational reform. It was soon caught up in the national movement, primarily because, as Renuka Ray (b. 1900), one of the leaders, reminisced, it was 'largely moulded and inspired by Gandhi through those who ran it.'[106] That is to say, women who were influenced by Gandhi and either actively joined or sympathized with the national political struggle shaped the contours of the AIWC and used it as a forum for advancing women's political, social and economic status/powers. The body also acted as a pressure group for women. For instance, it lobbied extensively for the passing of the Sarda Act of 1929. In 1930 it adopted a resolution in favour of complete gender equality in the matter of inheritance and control over property. This organization had branches all over India. The Bengal branch had generations of capable leaders like Sarala Ray, Renuka Ray, Phulrenu Guha and Ashoka Gupta, all of whom were freedom fighters.[107]

---

[105] Although Cousins took the initiative, it was the response from the Indian women themselves which made the task feasible. Papanek rightly observes that it would be 'wrong' to assume that a growing awareness of gender inequality in South Asia was 'simply the result of so-called western influence'. Hanna Papanek, 'False Specialization, and the Purdah of Scholarship', *Journal of Asian Studies*, vol. 44, no. 1 (Nov. 1984), p. 133.

[106] Renuka Ray, Transcript of Oral Interview (Nehru Memorial Museum and Library). A freedom fighter, she is currently the chairperson of Women's Co-ordinating Council, an umbrella body of women's organizations in Bengal. For confirmation of this view, see Kamaladevi Chattopadhyaya, Transcript of Oral Interview (Nehru Memorial Museum & Library). Kamaladevi was one of the leading women whose idea was to make women's movement a part of the freedom struggle.

[107] Phulrenu Guha, freedom fighter, an ex-Member of Parliament is one of the authors of the Report of the Committee on the Status of Women (New Delhi, 1974). Ashoka Gupta, also a freedom fighter, was the former President of the AIWC.

The basic limitation of these early twentieth-century women's organizations was their middle class character and the inability to involve the vast majority of women living in rural Bengal. All their aims and endeavours were clearly related to middle-class urban aspirations, their piecemeal schemes of uplifting the rural or urban poor notwithstanding.

Yet these women's organizations can claim a twofold importance in women history. First, they signified the transfer of leadership of women's movements from men to women. Issues and questions were raised from women's angles rather than those of men. Equally, they provided a platform for women and generated a belief that the responsibility of regenerating women belonged to women themselves.[108] This comprehension is the genesis of bonding among women and of the emergence of feminism in an embryonic form.

Second, women political activists, even if not informed with a conscious feminist ideology, were intimately associated with women's organizations, thereby establishing a link between the freedom struggle and women's movement.[109] Women leaders of national standing were ably assisted by ordinary women workers in different states. Women's experiences in the political campaigns of the 1920s and in the Swadeshi movement had given them 'a taste of agitational politics' and a self-confidence to champion their own cause.[110]

---

[108] For instance, one woman wrote in *Bangalakshmi*, vol. 6, no. 1 (1930), 'It is women, not men, who must carry the call for awakening to the door of every woman'.

[109] It is worth noting that women political leaders persuaded the Indian National Congress to create a women's section of the Congress. Some of them such as Hemaprabha Majumdar and Urmila Debi, built up women's political associations for the freedom movement. These gave women an experience of organizing woman power. They also helped to organize the All India Women's Social Conference in conjunction with the regular Congress session. It was at the Social Conference that Sarojini Naidu declared as early as 1906 that Indian men had deprived women of their due rights. And yet, 'it is not you, but we who are the makers of the nation.' *Modern Review*, vol. 1, 1907, p. 213.

[110] Given the contemporary social setting in which they operated, the members of various *samitis* exhibited considerable initiative and self-will in carrying out their extra-domestic activities. Consequently, an articulate female elite

(ii) Women's Writings

If literature be a reflection of society, it can be claimed that a new set of values was emerging among a section of women during the years of the freedom movement under review. This was specially represented in thoughtful essays authored by women in women's journals. Significantly, those journals which were politically oriented, or were edited by women political activists, were more feminist in outlook[111] than those whose chief purpose was 'to educate' women (e.g. *Bamabodhini Patrika* or *Antahpur*). Women political leaders used these journals as conduits for communicating their thoughts, both political and social.[112] In this article, I will discuss three of these journals, *Jayasree*, *Suprabhat* and *Bharatamahila*, each of which was edited during our period of study by politically active women, respectively, Leela Roy, Kumudini Bose (Mitra) and Sarajubala Datta (who belonged to the Anushilan group of *biplabis*). It is obviously not possible to refer to all the pieces published in these journals. Only a selective representation will be attempted.

---

emerged which attempted to define women's issues and find solutions. See G.H. Forbes, 'In Pursuit of Justice', *Samya Shakti*, vol. 1, no. 2 (1984), p. 37. Patricia Caplan, *Class and Gender in India* (London, 1985) is a noteworthy study of women's organizations in the context of Madras.

[111] For instance, *Bharatamahila* declared that its objective was to motivate women to work along with men in every field from politics to science.

[112] This is true of areas outside Bengal as well. Three women's journals, *Grihalakshmi*, *Sri Darpan* and *Chand*, published from Allahabad, a centre of middle class nationalist movement in northern Indian, contained many feminist articles, indicating the growth of feminist consciousness along with political consciousness Uma Nehru's articles were perhaps among the most articulate. To give an example, in the May 1918 issue of *Sree Darpan* she addressed a crucial question to the nationalist leaders. 'The loss of national freedom has made you so depressed, so anxious and so sorrowful. Consider then the enslavement of those who have lost not just political freedom but whose body, soul and spirit have been enchained. How can their hearts ever be joyful?' See Vir Bahadur Talwar, 'Feminist Consciousness in Women's Journals in Hindi, 1910–20' in Sanghari and Vaid, eds., *Recasting women*, pp. 204–32, esp. pp. 210 and 225.

Contributions by women political leaders clearly indicate their awareness of and resentment against gender asymmetry. For instance, Saraladebi Choudhurani wrote in *Suprabhat*, 'Lack of self-confidence and abuse of our power is most reprehensible. The Scriptures have described women as embodiment of strength and not as weaklings. In reality, women are the creators, the protectors and the destroyers, not men'.[113] Many women felt aggrieved at the apathy of the male political leadership to women's issues. Kumudini Bose sarcastically remarked, 'War drums are rolling to summon men to the fight for the country's freedom. Is this why (because of the noise) the anguished cry of women does not reach anybody's ears? If men choose to remain indifferent to women's grievances, then it must be left to the women to find their own strength to protect their interests.'[114] Sarajubala Datta shared similar sentiments. In her editorial column in *Bharatamahila* she questioned the integrity of the promises held out by the male leaders. In their writings and speeches, they propagated the need for the 'awakening of women' for the emancipation of the country. 'In actual terms, what have they done for us?' This was perhaps the first articulate formulation of the interests of women as opposed to men, as a group. The editor also ventured to question Rabindranath Tagore, who dominated the Bengal cultural scene throughout the first half of the twentieth century. Referring to a mammoth meeting at a provincial conference held at Pabna under Tagore, she mentioned that about five hundred women had attended it. 'And yet Tagore's speech made no reference to women and contained no message for them.'[115] Urmila Debi, though less radical, also complained that women of India had so far been kept out of all national movements. Steeped in ignorance, they were totally oblivious of their strength.

[113] Saraladebi Choudhurani, 'Narir Karya' (Role of Women), *Suprabhat*, vol. 3, no. 9, 1909. See also her provocative article 'Sinher Bibara' (In the Lion's Den), *Bangabani*, a political journal, vol. 1, no. 1 (1923–4).

[114] Kumudini Bose further asserted, 'As education is the basis for women's advancement, so is the emancipation of women its soul.' K. Bose, 'Bharate Narir Unnati' (The Progress of Women in India), *Bharatamahila*, vol. 7, no. 8, 1912.

[115] Editorial, *Bharatamahila*, vol. 4, no. 1, 1908 and vol. 3, no. 11, 1907.

The same downtrodden women were now being asked to help men.[116]

Political consciousness made many a lesser known woman comprehend the indignity of social subjugation. In an interesting short story which appeared in *Jayasree*, a woman while entering the prison van told another woman, 'Upto now we were confined to a small *sasurbari* (father-in-law's house), let us go to a big *sasurbari*' (a popular term for jail).[117] Spoken in a light vein, these words are nevertheless telling.

An anonymous article published in *Bharatamahila* during the heyday of the Swadeshi movement bluntly declared that 'the extent of deprivation of women by men has no parallel anywhere else in the world. The present status of India as a subjugated nation and her disgrace are no doubt an atonement for the grievous inequality.'[118] Said one Lalita Ray in the same journal, while discussing the role of women in the freedom movement, 'As long as women remain subservient to men, and men their masters, there is little hope for our country to see better days.[119]

Men were totally preoccupied in their struggle against colonialism. Who would fight the battle against patriarchy? The answer, according to Chapala Debi, was obvious. 'We, women, have to think of ourselves',[120] The cue was taken up by Susmita Debi. In the context of the national movement, she wrote:

[116] Urmila Debi 'Praner Katha' (From the Heart), *Banglar Katha*, a political weekly, 4 Nov. 1921.

[117] M. Debi, 'Bahirer Ahban' (The Call from Outside), *Jayasree*, vol. 1, no. 2, 1338 BS/1931 AD.

[118] Anon, 'Bangladesher Dasha' (The Hopeless Condition of Bengal), *Bharatamahila*, vol. 3, no. 2, 1907.

[119] Lalita Ray, 'Deshsebaye Narijati' (Women Serving the Country), *Bharatamahila*, vol. 5, no. 3, 1909. In this article the author posed a fundamental question. 'It is the belief of many that women must remain confined to their homes. What does one mean by home, may I ask? A home is where one is born, in which one lives and breathes one's last. Yet it is this home which suffers the most neglect by men. Places of work, temples for worship, and various other such establishments have gone through a process of reformation. But no such effort is visible when it concerns the home, only because it is the domain of women.'

[120] Chapala Debi, 'Amader Kartavya' (Our Duty) in *Suprabhat*, vol. 7, no. 8, 1913.

I do not suggest that the term femininity connotes some particular characteristics of women. Most women in our country live in an unnatural ambience. They have a separate existence isolated from men. This is what I call femininity. This is what has kept women as women and not allowed them to develop as human beings . . . . All the energies of women, their intellect, their strength, their skill, are devoted to catering to the comforts of men . . . . In their desires or aspirations, in fact in everything that women wish to do or accomplish, they meet with resistance at every step.[121]

The message was unambiguous. The call was for women's solidarity in the face of hostility. Anindita Debi, a regular contributor to *Jayasree*, drew a subtle comparison between the women's movement against patriarchy and the male-led movement against colonial domination.

'The path to political liberty . . . will be more smooth if we acquire self confidence in sufficient manner . . . . And this is true for the women also. They will find it easier to take their place in the larger world if they enter it with confidence and are able to prove themselves by the application of their knowledge and authority.'[122]

What distinguished the contributions of these politically aware women from those of their nineteenth-century counterparts was a change in tone, from a negative to a positive approach, from regret to demand, from grudging acceptance to direct questioning. Apart from sharp criticism of the systems of polygamy or child marriage, a whole series of new questions was asked.

Was the institution of marriage as it existed fair to women? Should women remain content, confined to the home? Were marriage and motherhood indispensable to a woman's life?[123] Alterna-

---

[121] Susmita Debi, 'Meyeder Meyelitya' (Femininity), *Jayasree*, vol. 1, no. 7, 1931.

[122] Anindita Debi, 'Uro Megh' (Fleeting Clouds), *Jayasree*, vol. 1, no. 6, 1931.

[123] For instance, Anindita Debi writing under the pseudonym 'Banganari' posed an important question, in *Jayasree*, vol. 1, no. 1 (1931). 'A wife is asked to accept her husband regardless of whether he is a good man or bad. The reverse concept is not applied . . . A mother has to look after the children, but a father,

tive ideologies were being projected. The debate between old and new ideas was depicted by Kamini Roy, an author and suffragist, in a poem.

> Grandmother: Men and women are different from one another and are mutually complementary. How can there be absolute equality between them? . . . . You are a mother, a wife, a sister, the nerve-centre of home . . . . If you get involved with the sordid business of the outside world, you will lose your femininity.
>
> Granddaughter: The young generation does not accept the doctrine that a woman's only destiny is wifehood and motherhood . . . nor that her only place is in the home . . . . Why should a woman be confined to home and denied her rightful place in society? . . . . Women of today desire, without fear or inhibition, all round self-development.[124]

Conclusion

The first stirrings of political consciousness among Bengali women were articulated through the national movement. Once this process

---

because he is a man, has to go out to earn the family bread. But that should hardly be a ground for the woman to be a loser in terms of the conjugal rights. Is this true award for motherhood?' As early as 1910, Satadalbashini Biswas, one of the regular women contributors to journals, had raised similar points. She went on to argue, 'Admittedly a husband is the mainstay in a woman's life, but educated women these days do not accept that they must submerge their personality totally in their husbands. They know that God has equipped them with the same faculties as men, and they do not think it right that all their energies should be devoted to looking after their husbands. In fact, they feel the urge to employ their gifts to serve the outside world.' S. Biswas, 'Nari Shaktir Apachay' (Misuse of Women's Strength), *Bharatamahila*, vol. 6, no. 2, 1910.

[124] Kamini Ray, *Thakurmar Chithi* (A letter from a Grandmother, Calcutta, n.d.).

began, issues of gender could not but arise in the minds of politicized women. It was not possible for the feminist consciousness to transcend all the socially constructed barriers and develop radical potentialities. Nor did the women leaders of the period envisage any such possibilities. Predictably, therefore, active participation of women in the freedom struggle did not entail any reordering of the patriarchal structure of society. The periodic outbursts of solidarity of women in the different phases of the movement did not produce its own discourse untainted by subversive social intervention. The cue for women's upliftment came initially from men. This set an implicit limit to the aspirations of women. For the more sensitive women, however, participation in the freedom movement meant a protracted struggle against two different badges of servility: colonialism and patriarchy.

Even though the second struggle remained largely inconclusive, a determined start was made in the period under review. Active involvement in the movement helped to bring about a remarkable shift in women's perspectives towards life, their world-view, self-image and ambitions. Above all, it refashioned women's personality. Striding along a path which had traditionally been an exclusively male domain, the path of politics, instilled in their collective personality an element of grit and determination which eventually won grudging admiration from their male counterparts.

This new woman found representation in contemporary literature. The writings of women have already been referred to. Among the male writers who took note of the new phenomenon, were Rabindranath Tagore and, later, Saratchandra Chatterjee, the two leading authors of the time. In Tagore's short story *'Aparichita'* (The Unknown Woman), written against the background of the period after Swadeshi movement, the reader comes across a marvellous new creation — an unmarried young woman who has rejected the notion that her only future is that of a housewife. She asserts herself against racist humiliation in a public railway carriage. She startles men, who are not yet familiar with the type. Written in the first person, the story begins with a description of how the narrator's marriage with Kalyani, the daughter of a certain Shambhunath Sen of Kanpur, was cancelled on the day of the wedding because of a dispute over the dowry. He meets Kalyani some years later in a railway carriage and is enchanted by her looks, her voice and her deportment.

> The train came to a halt at an important station. An army general with his entourage was going to board it. But all the coaches were full.... A few minutes before the train was scheduled to leave, a local official of the railway attached reservation slips to our two berths and asked us to vacate the coach. 'Please move to another coach', this official told me, 'the berths were reserved earlier for the General Sahib'. I stood up in great consternation, but the girl spoke up in Hindi. 'No, we will not leave.... This coach had no earlier reservation. That is a lie'. And then she tore off the two reservation slips and threw them on to the platform.
>
> Meanwhile the General and his attendant had already reached our compartment, and he had asked his attendant to put his luggage into the compartment. Then he looked at the girl, listened to what she had to say, and obviously read the expression on her face, for he drew the station master aside and spoke to him. What he said I do not know, but what ensued was that the train was detained, and another coach was attached for the General before we resumed our journey. The girl then went back to her companions and started merrily munching nuts, and I, thoroughly shamefaced, looked out of the window to watch the passing landscape.
>
> We reached Kanpur where the young woman was getting off.
>
> A servant had come to receive her. My mother could not restrain herself and asked her name. 'Kalyani', she replied...
>
> 'And your father'?
>
> 'Shambhunath Sen. He is a physician.' She got off.
>
> Later, I defied my uncle's strictures, ignored my mother's wishes, and visited Kanpur. I met Kalyani and her father. I humbled myself, I apologised to them. I could mollify the father, but Kalyani was adamant.
>
> 'No, I will never marry', she affirmed.
>
> 'Why not?' I asked.
>
> 'That is what my mother desires'.

I realised that she was not talking about the mother who had borne her but the motherland.[125]

Admittedly the voice of Kalyani did not find resonances in ordinary middle class households. As a role model, her standard was far too exacting. Most women of her class were malleable, and unwilling to exchange the restrictive security of home for a rough ride through the world. Yet the emergence of a new type of personality and a new form of consciousness, linked with political awareness, can be detected. While it would be wrong to undervalue the impact of the new ideas, it would be unhistorical to exaggerate the extent of women's perceptions of gender asymmetry or of their will to demolish patriarchy. Their goals were still unclear; they had not yet established any linkages with lower caste and working class women, and were yet to come up with an appropriate gender-specific agenda for political action.

Herein lies the strength as well as the limitations of feminist consciousness in Bengal during 1905–1929. Involvement in the freedom struggle had taught women the basics of agitational politics, and the breaking of the carapace of traditional domestic life had widened their horizon. They had begun, as their writing indicates, slowly to comprehend the reasons for their oppression and to perceive the need to organize their own associations as a source of strength. In short, they came out with a new personality of their own. Beyond this, however, the growth of feminist consciousness was tardy. Participation in the freedom movement whetted their appetite; it did not satisfy them. This is the context of Hena's anguished tirade. 'For us the liberation of the country makes little sense if we, women, are to be kept shackled inside our homes'.[126] Viewed in a broader context this tone of unfulfilled expectation was implicit in the logic of the freedom movement. It achieved much but left many things undone. Yet, we may be unequivocal in asserting that the roots of women's struggle of today can be traced back to the turn of the century and the following three decades.

[125] Rabindranath Tagore, 'Aparichita' in *Rabindra Rachanavali Birth Centenary Volume*, VII, pp. 680–2. Translated by Sukhendu Ray.
[126] Shantishudda Ghosh, *'Pather Ingit'*.

7
Women's Work in Bengal, 1880–1930: A Historical Analysis

*Mukul Mukherjee**

I

Work participation rates of a given population and the distribution of that population across employment avenues have emerged as important indicators of socio-economic change. This has generated a large number of studies on the working population of India, with special emphasis on its employment pattern and occupational structure. Most of these studies have the following features:

(i) analysis and findings are predominantly at the macro level, so that regional variations tend to merge into the all-India picture;

(ii) being primarily concerned with the latest developments in the employment and occupational structure, they do not usually consider historical trends and

(iii) rarely do they have a special focus on women's work and occupational distribution even though these are now recognized to have significant implications not only for women but for society as a whole.[1]

---

* Paper presented at Seminar on Perspectives on Women, Women's Studies Research Centre, Calcutta University, 28 August 1991 and based partially on Part III of my Ph.D. thesis ('Some aspects of Economic Change in Bengal, 1870–1930', Delhi University, 1982).

[1] In recent years there have been valuable contributions to the study of women's work and occupational structure in India. These are mostly based on census-NSS data for the period 1971–81 and concentrate mostly on all-India

Though the last two decades have seen a good crop of micro level studies, these are generally socio-economic surveys of small, often village-specific communities at fixed points of time and for this reason can scarcely be used for arriving at valid generalizations.[2] There is thus, a need for looking at work participation and occupational structure/employment patterns in India from a fresh approach that integrates all the three dimensions mentioned above: the regional context, the accent on women's role in the economic life of the region studied and the longitudinal perspective that brings out regional time-trends. This paper is a modest attempt to address this need and to show how women's work participation/employment pattern has evolved over time in the regional economy of Bengal during five decades in the colonial era: 1880–1930. These decades represent an exciting period of transition: the political back drop was in flux with the mounting opposition to colonial rule and the momentous impact of the Swadeshi movement; in the social arena women were gaining exposure to the public domain and the

---

rather than regional trends or patterns. To cite a few: Asok Mitra et al., *The Status of Women: Household and Non-household Economic Activity* and *The Status of Women: Shifts in Occupational Participation 1961–71* (New Delhi, 1979); K.C. Seal, 'Women in the Labour Force in India: A Macro-level Statistical Profile', paper presented at Workshop on Women in Indian Labour Force, ILO-ARTEP, 1980; Mukul Mukherjee, 'Women in Agriculture in India: A Statistical Overview', paper presented at second National Conference on Women's Studies, Trivandrum, 1984; Jeemol Unni, 'Change in Women's Employment in Rural Areas 1961–83', *Economic and Political Weekly* (EPW), 29 April 1989; Nirmala Banerjee, 'Trends in Women's Employment 1971–81', EPW, 29 April 1989; Pranab Bardhan, 'Some Employment and Unemployment Characteristics of Rural Women: An Analysis of NSS Data for West Bengal 1972–3', EPW, 25 March 1978.

[2] Many references including Govt. surveys will be found in Suchitra Anant, S.V. Ramani Rao et al., *Women at Work in India* (New Delhi, 1986) and *Bibliography on Women at Work in India: An Update* (New Delhi, 1987). To cite a few again: Kumaresh Chakravarty and G.C. Tiwari, 'Regional Variations in Women's Employment: A Case Study of Five Villages in Three Indian States', ICSSR (New Delhi, 1975); M. Atchi Reddy, 'Socio-economic Conditions of Women Construction Workers in Hyderabad', paper presented at Workshop on Women and Work, Hyderabad, 1985; Maria Mies et al., *Indian Women in Subsistence and Agricultural Labour* (ILO, Geneva, 1986).

economic arena saw the rise of a modern industrial sector offering a new range of employment opportunities for men and women.

This paper is divided into five parts. After this brief introduction, the second section outlines the methodology followed while the third brings out the trends and patterns of women's work in Bengal during our chosen time span. The fourth section discusses the factors underlying the low levels of female work participation in Bengal and concluding observations are presented in the last section.

II

At the outset we must acknowledge our debt to the author of the 1951 Census Report for West Bengal, Asok Mitra, who makes a seminal contribution not only by looking at the occupational statistics of the state from a historical perspective but also by marshalling data on women's employment.[3]

Most of the data presented in this paper too are derived from Bengal Census Reports starting from 1881. (Bengal here refers to Bengal Proper or the five administrative divisions of Burdwan, Presidency, Rajshahi, Dacca and Chattagram.)

We are conscious that the actual numbers of gainfully occupied women must have been higher than those reported in the various census counts, because of the known imperfections inherent in such counts with reference to women's work. There is now an extensive literature on the undernumeration of women in censuses and large scale surveys.[4] It is interesting to note that some of the issues highlighted in this literature were anticipated almost a century ago

---

[3] Census of India (COI) 1951, vol. VI, *West Bengal, Sikkim and Chandernagore*, Part I-A (Report), pp. 507–35; Asok Mitra, *India's Population: Aspects of Quality and Control*, vol. I, Part III (section 5) (New Delhi, 1978).

[4] See, for example, Nata Duvvury, 'Women in Labour Force: A Discussion of Conceptual and Operational Biases with reference to Recent Indian Estimates', paper presented at the National Workshop on Visibility of Women in Statistics and Indicators, SNDT University, Bombay 1989 and Devaki Jain and Nirmala Banerjee, eds., *Tyranny of the Household: Investigative Essays on Women's Work*, Part Four (New Delhi, 1985).

by perceptive observers connected with the Indian Census. Commenting on cultural biases that often distorted data on women, the 1901 Bengal Census admits: 'among many classes of the community it is not considered respectable that a woman should help to augment the family income and the return of actual workers is vitiated in consequence'.[5] Similarly, conceptual biases adversely affecting women are firmly entrenched in century old census norms (for example, 'women were not to be entered as employed unless they were employed on special work of a distinctly definite character').[6] Again, occupational data recorded in the 1891 Census could not be used in our tables on account of a curious instruction issued to enumerators regarding occupational classification: 'In case of children and women who do not work, enter the occupation of the head of the family or of the person who supports them but do not leave this column unfulfilled for any one, even an infant'.[7] As the author of the 1891 Bengal Census Report pithily observes, 'The immediate result of the above-quoted order was to absolutely obliterate all female occupations'.[8]

However, despite the limitations of census data and the paucity of alternative source material, we believe that available information can still be used to sketch the dominant trends and modes of women's work participation in Bengal during the period under study. Accordingly this paper attempts to portray two important characteristics of the female population of Bengal from a historical perspective: (i) the size and proportion of workers in the female population — referred to in the earlier censuses as the 'gainfully occupied' — and (ii) the distribution of this work force according to their livelihoods/occupations/spheres of employment corresponding mainly to the 'industrial distribution' of the work-force referred to in the post-independence censuses.

A uniform procedure has been followed in estimating the size and distribution of the gainfully occupied population according to census data. For the years 1881, 1901, 1911 and 1921 the working

[5] COI 1901, vol. VI, Part I, p. 481.
[6] Census of Bengal (COB) 1881, vol. I, para 421.
[7] COI 1891, vol. III (Report for Bengal), para 361.
[8] Ibid.

population is taken as the total number of persons recorded as 'earners' and 'working dependants'. In the Bengal Census Reports of 1881–1931 livelihoods/occupations are divided into a number of major categories designated as 'classes' — which are in turn disaggregated (in descending order) into subclasses, orders, suborders and groups. Two conventionally non-working sub-classes have been excluded from our estimates of the working population: (i) persons living on own income and (ii) persons following 'unproductive' or 'disrespectful' occupations. Inter-censal comparability is maintained by using a chronological reference chart which was formulated to identify a given occupation in the relevant categories/sub-categories in each census reviewed.[9] This provides a common classification code for mapping the occupational distribution of the work force over time.

Our Appendix Table presents detailed and gender-specific data on the occupational distribution of the Bengal working force during 1881–1931.

III

Income generating activities pursued by women in Bengal can be classified into three main types:
  (a) those which were followed by women independently, without reference to the occupations of their male relatives (e.g. rice husking, fuel gathering, domestic service);
  (b) those that were subsidiary to the family occupation of the chief earner/head of the household (e.g. work connected with textiles, pottery etc. and trade connected with agriculture, fishing, dairy farming) and
  (c) those in which men and women generally worked together, participation being on almost equal footing (e.g. mining, plantation labour, basket weaving and sometimes work in agriculture).

---

[9] Mukul Mukherjee, This chart is presented in 'Some aspects of economic change in Bengal, 1870–1930', unpublished Ph.D. Thesis, Delhi University, 1982, pp. 308–18 (Table AI:27).

There are indications that most of the traditional livelihoods of Bengal called for participation of women. Thus, apart from women engaged in rice processing or yarn spinning, keen observers like Hunter or O'Malley would note that 'Bauri females arrange the betel leaves into bundles before they are taken to market . . . Kumhar women assist in preparation of earthen pots . . . Malakar females prepare artificial flowers while Goala and Myra females share to a large extent in the individual pursuits of their caste . . . Namasudra and Sheikh women help in gathering and husbanding paddy';[10] 'among Jaliyas the man catches fish while the woman takes them to the market and sells them'.[11]

A good number of these economically active women may not have enjoyed a readily identifiable personal income or achieved entry in the census schedules which furnish our source material. But most of them would have been contributing significantly in maintaining the economic equilibrium of their households.

What captures attention when the Bengal working force is disaggregated by gender, is a striking asymmetry — both in the level and in the pattern of work participation as between men and women. In Table 1, concerned with the level of participation, this asymmetry is reflected in (i) the much smaller size of the female work force (FWF), numbering between 1.7 and 2 million — as compared to the male work force (MWF) which rose from about 11 million to 14 million between 1881–1931; (ii) the conspicuously low sex ratio of workers (females per thousand males) in successive decades (iii) only 7–10 per cent of the female population being recorded as workers while the worker–population ratio for males was usually about 60 per cent and (iv) the sharp fall in numbers disturbing the expected uptrend in the size of the FWF towards the end of the nineteenth century as contrasted to the steady growth of the MWF during 1881–1931.

When we look at the trends of women's work participation rates in Bengal from the macro perspective, there is another divergence:

---

[10] W.W. Hunter, *Statistical Account of Bengal* (Indian Reprint, Delhi, 1973), vol. II, p. 89. (First published in 1877.)

[11] L.S.S. O'Malley, *District Gazetteer, Chittagong*, 1980, p. 113.

these rates have not only remained much lower *vis-à-vis* men in Bengal, but also substantially below the all-India averages for women, which as Table 1 shows, veer around 30 per cent.

In fact, historically, Bengal seems to have had one of the lowest female participation rates amongst all the provinces of British India, although male participation trends show no such trend.[12] This comes out clearly in Table 2 which features West Bengal but nevertheless serves to project the Bengal proper situation in the all-India context.

Let us now look at the occupational structure of the Bengal economy during the period under review. The special tabulation presented in the Appendix shows that a cluster of thirty occupations continued to be the mainstay of women's livelihood in Bengal right up to the 1920s, accounting for about 95 per cent of the FWF. Apart from agriculture, other numerically important occupations include making and selling dairy products, foodstuffs and fuel items, textile spinning and weaving, basket making and allied crafts, work in mines and plantations and towards the end of the period, domestic service. A decade later women's employment shows signs of expanding beyond the traditional terrain and the share of these older occupations in the FWF drops to 82 per cent.

Other dimensions of the asymmetry mentioned above relate to the occupational patterns of men and women. Table 3 shows that at the all-India level there seems to be no significant difference between men and women as regards the basic division of workers between agriculture and non-agriculture. For India as a whole and for the whole period, more than two-thirds of both men and women workers are concentrated in agriculture, the percentage for women being consistently higher — between 70–75 per cent. In Bengal the picture is quite different: though an overwhelming proportion of the MWF (65–70 per cent) was predictably attached to agriculture right up to 1931, this figure was much lower in the case of the FWF and more volatile, fluctuating between 23 per cent and 48

---

[12] J. Krishnamurty, 'The Industrial Distribution of the Working Force in India, 1911–1961; A Study of Selected Aspects', unpublished Ph.D. Thesis, Delhi University, 1970, p. 244.

per cent during the five decades preceding 1931. While the sex ratio in the work force in agriculture is usually less than 75, the comparatively high presence of women in occupations other than agriculture is shown by sex ratios of 300 and above in this section.

The occupational distribution of women workers in Bengal, then, has been less lopsided and more significantly associated with industry, specially household industry. This is borne out further by Table 4 which shows the distribution of men and women workers by five broad areas of work: production of raw materials, industry, transport, trade and services. In almost all instances the percentage share of FWF in the last four areas has remained consistently higher *vis-à-vis* males, particularly in industry, which has never claimed more than 13 per cent in the MWF while the involvement of FWF in industry varied between 15 to 53 per cent.

The gender related asymmetry in employment patterns is brought out in yet another trend. This is shown in Table 5 where we estimate the temporal variations in the sex ratio of workers in selected occupations. Initially, in quite a few fields women outnumber men. But a woman-biased regression appears during the last two decades in the sense that with changes in production processes and decline in traditional crafts and callings, the sex ratio is transformed in certain types of work, giving more and more weightage to men. This happens at least in four broad areas: basket making and allied activities, making and selling of ordinary fuel, making and selling of foodstuffs and occupations related to jute textiles. In contrast, except for the unexalted area of domestic service, there seems to be no other occupation where a male-oriented work force became female intensive over time.

According to our data in Table 5 the highest sex ratio of work participation is to be found in manual rice husking i.e. processing of paddy by the time-hallowed contraption of the wooden *dheki*. And this brings us to another extremely significant but little known fact that is contrary to common assumption: leaving aside cultivation, rice husking by *dheki* has been the single most important means of livelihood for women of colonial Bengal. Even according to conservative census counts, this occupation supported more than two lakh women at the turn of the century as shown in Table 6.

It is surprising that very little attention has been paid to this important household industry which had virtually been a women's monopoly in Bengal. Probably this has happened because standard literature on the economic history of Bengal tends to emphasize textile-based occupations, specially cotton hand spinning, as almost the only form of significant economic activity for women outside agriculture. 'Textile industries occupied the most important place in the life of the people. The Cotton Manufacturing Industry was the most widespread of all';[13] or again, 'Weaving and Spinning had become national occupations, peculiarly suited to the mode of Bengali village life'.[14]

Throughout our period of study, however as Table 7 shows, 15–32 per cent of the FWF found employment in making and selling foodstuffs — primarily rice husking — while the corresponding figure for textiles never exceeded 12 per cent.

We have discussed elsewhere the significance of manual rice husking in the Bengal economy and the grave implications of its eventual collapse but we must note here that as more and more paddy flowed into the rice mills and the widely dispersed rice husking machines were worked and controlled by men, women gradually lost an important means of survival and the modern processing technology gave them very limited sustenance by way of compensatory employment.[15] This is again prominent in census data for later decades. According to the 1981 census, only 15,000 women in West Bengal were employed in 'grain processing' which included both mechanical and manual rice husking.[16]

---

[13] H.R. Ghosal, 'Changes in the Organisation of Industrial Production in Bengal Presidency in the Early Nineteenth Century', in B.N. Ganguly, ed., *Readings in Indian Economic History* (Bombay, 1964), p. 124.

[14] D.B. Mitra, *Cotton Weavers of Bengal* (Calcutta, 1978), p. 35.

[15] Mukul Mukherjee, 'Impact of Modernisation of Women's Occupations: A Case Study of Rice Husking Industry of Bengal', in J. Krishnamurty, ed., *Women in Colonial India: Essays on Survival, Work and the State* (Delhi, 1989), and Mukul Mukherjee, 'Mechanisation in Food Processing and Women's Employment', in Mira Savara and Divya Pandey, eds., *Between the Farm and the Thali: Women and Food Processing* (Bombay, 1990).

[16] COI 1981, Series-I India, Part III–B (i), Table B–12.

This particular occupation of rice husking, then, probably provides the most dramatic example of the vulnerability of women's employment in the face of technological change ushered in by modern industry.

Lastly we come to trends in women's work in the newly emerging factory sector including cotton and jute mills, oil mills, paper mills, sugar mills etc. and the new industries like engineering works, printing presses and railway workshops. The Census Report for 1921 published a special set of data on 'Industrial Statistics' in Bengal.[17] According to these data about 7.6 lakh men and women were working in about 2800 industrial establishments, each employing ten or more workers, with or without power.

Table 8 shows that if plantations and collieries are excluded, 1921 figures for male and female industrial employment in Bengal approach 4.6 lakh and 65,000 respectively. The gender composition of employment in modern industry is thus about 140 women for 1000 men, women's share being about 12 per cent of total employment in this sector. In a number of new industries like iron foundries and printing presses, where total employment in each industry varied between 10,000–15,000 women's average share was less than 8 per cent. In certain other areas, women's entry was only notional; for example in about eighty establishments connected with engineering and brass works, only about thirty women workers are shown against 20,000 men. These figures indicate that women's tenuous foothold in modern industry during the period under review could barely compensate for their displacement in other sectors.

Of the broad trends in the women's occupational structure in Bengal noted above, two merit more attention and analysis: (i) the strikingly low incidence of women workers in agriculture specially and (ii) in gainful employment generally. The lack of resilience in the female occupational structure is evident in the low work force/working-age population ratio i.e. the proportion of working women in the female population aged 15–59 years. This ratio,

---

[17] COI 192, vol. VI, Part II, Table XXII.

again, declines over time from about 19 per cent in 1881 to less than 14 per cent in 1931.

At first sight these unfavourable trends appear to be paradoxical. The evolving Bengal economy would seem to warrant rising employment levels for women on account of the following reasons:

(i) Bengal has always specialized in rice cultivation where sowing and transplanting are integral processes and so far as these activities are concerned, women are traditionally regarded as more efficient performers;[18]

(ii) growing diversification of production and the rise of new industries is expected to yield growing employment opportunities for both the sexes;

(iii) there was an increasing need to augment family income in the face of a secular rise in the costs of living (this need being reinforced by a much wider variety of goods and services being available for money);

(iv) a slow but secular improvement in general health and literacy probably had a favourable effect on women's working capacity.

In this context we must remember that the actual numbers of women workers must have been higher than those reported in the various censuses — because of the known shortcomings of census data so far as enumeration of women is concerned. But this alone obviously does not provide an adequate or wholly satisfactory answer and we need to look more carefully into the factors underlying the low profile of the female work force in the context of the over-all socio-economic environment of this region.

Agriculture

Turning first to agriculture, there is the general premise often articulated in official discourse that by and large the rural com-

[18] Women are supposed to withstand better the fatiguing postures and movements required for transplantation work. Also, women labourers are preferred because they are more adept at uprooting and handling the saplings and replanting them in straight rows which, in turn, facilitates weeding and reaping. See Arun Mukhopadhyay, *Agricultural Extension: A Field Study* (Calcutta, 1971), p. 130f.

munity of Bengal enjoyed a state of comparative prosperity and the common peasantry derived their livelihood with minimum physical exertion. This, by implication, obviated women's participation in agriculture.

A typical comment sums up the life style of the supposedly typical farming family: 'The life of the cultivator in East Bengal is in many ways a very happy life . . . He can produce the food of his own family and sufficient to purchase everything else which he requires from a few acres of land that he can cultivate unaided without overwork'.[19] Again, with reference to Khulna District: 'A significant indication of the comfortable circumstances enjoyed by the majority of agricultural population is that as a rule, they do not plough their lands or cut paddy themselves but employ labourers imported from other districts. Even the small cultivator is in the habit of doing little or no work himself'.[20]

If we accept the postulate of initial rural prosperity in large areas of Bengal, paucity of women in the work force ceases to be a mystery. The postulate itself, however, is highly simplistic.

(i) One clue may be found in the somewhat different supply structure of agricultural labour in Bengal, resulting in a comparatively limited need for female participation. This is brought about by a set of special circumstances prevalent in Bengal. In certain districts it was observed,

> It is the higher classes of agriculturists only that engaged hired *krishans* but the generality of cultivators manage their affairs by *pali* labour or in other words, they assist each other in the cultivation of their fields without any charge.[21]

A co-operative labour exchange system functioning in different parts of Bengal, thus, implied a reduced need for mobilizing female labour. There is evidence that this system (known variously as *ganta*, *gati* or *pali*) survives even today. For example in a village survey in Burdwan district in 1961, it was found that out of sixty-eight

[19] J.C. Jack, *Economic Life of a Bengal District* (London, 1916), p. 38.
[20] L.S.S. O'Malley, *District Gazetteer, Khulna* (Calcutta 1908), p. 111.
[21] Gopal Chunder Das, *Report on the Statistics of Rangpur for the Year 1872–73* (Calcutta, 1874), para 172.

agriculturist families of various castes, thirty-one depended on *ganta* for supply of extra labour during peak seasons.[22]

Apart from local arrangements of *pali* labour, inter-district migration of male workers was also customary during the peak agricultural season. These short term movements were made possible by the staggered crop cycle observed in different parts of Bengal, due in turn to localized geophysical conditions. Deltaic tracts in the littoral districts (24 Parganas, Khulna, Bakergang) for example, started their crop cycle usually two months later.[23] Migration from Jessore and Nadia towards 24 Parganas and from Santhal Parganas to Dinajpur seems to have been common.[24] Also notable was 'the annual exodus of husbandmen' from Faridpur to parts of Dacca district.[25] Hiring migrant male labour, thus seems to have been the preferred mode of securing additional labour rather than increased work participation by rural women.

(ii) Various studies have shown that female labour is used extensively for weeding. The chief crop of Bengal is rice, which however, requires limited weeding and this reduced total labour requirements in Bengal agriculture.[26] Besides, the activity of weeding could be unacceptable sometimes to Bengali women for cultural reasons:

> There is no taboo on women's doing it (weeding) but men are preferred for this job because during weeding, when the weeds have been pulled out from under a bunch of plants, the operator kneels and gives a blow near the base of the plants with his knees to harden the earth disturbed during weeding. Women cannot

[22] J.C. Sen Gupta, *Village Survey Monograph: Kamra* (Burdwan district), COI 1961, Part IV, nos., p. 16.

[23] *District Gazetteer, Khulna*, p. 111.

[24] Letter of SDO, Basirhat to Collector 24 Parganas, dt. 28 August 1885 as quoted in W.W. Hunter, *Movement of the People and Land Reclamation Schemes*, 1889; *District Gazetteer, Dinajpur*, 1910, p. 78.

[25] J.C. Jack, op. cit., p. 42.

[26] 'Ordinarily the cultivator gives one weeding and thinning to his *aus* crop . . . . There is no need of weeding and thinning operations in a transplanted *aman* field. As it is covered with water, no weeds as a rule grow': K.B. Saha, *Economics of Rural Bengal* (Calcutta, 1930), p. 25f.

do it due to their saris clinging to their legs in wet fields and it would be held indecent to raise [the sari] to the knees.[27]

(iii) Since the nature and duration of agricultural operations are determined in a significant way by climatic/geophysical characteristics of a particular region, the extent of irrigated area *vis-à-vis* area under rainfed cultivation would appear to be an important variable influencing women's work in agriculture, particularly as wage labour. This is because irrigation not only leads to increased demand for female labour in agriculture by promoting transplantation, it also indirectly raises the total demand for agricultural labour (including female labour) by enhancing yields and harvests. Thus one would expect a noticeable association between irrigated rice area and use of female labour in agriculture. This hypothesis has been recently explored by Geeta Sen.[28] Using regression analysis on district level data from the 1971 census for examining the incidence of women agricultural labourers in the rural female population, she finds that 'the proportion of women agricultural labourers in the female population appears to vary systematically, inter alia, with the extent of irrigation, indicating possibly that it is not paddy cultivation per se, but irrigated paddy cultivation that increases incidence of female labourers'.[29] We must point out here that Bengal agriculture was mainly dependent on rainfall and inundation and even in the late 1930s, irrigated rice area accounted for less than 1 per cent of the gross area under rice.[30]

(iv) In areas growing transplanted *aman* rice, it is very likely that women in agricultural households have always participated in the preparation of seed beds and the replanting of seedlings in rice fields. But these activities occupy an extremely small fraction of time in the crop cycle, ideally five days according to Bengali

[27] Gauranga Chattopadhyay, *Ranjana: A Village in West Bengal* (Calcutta, 1964), p. 119.
[28] Geeta Sen, 'Paddy Production, Processing and Women Workers in India — The South versus the North-east', in International Rice Research Institute, *Women in Rice Farming* (Manila, 1985).
[29] Ibid., p. 393.
[30] *Rice Marketing Committee Report*, 1941, Appendix IV, as cited in Geeta Sen, 'Paddy Production and Women Workers in India', Table 21.3.

proverbs, in the month of Ashadh (corresponding to 15 June to 15 July).[31] Many women workers remained 'invisible' in an enumeration like the decennial census because the 'usual status' approach of such enumerations would not take into account this purely seasonal but by no means insignificant economic activity. Thus the time bias of the census (being conducted in the slack season in March) would tend to reinforce its implicit gender bias mentioned earlier, in understating female participation in agriculture.

Perhaps intensive studies probing labour input in agriculture by sex and task may provide a better guide to actual activity levels of women rather than census figures which relate to a slack period in rural Bengal in the wake of the *Kharif* harvest. Thus the traditional pattern of women's participation in agriculture seems to be represented more plausibly in some Type studies conducted in West Bengal during later decades. In one such study female labour accounts for about 16 per cent of the person-days required for the peak harvesting season.[32] According to another, the ratios of working hours of men and women during the reference week were 42:42; 40:38 and 34:30 in three villages surveyed in Bankura district, which has a large component of Scheduled Castes and Tribes.[33]

The Bankura study also points to an important qualification to the general pattern of women's work observed in agriculture. Female participation rates may be appreciably higher in localities with proportionately large populations of Scheduled Castes and Tribes with their distinctive mores and manners of living. In these pockets the working force may be equally divided between the sexes, even in agriculture. Recent sociological studies confirm this trend.[34] For

---

[31] For example, *'Ashadher panch dine rope jadi dhan/Sukhe thake krishi kariya, bare samman'*; i.e., 'prosperity is assured for those who transplant their paddy during five days in Ashadh'.

[32] R.K. Som and G.C. Bhattacharya, 'Type Study on Peak Period in Harvesting *Aman* Paddy, West Bengal, December 1954–January 1955', *Sankhya*, vol. 22 (1960), p. 131.

[33] Govt. of India, Labour Bureau, *Report on Intensive Type Studies on Rural Labour in India—Bankura (1968–69)*, 1975, Table 6.3.

[34] See, for example, Shyamalkanti Sen Gupta, *The Portrait of Mahali Economy in Midnapore* (Calcutta, 1969), chapters III and IV; Satyabrata Chakrabarti,

the earlier decades one may refer to district level census figures for men and women workers cross-classified by castes and tribes, besides occasional evidence from official archives such as the Dufferin Enquiry Report of 1888. 'Women working as day labourers will almost invariably be found to [belong to] Kols, Dhangars and ... Sontals. No women of ordinary cultivator classes in Bengal would work in fields except under pressure of dire necessity.'[35]

General Propositions

After discussing a special set of conditions making for the observed low participation of women in agricultural work in Bengal, we may now consider some general propositions which might lead to a better understanding of the dimensions of women's work in Bengal.

In the first place we must realize that at least one possible demographic explanation is of no relevance for our purposes. Differences in work participation rates may sometimes be linked to differences in age-structure as between various segments of the population. So far as Bengal is concerned, there was no significant divergence between men and women in regard to the ratio of their working-age population to total population (at least upto 1941) which could lead to divergent occupational trends.[36]

Regional value systems play a very important role in the domain of women's work anywhere, specially in an underdeveloped economy with a pervasive rural milieu. In the Bengali context popular perception of status tended to be negatively associated with 'visible' work participation by women, particularly in outdoor agricultural activity. Orthodox mores denigrated exposure to and contact with non-family males and even certain categories of male relatives. Socio-cultural norms therefore discouraged many types of open work participation on the part of women and produced strong

---

'Santal Women in Agriculture: Observations in a Bengal village', in Indian Anthropological Society, *Tribal women in India* (Calcutta, 1978).

[35] *Report on the Condition of the Lower Classes of People in Bengal* (Dufferin Enquiry Report) (Calcutta, 1888), para 7. (Letter of Commissioner, Burdwan Division to Secy., GOI, Revenue Dept., dt. 16 April 1888.)

[36] See Age Distribution Tables in relevant Census Reports, specially COI 1931, vol. V, Part I, p. 123.

motivation — on the part of both sexes — to restrict women's economic activities to household industries as far as possible. As Boserup remarks, the 'advantages' of women's employment in home industries is emphasized not only in Bengal and other parts of India but also in many developing countries of Africa and Latin America.[37]

Not only did cultural conventions influence the low incidence of female labour in the agricultural working force of Bengal, they also worked against accelerated absorption of women in the non-agricultural sector in the early phase of economic transition, particularly in the new mills and factories. The working conditions in these industrial units localized around the metropolis were no doubt onerous, particularly for women workers, but there was another, equally serious disincentive: the factory job never quite achieved the status of a respectable livelihood for ordinary Bengali women. Thus, in the course of her pioneering investigation of women workers in the Bengal textile factories in the 1920s, Dagmar Curjel noticed a 'marked reluctance among ordinary respectable Bengali women around Calcutta to take up factory work' and the mill-hand's job was probably the last resort for the helpless, most such jobs being usually held by widows or by women of 'doubtful reputation'.[38]

This is in sharp contrast to the situation prevailing in contemporaneous China or Japan where the number of women textile mill workers far outweighed that of men.[39] Recent research has shown that right from the initial stages of industrial development following the Meiji Restoration, Japanese entrepreneurs favoured female labour in textile mills and sought to propagate the 'benevolence' of factory owners to their 'daughter-workers'.[40] These young workers

[37] Ester Boserup, *Women's Role in Economic Development* (London, 1970), p. 115.
[38] Dagmar Curjel, 'Women's Role in Bengal Industries', *Bulletin of Indian Industries and Labour*, no. 31 (1923), Calcutta, p. 7.
[39] Arno Pearse, *The Cotton Industry of China and Japan* (Manchester, 1929), pp. 94 and 175.
[40] Peter Custers, 'Women's Labour in the Japanese Economy', EPW, 1–8 June, p. 1416.

came from poor families, in many cases enticed by recruitment agents who often acted as money lenders. We have no precise information on the average period of time spent by these women as captive labour confined in well-guarded mill dormitories. But there is evidence to show that at least till the 1930s, young village women accounted for as much as 80–90 per cent of the workers in the silk and textile mills of Japan.[41] In the Bengal context, the newly emerging industrial sector did not generate similar pressures on the demand side which could be a counterpoise to some of the constraints depressing the supply of female labour. (Demand for mill labour in Bengal was largely met by a steady flow of migrants from Bihar and Uttar Pradesh and the displaced artisans from rural Bengal.)[42]

Furthermore, even during the later phase of economic transition a large number of women probably forfeited access to a widening range of employment opportunities due to pervasive illiteracy. The literacy rates for women in Bengal were about 1 per cent and 3 per cent in 1901 and 1931 respectively. Tables show the relative paucity of women in selected areas of employment in Bengal during 1911–31. In contrast, enumerations carried out in the USA in the early decades of the twentieth century shows the very different trends in the distribution of the female working force in a fast-developing western economy. The following occupations in the USA gained more than 50,000 women workers each between 1910 and 1940: (i) stenographers, typists, clerks; (ii) saleswomen; (iii) teachers; (iv) book-keepers, accountants and cashiers; (v) proprietresses, managers and officials.[43]

The 1931 census in Bengal recorded only 8000 women working as clerks, cashiers and accountants and less than 4,000 were

---

[41] Ibid.

[42] At the turn of the century Hindi-speaking (upcountry) population accounted for 50–65 per cent of the industrial work force in the three districts of 24 Parganas, Howrah and Hooghly. See COI 1901, vol. VIA (Bengal), Part II, Table X and COI 1911, vol. V, Part I, p. 79.

[43] J.M. Hooks, *Women's Occupations Through Seven Decades* (Washington, 1947), p. 63.

employed in public administration while the comparative figures for men were about 2 lakhs and 50 thousand.

Let us now explore some of the implications of modernization. As an agriculture-bound backward economy is exposed to modern industrial techniques, several kinds of changes take place. While male employment in many sectors may move in the same positive direction, there may be no uniform impact for women. Instead, time-worn technologies usually have serious consequences for the economic situation of large segments of rural women.

Again, if widening contact with advanced economies and international market forces is thought of as another aspect of modernization, its consequences are not identical for all areas of female economic activity. Employment of women was adversely affected in cotton and silk textile production in the wake of a changed pattern of international commodity flows. On the other hand the expansion of jute cultivation and the establishment of jute mills together with a buoyant market for gunny did open new avenues of employment for women but their impact was not strong enough for neutralizing the adverse trends.

One of the characteristics of a traditional economy is the lack of sharp differentiation between the makers and sellers and trade is, in most cases, synchronous with manufacture. In such a model, production and sale of textiles, pottery and food items (including fish, dairy products, agricultural products) is usually typically carried out by the same family as a single unit, the woman perhaps taking a more active role in the disposal of the goods concerned. Other things remaining the same, a large number of women would be without visible economic activity as trade evolved into a distinct occupation with predominant male participation. This kind of change is also associated with modernization in which women did not emerge as the gainers. The general trend is indicated by census data on 'Female Sellers of Cardamom, Betel Nut, Vegetables, Fruit and Areca Nut in Bengal'. While about 28,000 such sellers were enumerated in 1911, by 1931 their number had dwindled to about 4,500.

Lastly, impediments to women's employment may also be related to institutional changes. If modernization is interpreted in terms of heightened public awareness of social problems and increased state involvement in social welfare, these may lead paradoxically to reduced work opportunities for women. Coal mining legislation prohibiting underground work for women, maternity benefit provisions applicable to industrial establishments, and legal restrictions on maximum load of jute bales to be carried by women provide ready examples.[44] When the miner and his wife both worked underground cutting and loading coal, the pair could jointly produce three tubs of coal whereas a single man, working unaided, can produce only one tub.[45] Even if surface jobs were available for some of the displaced women miners, the low daily rates were unable to compensate fully for the loss of joint mining income. As Simmons observes, 'It is highly ironic that this particular piece of legislation had the effect of causing a great deal of suffering and hardship to those whom it was supposed to benefit'.[46]

IV

The central proposition that emerges from this review is that women of Bengal played an important role in the economic life of the region, particularly in the household industries sector but the overall level of their work participation as recorded in the census has remained one of the lowest amongst British Indian Provinces, and a striking asymmetry has persisted in the work participation trends and patterns of men and women in Bengal. Some other insights are: (a) even though Bengal specialized in the cultivation of transplanted rice, and transplantation is generally considered to be the work of women not even half the female working force in Bengal was found to be engaged as cultivators or agricultural labourers during the period under review. This suggests that in the case of

[44] GOI, Dept. of Social Welfare, Ministry of Education and Social Welfare, *Towards Equality: Report of the Committee on Status of Women in India* (Delhi, 1974), p. 148.
[45] Radhakamal Mukherjee, *The Indian Working Class* (Bombay, 1945), p. 79.
[46] Colin Simmons, 'Working Conditions, Accident and 'Protective' Legislation in the Indian Coal Mining Industry in the Pre-independence Period', *Bengal Past and Present*, January–June 1970, p. 195.

women, the occupational distribution was less skewed as compared to men. (b) an interesting feature of the occupational distribution of the women of Bengal, brought out by this study, is the extremely important status of the occupation group linked to processing and selling foodstuffs. This serves to displace the popular notion regarding the superiority of textiles as a traditional source of women's livelihood in Bengal. (c) well into the twentieth century manual rice husking remained one of the few activities capable of providing an independent as well as respectable livelihood for needy women from all strata of society and (d) by and large modern technology had a differential impact on the occupational structure of men and women. This is brought home forcefully in women's historical experience in rice processing in Bengal. It has been observed that 'The status of any given section of population is intimately connected with its economic position which (itself) depends on rights, roles and opportunities for participation in economic activity'.[47] This study thus points to a significant aspect of the Bengal economy during the period under review: the rise of modern industry has negative implications for the status of women.

Analysing cross-country employment data from UNO records around 1950, scholars have found that female activity rates show a U-shaped trend, decreasing during the early stages and rising again during the later stages of development.[48] It is quite possible that the particular period of our study, with unfavourable trends in female work participation in Bengal represented these early phases. According to the 1981 Census data, however, the proportion of main workers in the female population of West Bengal was only 6 per cent as compared to the all-India figure of 14 per cent.[49] So, whether or not a reversal in trends had taken place in the interim period can only be ascertained by a detailed study of work participation data from recent censuses and National Sample Surveys.

[47] *Towards Equality*, p. 148.
[48] J.N. Sinha, 'Dynamics of Female Participation in Economic Activity in a developing economy', as cited in Leon Tabah, ed., *Population growth and Economic Development in the Third World* (Liege, 1975), p. 73.
[49] Govt. of West Bengal, *Economic Review 1989–90: Statistical Appendix*, Table 2.3.

Table 1
Male and Female Working Force in Bengal
(MWF and FWF): 1881–1931

Year	Workers (thousand) F	M	WF as % of population F	M	Sex ratio of workers (females per 1000 males)
1881	1827	11172	10.1	61.4	163.5 = 164
1901	1697	12793	8.2 (31.7)	59.5 (61.9)	138
1911	1947	13972	8.8 (33.7)	57.8 (61.9)	152
1921	2058	14063	9.1 (32.7)	58.2 (60.5)	155
1931	1792	12398	7.4 (27.6)	47.6 (58.3)	156

Note: Figures in brackets refer to All-India percentages.
Source: Census Population and Occupation Tables in relevant years; Asok Mitra, *India's Population: Aspects of Quality & Control*, vol. I, p. 439.

Table 2
Trends in Female Participation Rates in India 1911–1961
(Percentages)

(1)	1911 (2)	1921 (3)	1931 (4)	1951 (5)	1961 (6)
Andhra Pradesh	41.6	37.5	30.3	21.2	41.3
Assam	39.0	37.5	35.5	30.7	31.8
Bihar	34.7	35.9	26.1	20.7	27.1
Gujarat	30.0	24.1	28.6	28.0	27.9
Kerala	28.0	24.1	38.4	18.1	19.7
Madhya Pradesh	47.9	46.8	37.5	37.9	44.0
Madras	36.5	29.2	23.1	12.7	31.3
Maharashtra	39.8	37.0	30.3	33.3	38.1
Orissa	30.4	33.2	30.0	18.8	26.6
Rajasthan	45.4	46.2	38.3	38.3	35.9
Uttar Pradesh	33.3	37.3	29.8	23.6	18.1
West Bengal	18.8	17.4	13.2	11.6	9.4
India	33.9	32.8	28.4	23.3	28.0

Source: J. Krishnamurty, 'The Industrial Distribution of Working Force in India 1911–1961: A Study of Selected Aspects', Ph.D. thesis, Delhi University, 1970, p. 245.

Table 3
Men and Women in Agricultural and
Non-Agriculture Working Force in Bengal (AWF and NWAF): 1881–1931

Year	AWF (thousand) (ordinary cultivators and agricultural labourers) F	M	AWF as % of WF F	M	Sex ratio (SR) in AWF	SR in NWAF (NWAF = Total WF excluding AWF and general labour)
1881	414	7210	22.7	64.5	57	398
1901	458	8319	27.0 (71.3)	65.0 (65.2)	55	300
1911	689	9499	35.4 (73.9)	68.0 (68.5)	72	313
1921	983	9827	47.8 (75.5)	69.9 (69.8)	100	237
1931	508	8073	28.3 (72.3)	65.1 (68.7)	62	296

Note: Figures in brackets refer to all-India percentages.
Source: Census Occupation Tables in relevant years; Asok Mitra, op. cit., p. 441.

Table 4
Sectorwise Distribution of Male and
Female Workers in Bengal (%): 1881–1931

Year	Production of raw materials F	Production of raw materials M	Industry F	Industry M	Transport F	Transport M	Trade F	Trade M	Services F	Services M
1881	26.1	66.0	52.7	13.1	–	–	–	–	5.1	13.3
1911	49.7	75.1	26.3	8.1	11.2	5.3	–	–	14.6	6.7
1921	61.4	75.4	19.1	8.0	8.6	5.6	–	–	7.3	5.5
1931	46.1	73.0	15.5	7.2	8.0	6.3	–	–	25.1	6.7

Notes: (1) The 1881 percentages for 'Production of raw materials' would differ from those in the later censuses as the former do not include fishing and mining as in 1911, 1921 and 1931. Similarly 'industry' in 1881 would be somewhat inflated on account of inclusion of fishing, mining and some trade.
(2) The tertiary sector (transport, trade and services) is not subdivided in 1881 census tables.

Table 5
Women Workers in Bengal in
Selected Areas of Employment ('00): 1881–1931

		1881	1901	1911	1921	1931
1.	Producing and selling ordinary fuel	210	208	276	119	39
2.	Making and selling dairy products	–	215	223	166	182
3.	Silk worm raising	–	301	141	23	5
4.	Cotton textiles	1703	462	450	519	357
5.	Silk textiles	–	34	94	36	10
6.	Jute textiles	435	262	508	542	388
7.	Basket making and allied handicrafts	617	454	429	297	198
8.	Medicine	121	126	152	105	113
9.	Industries	3	12	18	26	50
10.	Domestic service	1337	801	1107	1158	4198
11.	Rice husking	–	2131	2703	1696	1311

Source: Mukul Mukherjee, 'Impact of Modernisation on Women's Occupations: A Case Study of Rice Husking Industry of Bengal', J. Krishnamurty, ed., *Women in Colonial India: Essays on Survival, Work and the State* (Delhi, 1989), p. 184.

Table 6
Sex Ratio in Selected Areas of
Employment in Bengal: 1881–1931
(Women per thousand men)

	1881	1901	1911	1921	1931
1. Pasture and agriculture	65	71	85	115	89
2. Making and selling food staffs	1317	617	747	530	467
3. Rice husking	22283	27305	10872	13412	7822
4. Total textiles	725	375	307	270	206
5. Cotton textiles	664	260	312	337	262
6. Jute textiles	1266	316	278	217	168
7. Jute Mills	–	–	206	200	–
8. Producing and selling ordinary fuel	2274	1925	633	760	694
9. Basket making and allied crafts	–	1061	1161	775	559
10. Sanitation	324	378	343	390	250
11. Instruction	2	1	49	64	73
12. Plantation	76	674	724	778	792
13. Domestic Service	316	683	469	359	1114

Source: Occupation Tables in Census Reports of relevant years.

Table 7
Distribution of Male and Female Working Force in
Selected Occupations in Bengal (%): 1881–1931

Year	Pasture and agriculture M	F	Making and selling food stuffs M	F	Textiles M	F	Selected Services M	F
1881	66.0	26.1	4.0	32.3	2.7	11.9	5.3	8.5
1901	70.2	35.2	5.7	26.7	2.2	6.3	2.6	7.8
1911	73.3	44.9	4.9	26.1	2.5	5.5	10.9	7.4
1921	74.1	58.3	4.8	17.2	2.9	5.4	3.5	6.4
1931	71.5	44.4	4.8	15.4	3.0	4.3	4.7	24.5 (9.7)*

Notes: (i) Selected Services = Religion + Medicine + Instruction + Domestic Service.

(ii) * % obtained if working dependants are excluded from the total number under Domestic Services.

Source: Relevant Census Occupation Tables.

Table 8
Men and Women Workers in Selected Industries in Bengal: 1921

Industry	No. of establishments	Women	Men
1. Cotton spinning and weaving mills	18	1955	11780
2. Jute presses	188	772	9870
3. Jute mills	62	47090	237670
4. Engineering works	48	20	18688
5. Iron foundries	60	2415	13300
6. Glassware and earthenware	421	6143	30713
7. Chemicals	194	1240	16620
8. Oil mills	104	231	3832
9. Paper mills	5	673	4055
10. Rice mills	137	1570	2742
11. Sugar mills	51	30	1880
12. Printing Presses	243	38	14079
13. Workshops including Railway Workshops	93	776	50428

Source: Census of India 1921, vol. VI, Part II Table No. XXII.

Table 9

Male and Female Working Force in Selected Sectors in Bengal ('000): 1911–1931

	1931 M	1931 F	1921 M	1921 F	1911 M	1911 F
1. Tea Plantation	141.6	111.8	110.7	107.4	95.8	91.8
2. Education	68.6	5.0	41.1	2.6	37.4	1.8
3. Health	56.4	11.3	46.3	10.4	41.5	15.2
4. Cashiers, Accountants, Clerks & Other Employees	195.8	8.1	160.0	3.4	76.8	1.1
5. Storekeepers and Shop	135.3	7.0	51.1	3.1	—	—
6. Public Administration	48.9	3.6	—	—	—	—
7. Post, Telegraph, Telephones	10.6	0.03	14.0	0.1	—	—
8. Railway employees and labour employed in Railway Construction	67.0	1.8	71.3	3.4	—	—

Source: Relevant Census Occupation Tables.

Appendix

Male and Female Workers in Bengal in Selected Occupations, 1881–1931
(Hundred)

Occupations	1881 M	1881 F	1901 M	1901 F	1911 M	1911 F	1921 M	1921 F	1931 M	1931 F
(1)	(2)	(3)	(4)	(5)	(6)	(7)	(8)	(9)	(10)	(11)
1. Ordinary Cultivators	72100	4140	77474	3589	81901	4472	82930	7275	56574	2548
2. Agricultural Labourers	–	–	5721	994	13086	2416	15344	2555	24155	2529
3. Growers of Special Products	135	10	1168	788	1290	934	1409	1096	11746	1113
4. Stock-Raising	1474	574	2405	68	2602	113	1105	41	1110	54
5. Total Pasture and Agriculture	73785	4770	89764	5964	102458	8750	104254	11997	88688	7959
6. Mining	17	2	125	110	395	250	382	291	252	175
7. Producing and Selling Ordinary Fuel	92	210	108	208	207	276	162	119	147	39

Occupations	1881 M	1881 F	1901 M	1901 F	1911 M	1911 F	1921 M	1921 F	1931 M	1931 F
(1)	(2)	(3)	(4)	(5)	(6)	(7)	(8)	(9)	(10)	(11)
8. Fishing, including Dealing in fish	2399	1189	3078	1090	2917	1254	2674	883	1616	304
9. Making and Selling Dairy Products	—	—	600	215	667	223	483	166	759	182
10. Rice Husking	—	—	96	2131	99	2703	156	1696	98	1310
11. Dealing in Grain and Pulses	—	—	—	—	620	321	980	385	631	296
12. Total Making and Selling Food Stuffs	4484	5907	7328	4524	6806	5085	6693	3544	5917	2763
13. Silk-Worm Rearing	—	—	42	301	90	141	35	23	2	5
14. Silk Textiles	—	—	103	34	179	94	42	36	36	10
15. Cotton Handloom	—	—	1733	456	1342	431	—	—	—	—
16. Cotton Mill	—	—	43	5	99	19	—	—	—	—
17. Total Cotton	2566	1703	1776	462	1441	450	1540	519	1365	357

Occupations	1881 M	1881 F	1901 M	1901 F	1911 M	1911 F	1921 M	1921 F	1931 M	1931 F
(1)	(2)	(3)	(4)	(5)	(6)	(7)	(8)	(9)	(10)	(11)
18. Jute Mill	–	–	636	134	1789	368	–	–	–	–
19. Total Jute	344	435	830	262	1826	508	2494	542	2315	388
20. Total Textiles	3005	2179	2866	1074	3466	1065	4085	1104	3744	773
21. Basket Making and Allied Handicrafts	1566	617	428	454	369	429	383	297	354	198
22. Pottery Making and Selling	604	220	743	224	695	336	610	306	410	119
23. Brick and Tile Making	–	–	80	16	200	43	505	54	179	35
24. Building Industries	746	13	552	35	898	80	808	92	496	41
25. Hair Dressing	–	–	786	58	699	82	697	52	584	32
26. Washing and Cleaning	–	–	438	136	395	200	369	131	309	84
27. Road Transport	931	1	1026	13	2336	285	1529	139	1067	103
28. Rail Transport	15	–	3406	3	740	20	714	34	670	19
29. Sanitation	–	–	183	60	200	75	206	70	160	62

Occupations	1881 M (2)	1881 F (3)	1901 M (4)	1901 F (5)	1911 M (6)	1911 F (7)	1921 M (8)	1921 F (9)	1931 M (10)	1931 F (11)
(1)										
30. Religion	1044	93	1512	391	1182	173	904	22	779	30
31. Medicine	342	121	350	126	415	152	463	105	564	113
32. Instruction	254	3	292	12	374	18	411	26	686	50
33. Domestic Service	4224	1337	1173	801	2362	1107	3263	1158	3768	4198
34. General Labour (Unspecified)	8395	1733	10473	2050	4324	421	2263	506	3477	551
35. General Trade (Unspecified)	2048	474	833	69	341	27	511	31	1379	73

Source: Census Occupation Tables of relevant years.

8

The Role of Women in Economic Activity: A Study of Women in Rice Farming Systems in West Bengal

Bahnisikha Ghosh

I Introduction and Outline

The reduction of unemployment, poverty and destitution has been the major objectives of India's development policy. However, it took long to realise that such problems are often sex-specific and that alleviation of such conditions should be specially targeted at women. Policy-planners attempt to maximize welfare of households and assume that the welfare of individual members of the household would generally contribute to family welfare. However, it is now widely recognized that interests of men and women within a household do not always and necessarily coincide and benefits accruing to the male members do not necessarily reach the female automatically.[1] Moreover, households with female heads are among the poorest in the country,[2] perhaps suggesting a sex bias in economic well-being. Many of the development

[1] Bina Agarwal, 'Work Participation of Rural Women in the Third World: Some Data and Conceptual Biases', paper presented at the Technical Seminar on Women's Work and Employment (New Delhi, 1982); Amartya K. Sen, 'Gender and Cooperative Conflict', in Irene Tinker, ed., *Persistent Inequalities* (New York, 1990).

[2] G. Parthasarathy, 'Rural Poverty and Female Heads of Household: Need for Quantitative Analysis', paper presented at the Technical Seminar on Women's Work and Employment (New Delhi, 1982).

schemes in India seems to have been formulated without any special knowledge and appreciation of women's status as reflected in the intrahousehold sex-specific division of labour and income. As a result this half of the community was practically out of the direct focus of development programmes. The production-oriented programmes of rural development until very recently ignored women's employment needs, and planners took women for granted without assessing their specific roles in agriculture.[3] It is thus important to explore this sex-dichotomy in the process of development and focus specific attention upon women as a component of the household and national economy for effective development programmes. The broad objective of this paper is to attempt to examine the role and status of women as compared to men in economic activities.

The study focuses on rice-based farming systems in selected villages in West Bengal. Section II discusses problems of data and measurements for studies of economic contributions of women and indicates the source of data used here. Section III reviews women's work in economic production and home production, and Section IV makes an in-depth analysis of women's work in rice production. Section V analyses the major determinants of time allocation, Section VI examines the question of gender equity in consumption, nutrition and work and Section VII summarizes the conclusions.

II Problem of Data and Measurement[4]

The recognition that enhanced participation of women in the economic scene is a major correlate of improvement of their status, although of quite recent origin, is at last expected to lead towards a search for selective interventions in order to increase the economic opportunities and options open to them. For this purpose, it is essential to study and analyse past trends and predict future courses. A strong data base particularly on work participation by sex is a

---

[3] National Commission on Agriculture, *Report of the National Commission of Agriculture* (New Delhi, 1976).

[4] Bahnisikha Ghosh, *The Indian Population Problem: A Household Economics Approach* (New Delhi, 1990).

critical prerequisite for development and policy formulations. Unfortunately, the paucity of such useful data severely limits the quality of analyses in respect of labour force participation of women in Bengal and of rural women working in agriculture in particular. Conventional labour force statistics in developing countries have a systematic bias, both definitional and conceptual, that under estimates the contribution of women. Domestic work, primarily a responsibility of women in the household, is commonly excluded from censuses and national accounts. Also the substantial labour that female workers render in the fields has been invisible to the collectors of rural labour force statistics.[5] In India, female unpaid family helpers in agriculture are rarely included in the labour force. In most developing countries, including India, problems of definitions and procedure plague collection of labourforce statistics for the male and the female alike. However, the undercount of women and children in most population censuses has been disproportionately large. This has been due either to the adherence to the narrow definition of 'economic' activity proposed in International guidelines[6] or due to biases in the application of these guidelines. For example, farmers' wives and children (especially students) are strictly assumed to be non-workers and their labourforce characteristics are not even collected. In several empirical studies dealing with aspects of total agricultural employment, aggregation is done by counting female labour time as half or three-quarters of male labour time.[7] This *a priori* assumption is often sought to be justified by the fact that women usually receive half or three-fourths of male wage.[8] Insofar as such undercounting is not consistent across

---

[5] Ester Boserup, *Women's Role in Economic Development* (New York, 1970); Ruth B. Dixon, 'Counting Women in the Agricultural Labor Force', *Popular and Development Review*, vol. 18, no. 3 (New York, 1982).

[6] International Labour Office, *International Recommendations on Labour Statistics* (Geneva, 1976).

[7] A.S. Kahlon, S.S. Miglani and S.K. Mehta, *Studies in the Economics of Farm Management in Ferozepur District (Punjab): Report for the Year 1967–68* (New Delhi, 1973).

[8] P. Sanghvi, *Surplus Manpower in Agriculture and Economic Development* (with Special Reference to India) (Bombay, 1969).

countries or even within countries over time, these labour force statistics afford a shaky basis for purposes of analysing and comparing trends and variations.

In developing countries like India barely 10 per cent of workers are in the organized sector. In contrast to their western counterparts, women in agriculture here are mainly unpaid family helpers rather than wage earners, underemployed rather than formally unemployed, seasonal rather than regular members of the work-force. In situations where subsistence farm families sell little of their produce, members often work as exchange labour on neighbours' fields in addition to working on the family farm. Children and women traditionally look after livestock and take part in the processing of crops in their courtyards but do not go out to work in the fields. These tasks are treated virtually as extensions of house-work and the dividing line between domestic work for family's own consumption and 'economic' work is often blurred. This difficulty is compounded by the fact that women themselves often fail to report their 'productive' work as such, and include all these among their domestic chores. Moreover, the fact that women in these households often engage in small trades and crafts in slack seasons, classifying them not only as workers or non-workers but also as agricultural workers or non-agricultural workers becomes extremely difficult. Putting these women strictly within one category or the other by applying conventional definitions, therefore, results in a severe undercount.

In view of the above difficulties it becomes extremely important for the researcher to define what exactly are economic activities. According to United Nations definitions, economically active persons are 'all the persons of either sex who furnish the supply of labour for the production of goods and services during the time-references period chosen for the investigation'.[9] Included within economic activity are planting, cultivation and harvesting in anticipation of profit, preparing product for sale, tending of livestock, and repairing of farm equipment, while 'household duties such as

[9] J.G.C. Blacker, 'A Critique of International Definitions of Economic Activity', *Population Bulletin of ECWA*, no. 14 (1978).

the preparation of food and the care of chickens and other livestock which are used for consumption instead of for exchange' are excluded.[10] The problem of choice of the right definition is intractable because the choice involves arbitrariness in drawing a line between where domestic work ends and production begins. For example, how to classify such activities as tending of cows where the milk is partly sold and partly consumed within the household? Critics of conventional labour force statistics would suggest that even domestic work such as cooking and child care be included in national accounts of gross national product thereby recognizing the contribution of women in reproduction of the labourforce, and in the production of goods that would otherwise have had to be purchased. However, this would mean including all women between 5 and 59 years of age in the labour force and it would be difficult to assess the response of female economic activity pattern to socio-economic stimuli over time. The other extreme would be to count only those women who work under a rigid wage payment system, that is, in the modern sector.[11] The practices of censuses usually fall between these two extremes, the exact position depending upon an arbitrarily drawn dividing line, and on the selection of this dividing line depends the reliability of the data.

One method to minimize such problems of definitions and measurement is to use time allocation data. These comprehensive time-use studies have several advantages over other approaches. First, this approach does not require the investigators to apply *a priori* judgments as to what are economic uses of time. Second, male respondents often fail to see many of the duties performed by women as economic activities and may, therefore, claim that the

---

[10] Elise Boulding, Shirley A. Nuss, Dorothy Lee Carson and M.A. Greenstein *Handbook of International Data on Women* (New York, 1976); Ruth B. Dixon, 'Counting Women in the Agricultural Labor Force', *Popular and Development Review*, vol. 18, no. 3 (New York, 1982).

[11] J.G.C. Blacker, 'A Critique of International Definitions of Economic Activity', *Population Bulletin of ECWA*, no. 14 (1978); Ester Boserup, 'Employment of Women in Developing Countries', in Leon Tabah, ed., *Population Growth and Economic Development in the Third World*, vol. I (Belgium, 1975).

women do nothing other than domestic work. Detailed information on time-use by women in such cases might show that much of the work performed by them was actually economic activities yielding income or, at least, activity that saves expenditure that would have otherwise had to be incurred. The approach also has definite usefulness in cases where the work done by women is not specialized (that is, where women perform a variety of agricultural and non-agricultural tasks) and can provide important insights into how the women are actually allocating their time between different activities. These studies are also particularly relevant in situations where a large share of activities is non-marketed and/or non-monetized and where the reward for labour do not always reflect the value of that labour.

This paper uses time allocation data collected in a number of household surveys in 9 villages in Nadia District and 3 in Birbhum District in West Bengal.

III Women's Work in Economic Production and Home Production

Official data on employment fail to show that for women in low-income households, working long hours at any task that promises the slightest return, underemployment or unemployment do not necessarily mean idleness or leisure. Much of women's work (encompassing activities such as food processing, kitchen gardening, animal husbandry, provision of fuel, fetching of water, manufacturing for home use — all these in addition to cooking, child care, etc.) is lumped together under 'domestic work' which is specifically excluded from the definition of 'work' in UN census manual. This results in the exclusion of many women from the labour force. It is more appropriate to treat these as 'home production' activities and to show how individual men and women allocate their time to these activities as well as to activities that are conventionally termed as economic. This can help examination of the concept of 'work' and also of the relative contribution of women in the total volume of such work. Such a micro analysis is presented here.

The distribution of total time of the population of the sample villages has been studied for all activities excluding personal care, rest, recreation and sleep. The traditional 'economic activities' have been classified into agriculture and non-agriculture and the 'home production activities' are education, child care, house work and other activities.[12]

It would appear from Chart I that, on an average the male spends about 9.47 hours and the female about 9.53 hours per day on the activities considered. Out of this, the male allocates about 6.25 hours per day to economic activities and only about 3.22 hours to home production activities. The female, on the other hand, appears to spend the bulk of her time, that is, 8.18 hours per day on so-called 'home production' activities as education, child care, house work, and on activities such as sewing, knitting, mat-making, making cowdung cakes for home use as fuel and tutoring of own children. Thus, she participates in traditionally defined 'economic activity' for only 1.35 hours, more than two-thirds of which is spent outside the home, as hired labour. If activities such as house work, education, child care etc., were viewed as 'work' in the broader sense of the term, 'total work' performed by the female would be more than that by the male. This is due to the fact that the female spends much longer hours than the male in activities other than those strictly economic, which more than compensates for the excess of male over female hours in economic activities. In fact, the number of hours spent by the female on home production activities is fairly stable at about 5.5 hours per day, irrespective of variations in the number of hours she spends on conventional economic activities, while the time spent by the male on home production activities varies substantially. This implies that an extra hour of work in economic activity would be at the expense of hours in home production subsistence activities for the male, while it would only add to the total volume of work done by the female.

The above pattern of allocation of time shows that out of the total time of work, the proportion spent on economic activities is 66 per cent for the male and 14 per cent for the female (Chart II).

---

[12] Sudhin K. Mukhopadhyay, *Rice-Based Farming Systems Research: An Experiment at Kalyani* (Kalyani, 1990).

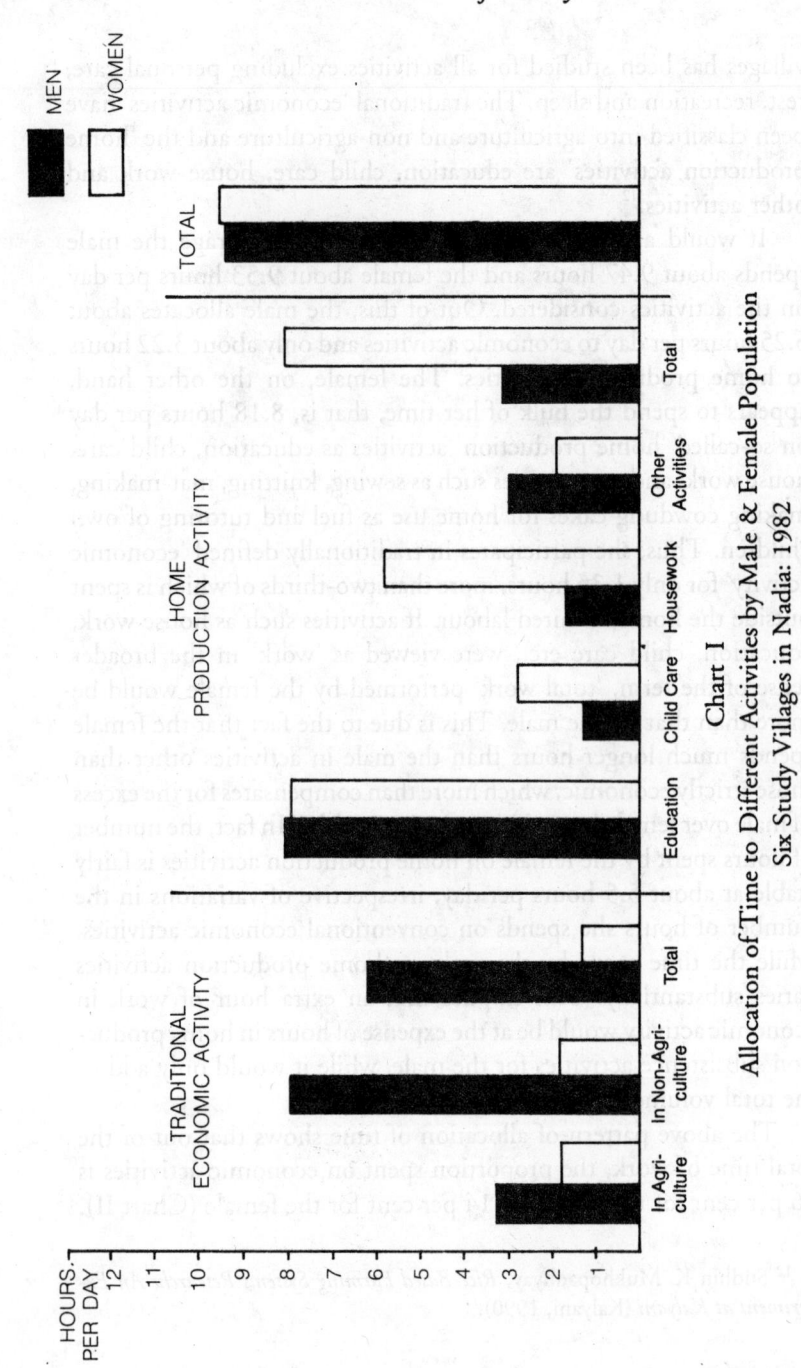

Chart I
Allocation of Time to Different Activities by Male & Female Population
Six Study Villages in Nadia: 1982

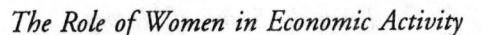

The Role of Women in Economic Activity   261

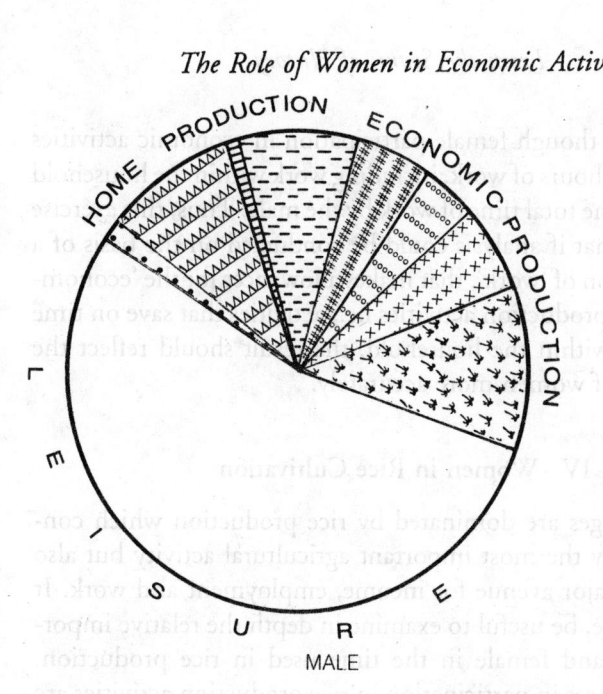

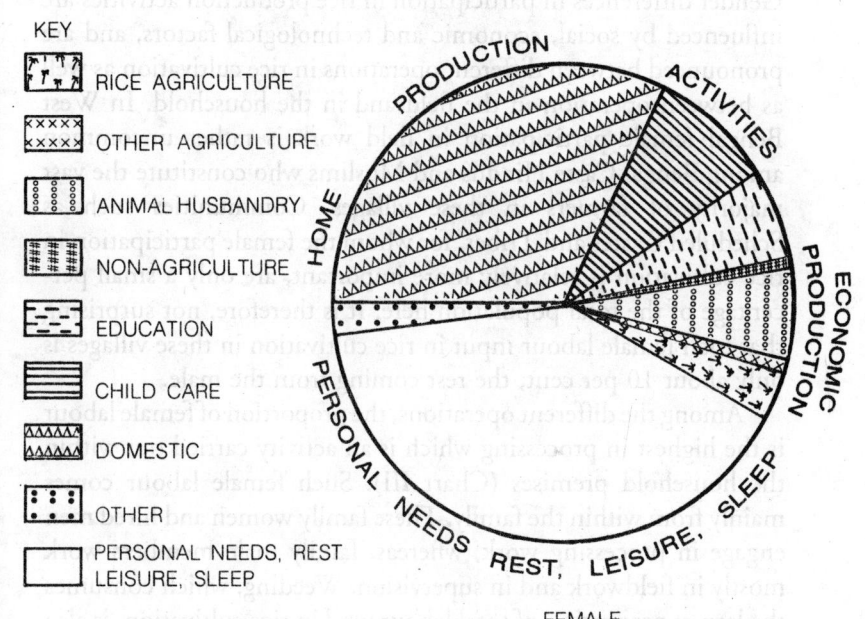

KEY

- Rice Agriculture
- Other Agriculture
- Animal Husbandry
- Non-Agriculture
- Education
- Child Care
- Domestic
- Other
- Personal Needs, Rest, Leisure, Sleep

Chart II
Allocation of Time to Different Activities: Male-Female Differential

However, even though female participation in economic activities is low, her total hours of work, including work within the household is no less than the total time of work by the male. Thus, this exercise clearly shows that if analysis could be conducted on the basis of a revised definition of 'work', that makes allowances for the 'economizing' of home production activities i.e., activities that save on time and resources within the household, the result should reflect the contributions of women more accurately.

IV Women in Rice Cultivation

The study villages are dominated by rice production which constitutes not only the most important agricultural activity but also provides the major avenue for income, employment and work. It would, therefore, be useful to examine in depth the relative importance of male and female in the time used in rice production. Gender differences in participation in rice production activities are influenced by social, economic and technological factors, and are pronounced between different operations in rice cultivation as well as between operation in the field and in the household. In West Bengal female participation in field work is rather uncommon among Bengal Caste Hindus and Muslims who constitute the vast majority of farmers in these villages. Communities such as Scheduled Castes and Tribes, for whom the female participation in rice cultivation is relatively more important, are only a small percentage of the total population here. It is therefore, not surprising that total female labour input in rice cultivation in these villages is only about 10 per cent, the rest coming from the male.

Among the different operations, the proportion of female labour is the highest in processing which is an activity carried out within the household premises (Chart III). Such female labour comes mainly from within the family. These family women and hired men engage in processing work, whereas, family male members work mostly in fieldwork and in supervision. Weeding, which consumes the largest proportion of total labour used in rice cultivation, is also the most important rice growing activity of the female, who are mostly hired rather than family labour. The second most important

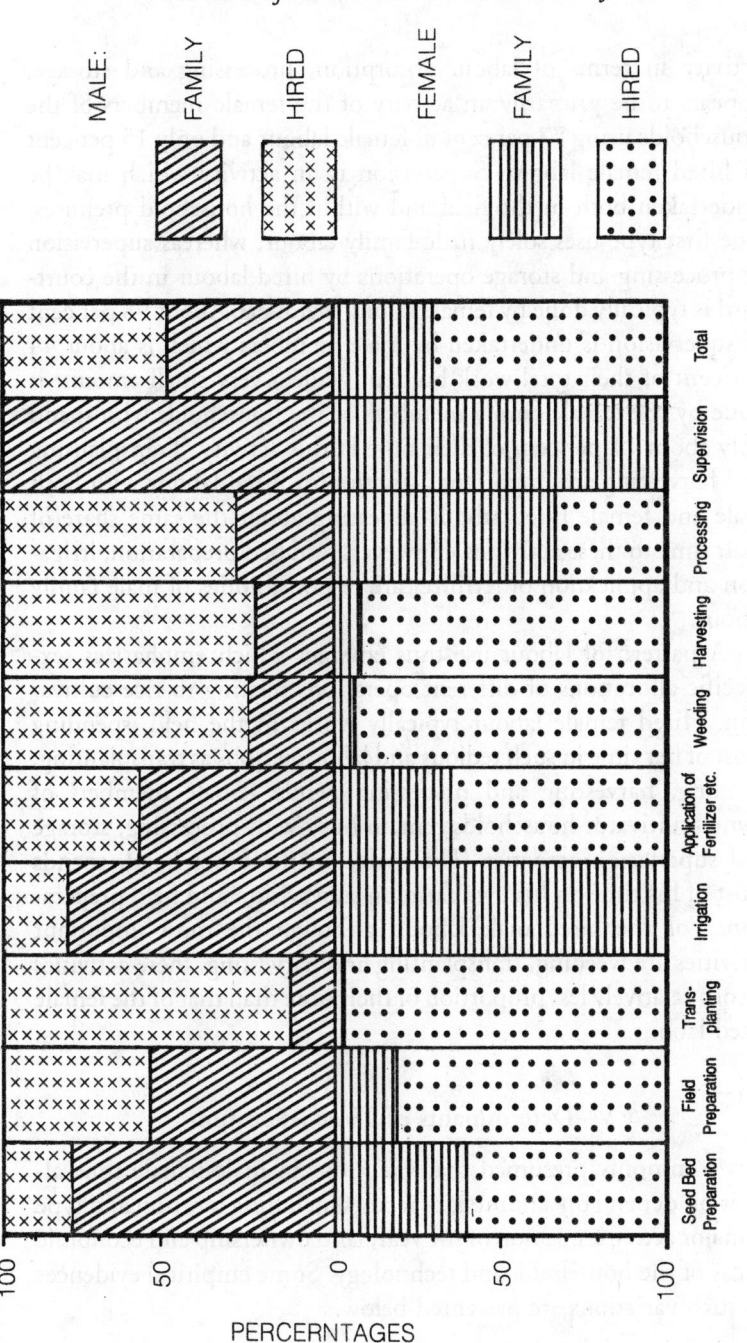

Chart III
Percent Distribution of Male & Female: Hired & Family Labour Use in Rice Operations

activity in terms of labour absorption, processing and storage, appears to be primarily an activity of the female members of the households using 77 per cent of female labour and only 15 per cent of hired female labour. Supervision is an activity which may be undertaken both in the field and within the household premises. The first type uses solely male family labour, whereas supervision of processing and storage operations by hired labour in the courtyard is typically done by female family members. About 98 per cent of supervision is undertaken by male members which is about 44 per cent of their total work burden, while a very small amount is done by the female family members of the households who spend only about 11 per cent of their time in this activity. Transplanting and harvesting are important activities for hired labour with both male and female hired labour allocating about the same share of their time to these activities. However, seed bed preparation, irrigation and application of fertilizer are responsibilities of male family labour.

A pattern of labour use thus emerges which emphasizes sex-specific allocations of different operations relating to rice cultivation. Hired female labour typically works in the field, spending most of her time in such tedious and laborious jobs as transplanting, weeding, harvesting and processing, while female members of owner-cultivator households remain busy with processing, storage and supervision activities. The male, on the other hand, spends most of his time on his own farm on supervision and field preparation. For the hired male labour, although the most important activities are weeding, transplanting and harvesting, these activities absorb relatively less proportion of their time than that of the female hired labour.

V Determinants of Time Allocation

It is commonly presumed that variations in male-female time allocation depend on a number of factors including location and type of major activities, season of the year, land ownership and economic status of the household, and technology. Some empirical evidences on such variations are presented below.

Year and Location

The data on time allocation discussed in the preceding pages refer to a cluster of villages in Nadia district in 1982. Since 1987 two villages of the cluster were subjected again to a series of repeat surveys at the interval of ten days. Data were collected on every tenth day on the basis of record keeping by 15 households in each village selected as stratified random samples. One of the villages is predominantly Hindu while the other is primarily Muslim. In a similar way, two other villages — one with mixed population and the other with exclusively tribal (Santhal) population — were surveyed in the district of Birbhum. The results (Tables 1 and 2) show that in the Nadia village between 1982 and 1987 there has been practically no change in the level and pattern of time allocation by the male and female for their work. However, between villages categorized by differences in communities, there is some variation. For example, in the Muslim dominated village the male-female differential in total work burden is relatively higher. Although the overall differences between the villages in Nadia and Birbhum are not significantly high, the male-female differences in the pattern of time distribution between traditional economic activities and home production activities shows that by and large economic production activities claim larger proportion of the total burden in Birbhum. This is more pronounced in the case of female. A comparison between the mixed population village and the tribal village shows that in the latter the female contributes more than 56 per cent of the work hours as compared with 52 per cent in the former. A comparison between economic production and home production in the two villages shows that the share of economic production in total work burden is greater for the female of the tribal population. Thus, although during the five years since 1982 there was no appreciable change in the labour and distribution of work burden for the male and the female in the villages studied, there are cross-sectional variations between locations and communities. By and large, the work burden is higher for the female across the different populations studied.

Table 1
Allocation of Time by Male and Female for Principal Crop Season
Hours per Head per Day: By Location and Community Type

Activities	\multicolumn{2}{c}{NADIA (Alluvial)}						\multicolumn{4}{c}{BIRBHUM (Laterite)}			
	Average of Study Villages (1982)		Village A (1987)		Village B (1987)		Village C (1987)		Village D (1987)	
	M	F	M	F	M	F	M	F	M	F
Economic Production	6.25	1.35	6.42	1.44	6.75	1.76	7.36	3.08	6.90	3.40
Home Production	3.22	8.18	2.98	8.26	2.45	8.38	2.50	7.58	2.07	8.12
Total Work Burden	9.47	9.53	9.40	9.70	9.20	10.14	9.85	10.66	8.97	11.52
Other Social and Personal Requirements, Rest & Sleep	14.53	14.47	14.60	14.30	14.80	13.86	14.13	13.34	15.03	12.47
All Activities	24.00	24.00	24.00	24.00	24.00	24.00	24.00	24.00	24.00	24.00

Note: Village A: Chanda (Nadia District): Mainly Hindu Sample
Village B: Sonakur (Nadia District): Mainly Muslim Sample
Village C: Ayanadanga & Mostala (Birbhum District): Mixed Population
Village D: Uparkhara (Birbhum District): Tribal Population

Table 2
Percent Distribution of Hours Spent by Male and Female for Principal Crop Season By Location and Community Type

(Village Survey in 1987)

Activities	NADIA (Alluvial)				BIRBHUM (Laterite)			
	Village A		Village B		Village C		Village D	
	M	F	M	F	M	F	M	F
Economic Production	26.75 (81.62)	6.00 (18.32)	28.12 (79.32)	7.33 (20.68)	30.67 (70.49)	12.84 (29.51)	28.75 (66.99)	14.17 (33.01)
Home Production	12.42 (26.51)	34.42 (73.59)	10.21 (22.62)	34.92 (77.38)	10.41 (24.79)	31.58 (75.21)	8.63 (20.31)	33.83 (79.69)
Total Work Burden	39.17 (49.21)	40.42 (50.79)	38.33 (47.57)	42.25 (52.43)	41.08 (48.05)	44.42 (51.95)	37.38 (43.78)	48.00 (56.22)
Other Social and Personal Requirements, Rest and Sleep	60.83 (50.52)	59.58 (49.48)	61.67 (51.64)	57.75 (48.36)	58.92 (47.54)	55.58 (48.54)	62.62 (54.65)	51.99 (45.35)
All Activities	100.00	100.00	100.00	100.00	100.00	100.00	100.00	100.00

Figures in parentheses denote respective shares of male and female in that activity

Seasonal Variation

Activities in rural households are very often influenced by seasonal variations. In order to test this effect of seasons on male-female differential in time allocation, data have been analysed for the busy season and lean season for the four villages in Nadia and Birbhum. The results show that there is almost invariably an increase in the total hours of work in the busy season compared to the lean season. The extent of increase is the highest in the tribal village and the lowest in the Muslim village. The reason presumably may be the preponderance of landless labour in the tribal community working as hired workers in the busy season and the absence of participation in field work by the Muslims leaving their hours of work relatively little changed. The work burden of women is relatively higher for both landless and land-owning households. The additional burden is of course due to the hours spent on home production activities by the female (Tables 3 and 4).

Land Ownership Status

A comparison between land-owners and landless households shows that members of the latter, both male and female, have larger work burden. The share of economic production in the total work hours is also higher for the landless, the female working relatively more (Tables 5 and 6 and Chart IV).

Effect of Technology

In order to examine whether technological change in agriculture has any differential impact on male-female labour use, the cultivators were classified in HYV (high yielding variety) and TV (traditional variety) rice growers. Such disaggregation of the cultivators and comparison with landless labourers shows (Table 7) that *total number of hours* worked on an average increases from 6.2 and 9.2 hours respectively for the male and female for the TV growers to 7.5 and 10 hours for the HYV growers. This is due to increase in agricultural activities, total economic production activities as well as total home production activities. The female for both the HYV and TV growers work longer than the male and this

Table 3
Allocation of Time by Male and Female for Principal Crop Season
Hours per Head per Day: By Season

(Village Survey in 1987)

Activities	Lean Season Village A M	A F	B M	B F	C M	C F	D M	D F	Busy Season Village A M	A F	B M	B F	C M	C F	D M	D F
Economic Production	6.30	1.02	6.35	1.77	6.89	2.25	5.83	2.76	7.10	2.16	7.29	1.74	7.76	3.63	7.68	3.92
Home Production	2.86	7.68	2.65	7.64	2.62	7.16	2.73	7.82	3.12	8.92	2.15	8.89	2.40	7.91	1.57	8.34
Total Work Burden	9.16	8.70	9.00	9.41	9.51	9.41	8.56	10.58	10.22	11.08	9.44	10.63	10.16	11.54	9.25	12.26
Other Social and Personal Requirements, Rest & Sleep	14.84	15.30	15.00	14.59	14.49	14.59	15.44	13.42	13.78	12.92	14.56	13.37	13.84	12.46	14.75	11.74
All Activities	24.00	24.00	24.00	24.00	24.00	24.00	24.00	24.00	24.00	24.00	24.00	24.00	24.00	24.00	24.00	24.00

Table 4
Percent Distribution of Hours Spent by Male and Female for Principal Crop Season By Season

(Village Survey in 1987)

Activities	Lean Season Village A M	A F	B M	B F	C M	C F	D M	D F	Busy Season Village A M	A F	B M	B F	C M	C F	D M	D F
Economic Production	26 (86)	4 (14)	26 (78)	7 (22)	29 (75)	9 (25)	24 (68)	11 (32)	30 (77)	9 (23)	30 (81)	7 (19)	32 (68)	15 (32)	22 (66)	16 (34)
Home Production	12 (27)	32 (73)	11 (26)	32 (74)	11 (27)	30 (73)	11 (26)	33 (74)	13 (26)	37 (74)	9 (19)	37 (81)	10 (23)	33 (77)	7 (16)	35 (84)
Total Work Burden	38 (51)	36 (49)	37 (49)	39 (51)	40 (50)	39 (50)	35 (45)	44 (55)	43 (48)	46 (52)	39 (47)	44 (53)	42 (47)	48 (53)	39 (43)	51 (57)
Other Social & Personal Requirements Rest & Sleep	62 (49)	64 (51)	63 (51)	61 (49)	60 (50)	61 (50)	65 (54)	56 (46)	57 (51)	54 (49)	61 (52)	56 (48)	58 (53)	52 (47)	61 (56)	48 (44)
All Activities	100	100	100	100	100	100	100	100	100	100	100	100	100	100	100	100

Figures in parentheses denote respective shares of male and female in that activity

Table 5
Allocation of Time by Male and Female for Principal Crop Season
Hours per Head per Day: By Land Ownership Status

(Village Survey in 1987)

	Land Owner				Landless			
	Village A		Village B		Village A		Village B	
Activities	M	F	M	F	M	F	M	F
Economic Production	6.24	1.52	6.60	1.20	8.64	2.65	6.69	2.18
Home Production	3.11	8.09	2.43	8.42	1.44	7.87	2.52	9.35
Total Work Burden	9.35	9.61	9.03	9.62	10.08	10.52	9.21	11.53
Other Social and Personal Requirements, Rest & Sleep	14.65	14.39	14.97	14.32	13.92	13.48	14.79	12.47
All Activities	24.00	24.00	24.00	24.00	24.00	24.00	24.00	24.00

Table 6
Percent Distribution of Hours Spent by Male and Female for Principal Crop Season Hours per Head per Day: By Landownership Status

(Village Survey in 1987)

Activities	Land Owner				Landless			
	Village A		Village B		Village A		Village B	
	M	F	M	F	M	F	M	F
Economic Production	26.00 (80.42)	6.33 (19.58)	27.50 (84.62)	5.00 (15.38)	36.00 (76.53)	11.04 (23.47)	27.87 (75.43)	9.08 (24.57)
Home Production	12.96 (27.77)	33.71 (72.23)	10.12 (22.38)	35.08 (77.62)	6.00 (15.47)	32.79 (84.53)	10.50 (21.22)	38.96 (78.78)
Total Work Burden	38.96 (49.31)	40.04 (50.69)	37.62 (48.42)	40.08 (51.58)	42.00 (48.94)	43.83 (51.06)	38.37 (44.41)	48.04 (55.59)
Other Social and Personal Requirements, Rest & Sleep	61.04 (50.45)	59.96 (49.55)	62.37 (51.00)	59.92 (49.00)	58.00 (50.80)	56.17 (49.20)	61.62 (54.25)	51.96 (45.75)
All Activities	100.00	100.00	100.00	100.00	100.00	100.00	100.00	100.00

Figures in parentheses denote respective shares of male and female in that activity

The Role of Women in Economic Activity 273

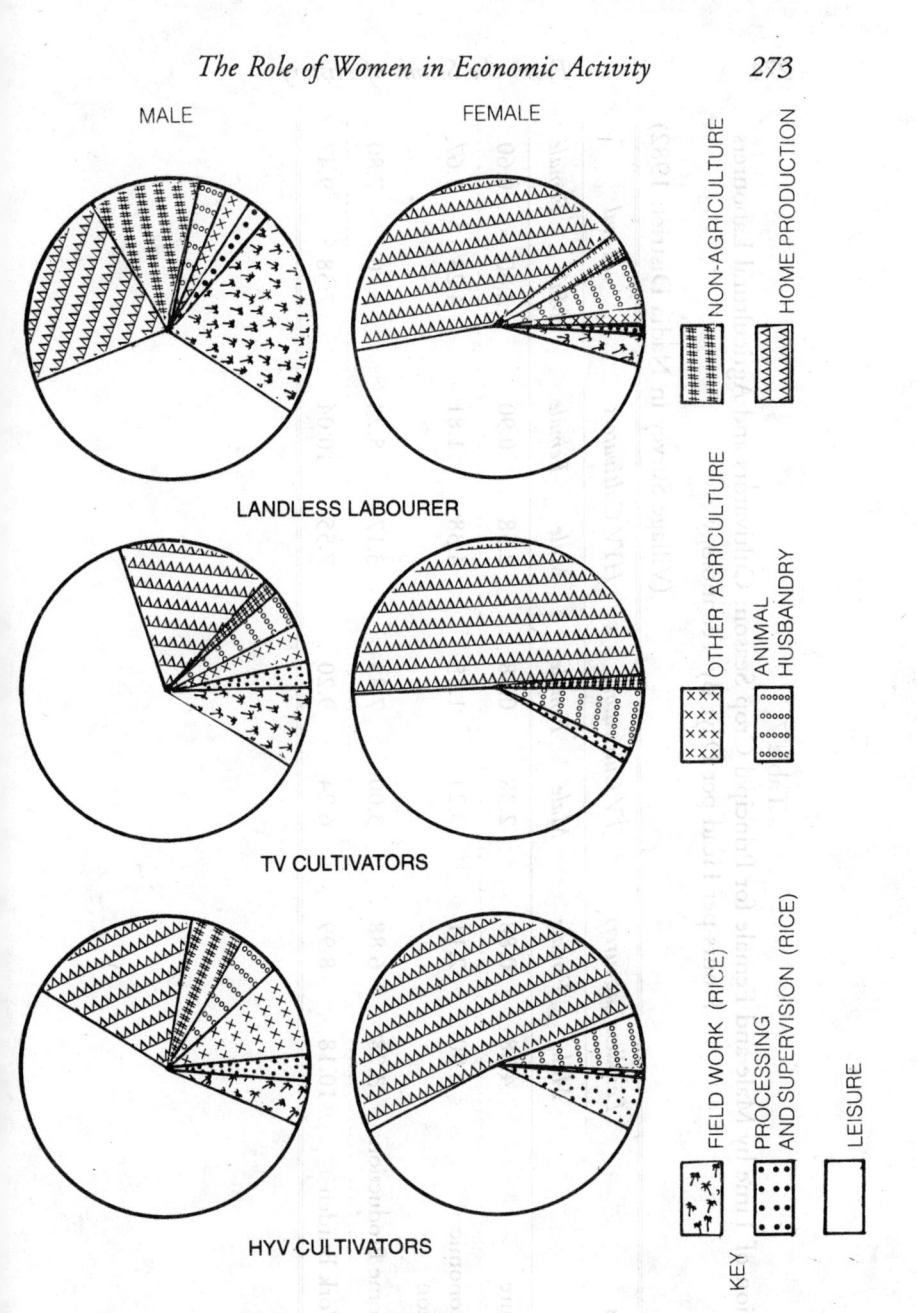

Chart IV
Gender Differential in Allocation of Time to Different Activities:
By Socio-Economic Groups and by Technology

Table 7
Allocation of Time by Male and Female for Principal Crop Season: Cultivators and Agricultural Labourers Hours per Head per Day: By Technology

(Village Survey in Nadia District: 1982)

Activities	Landless Labourers Male	Landless Labourers Female	TV Cultivators Male	TV Cultivators Female	HYV Cultivators Male	HYV Cultivators Female	Total Male	Total Female
Agriculture	4.38	0.88	2.38	0.18	2.58	0.90	2.80	0.60
Total Economic Production	6.90	2.11	3.24	1.35	4.38	1.81	4.28	1.67
Total Home Production	3.28	6.88	3.00	7.85	3.17	8.23	3.10	7.80
Total Work Burden	10.18	8.99	6.24	9.20	7.55	10.04	7.38	9.47

is due to their large participation in home production activities (Chart IV). However, in agricultural as well as total economic production activities, the number of hours worked by the female increased from TV to HYV.

The bulk of the increase in agricultural activity for the female from the TV to HYV is due to rice production and that also in processing and supervision (Table 8). For the male there is a small decline in the total number of hours worked for rice, as a result of the change to HYV. This may perhaps be due to the fact that the new technology has brought forth large volumes of output requiring more threshing, cleaning, parboiling, etc., where the short-duration modern varieties might require smaller hours to work on the field. When one takes into consideration the total rice-based farming system including non-rice crops and animal husbandry, the increase is more pronounced for the total labour requirement. There is very little gender-differential in this increased labour requirement for the farming system as a whole.

When one looks into the home production activities of the family including domestic chores, child care, education, etc., one notices (Table 9) that here also the work load of the female increases from 7.85 to 8.23 hours per day on an average as a result of change from TV to HYV rice cultivation. The corresponding increase for the male is only from 3 to 3.17 hours per day. The composition of this home production further suggests that the bulk of the activity is for the domestic chores of the female, whereas for the male it is for educational activities. It is noteworthy that as a result of the change to new technology there seems to be a spurt in educational activities for both male and female, the increase being relatively larger for the female.

A more rigorous test is undertaken here on the basis of data from a sample of 52 farms cultivating traditional variety and 26 farms growing high yielding variety of rice. A long-linear functional form is postulated and variations in total female labour use and proportions of female in total labour use are sought to be explained with the help of two equations with the following independent variables:

(i) farm size

Table 8
Allocation of Time by Male and Female in Agricultural and Allied Activities Hours per Head per Day
(Village Survey in Nadia District: 1982)

Activities	Landless Labourers Male	Landless Labourers Female	TV Cultivators Male	TV Cultivators Female	HYV Cultivators Male	HYV Cultivators Female	Total Male	Total Female
Agriculture: Rice								
Field Work	3.54	0.53	1.35	0.003	0.68	0.00	1.47	0.11
Processing & Supervision	0.35	0.09	0.42	0.17	0.41	0.84	0.41	0.41
Total Activity in Rice	3.89	0.62	1.77	0.17	1.09	0.84	1.88	0.52
Agriculture: Others	0.49	0.26	0.61	0.01	1.49	0.06	0.92	0.08
Total Agriculture	4.38	0.88	2.38	0.18	2.59	0.90	2.80	0.60
Animal Husbandry	0.48	0.85	0.61	1.12	0.76	0.91	0.64	0.98
Total Agriculture and Allied Activities	4.86	1.73	2.99	1.29	3.35	1.81	3.44	1.58

Table 9
Allocation of Time by Male and Female to Economic Production and Home Production Activities Hours per Head per Day

(Village Survey in Nadia District: 1982)

Activities	Landless Agricultural Labourers Male	Landless Agricultural Labourers Female	Farmers Cultivating TV Rice Male	Farmers Cultivating TV Rice Female	Farmers Cultivating HYV Rice Male	Farmers Cultivating HYV Rice Female	Total Male	Total Female
Economic Production: (Total)	6.90	2.11	3.24	1.36	4.38	1.81	4.28	1.67
Home Production:								
Education	0.67	0.38	1.33	0.63	1.53	1.62	—	—
Childcare	0.25	1.69	0.19	1.59	—	1.14	—	—
Domestic	2.33	4.81	1.22	5.13	1.42	5.15	—	—
Others	0.17	—	0.26	0.50	0.22	0.32	—	—
Total	3.28	6.88	3.00	7.85	3.17	8.23	3.10	7.80
Total Work Burden	10.18	8.99	6.24	9.20	7.55	10.04	7.38	9.47

(ii) expenditure per hectare on seeds (representing quality and plant population)
(iii) farm-yard manure and compost
(iv) commercial fertilizer
(v) insecticide, weedicide and plant treatment, and
(vi) technology.

The expected effects of seed and manure upon both total female labour and its proportion in total labour are positive because these tend to use more hours in animal husbandry, transplanting, weeding and harvesting — all female labour-intensive activities. On the other hand, the effects of fertilizer and plant treatment are expected to be negative since these are applied more by the male and they tend to displace female labour that would otherwise be needed for plant care and weeding. Farm size may have indeterminate effect through the interaction of a positive output effect and negative substitution effect. Technology in the form of a change from TV to HYV is likely to increase total labour including female labour use. But its effects upon the share of the female may still be indeterminate. The results (Table 10) conform to expected behaviour. It demonstrates that the transition to the new technology has a strong positive impact not only on total female labour use but also on the position of the female vis-a-vis that of the male. It also appears that the application of commercial fertilizer and plant treatment has strong negative effect upon female labour use, both absolutely and relatively to male. The effects of seed and farm size are not significant.

An additional test is provided here with the help of data from 75 farms cultivating TV and another 75 cultivating HYV rice in the districts of Hooghly and Birbhum in West Bengal.[13] A log-linear function, similar to the above, is fitted for three equations:

For (a) For the TV farmers;
    (b) the HYV farmers; and
    (c) farmers pooled together.

[13] Data for this analysis were taken from the secondary source of Farm Management Studies conducted by the Government of West Bengal. This will provide an additional check on the results obtained through the primary survey data.

Table 10
Labour Use Functions:
Household Survey Data (Nadia) Pooled (N=78)
Log Linear

(Village Survey in Nadia District: 1982)

Intercept/ Independent Variables	Total Female Labour	Proportion of Female in Total Labour
Intercept	1.74	−3.79
Farm Size	−0.02	0.07
	(0.13)	(0.12)
Seed	0.56	0.23
	(0.32)	(0.37)
Manure/Compost	0.25	0.04
	(0.16)	(0.15)
Fertilizer	−0.44*	−0.93**
	(0.14)	(0.23)
Plant Treatment	−0.31*	−0.32*
	(0.10)	(0.10)
Dummy (for Technology)	0.37**	0.11**
	(0.11)	(0.03)
R^2	0.42	0.28

Note: Figures in parentheses denote standard errors
* denote significance at 5% level; ** denote significance at 1% level

Variations in the share of women in total labour is explained in these functions with the help of six independent variables, mainly, area under crop, cropping intensity, farm business income, expenditure on labour, total value of output per hectare and technology. It is hypothesized that the proportion of female labour in a rice-based farming system would be positively affected by cropping intensity, farm business income and technology, whereas the effects of area, expenditure on human labour and total value of output per hectare would be indeterminate because of the simultaneous operation of both positive and negative effects. The results (Table 11) show that cropping intensity, farm business income and expenditure on human labour all exert positive effects upon the proportion of women in total labour in all the three equations. The coefficient for value of output per hectare is also significantly positive in the two equations representing the two technologies separately, whereas it is insignificant in the pooled equation. The effect of area is insignificant all through. The equation with the pooled data strongly demonstrates the positive impact of the HYV technology through the high and statistically significant coefficient for the dummy variable representing technology. The statistical exercise thus provides strong evidence in support of the hypothesis that the new HYV technology in rice cultivation has exerted a fairly strong positive impact on female labour use.[14]

VI Equity in Consumption, Nutrition and Work

A common hypothesis in the literature on women and development is that female members within the family enjoy a relatively smaller share of the total household consumption. This side by side with their higher work burden gives rise to a more pronounced sex discrimination in food consumption, health and nutrition, and status of women. Data have been collected on different items of consumption by each member of the households surveyed. Analysis of these data shows that the findings are, by and large, in agreement with the hypothesis of a relative intra-family disparity against women. Women are found to consume less than men, both in terms of the quantities of major food items, e.g., rice, fish, meat, milk, etc., and their calorie value. The data also show that the relative

---

[14] Bahnisikha Ghosh and Sudhin K. Mukhopadhyay, 'Gender Differentials in the Impact of Technological Change in Rice-Based Farming Systems in India', in Susan V. Poats, Marianne Schmink and Anita Spring, eds., *Gender Issues in Farming Systems Research and Extension* (Boulder, Colorado, 1988).

Table 11
Labour Use Functions: FMS Data (Hooghly and Birbhum)
Log Linear
Dependent Variable: Share of Women in Total Labour Use

Technology	Intercept	Area Under the Crop	Cropping Intensity	Farm Business Income	Expenditure on Labour per Hectare	Total Value of Output	Dummy for Technology	R^2
Local (N = 75)	−2.80	0.06 (0.08)	−0.18 (0.32)	0.20** (0.05)	0.21 (0.15)	0.54* (0.25)	—	0.44
HYV (N = 75)	1.07	0.81 (0.81)	0.91** (0.23)	0.20** (0.05)	0.37 (0.25)	0.16* (0.06)	—	0.53
Pooled (N = 150)	0.75	0.09* (0.04)	0.56** (0.14)	0.20** (0.03)	0.21 (0.13)	−0.01 (0.12)	5.10** (0.07)	0.46

Note: Figures in parentheses denote standard errors
* denotes significance at 5% level; ** denotes significance at 1% level

share of female in consumer expenditure in most cases[15] goes down in the lean season when income and food availability is relatively less. Similar gaps exist between the amounts of expenditure on purchased consumption goods incurred for the male and the female, between the seasons, as well as over the year (Tables 12 and 13).

Table 12
Percent Share of Male and Female in
Total Household Expenditure on Consumption Goods

	May-June M	May-June F	September M	September F	Average for Both Seasons M	Average for Both Seasons F
Village A	67.02	32.97	50.85	49.15	62.07	37.93
Village B	55.34	44.67	64.62	35.38	60.78	39.22
Village C	53.65	46.34	58.64	41.36	56.33	43.67
Village D	51.07	48.93	57.68	42.32	53.90	46.10

Table 13
Calorie Intake per Capita per Day for Landless Households

	May-June M	May-June F	September-October M	September-October F
Village A	3088	2418	2057	1497
Village B	2140	1185	1481	1002
Village C	2575	2336	2479	1976
Village D	2737	2552	2431	2187

[15] This is true for three out of four villages. In the remaining village the share of women is less than that of men in both seasons. But their relative position does not deteriorate in the lean season. The village, it may be noted, is generally better off economically and the level of expenditure per woman remains about the same in both seasons, although their share goes up in the lean season.

Food consumption in quantity or in calorie should be studied in the context of the requirement of the individual both for physical need and for work load. Data from the four villages show that the women not only have lesser total calorie intake compared to men, but they also suffer in regard to the physical consumption requirements justified by their work load. The index of equity between men and women in calorie intake per work-hour shows that in three out of four villages the work-calorie distribution is clearly against the female. In one village (village C) the distribution is just balanced (Table 14).

Table 14
Calorie Intake per Hour of Work Load and Equity in Calorie Intake

	Calorie Intake per Hour of Work M	Calorie Intake per Hour of Work F	Index of Equity* in Work-Calorie Distribution
Village A	286.46	219.46	0.97
Village B	372.21	275.02	0.94
Village C	256.70	203.53	1.00
Village D	288.83	207.26	0.91

* The Index is calculated by the following formula:

$$E = \frac{\text{Intake by Female}}{\text{Requirement by Female}} \div \frac{\text{Intake by Male}}{\text{Requirement by Male}}$$

$E \gtreqless 1$ Denotes respectively Pro-Female, Fair and Pro-Male distribution

As discussed earlier, an additional repeat survey was conducted for 30 selected farm households in two villages in Nadia. Data were collected for each member of the households regarding their consumption and time-allocation and also on household transaction. Each household was visited and data collected from it on every tenth day for one whole year, 1987–1988 (i.e., 36 times during the year). These data show variations around the year in the levels of calorie consumption and hours worked by the male and female members of the household. These have been summarized for two size classes of farmers, small and big, and averages have been calculated for each month. Results of this analysis for 12 months (Charts V–A and V–B and Table 15) support the conclusions derived earlier about the differences in work-consumption relationship between male and female household members. The male would have a higher level of calorie consumption than the female throughout the year for both small and big farmers. When total work is concerned, the average number of hours worked per day by the male is higher than that by the female only during September to January for small farmers. This is the busiest period in the rice farming system beginning with the preparation for *Rabi* crops through to *Aman* (*Kharif*) rice harvesting and transplanting of *Boro* rice. For the small farmers the proportion of their own household labour is larger than that for the big farmers, who during this season use hired labour and to that extent have lower hours of work by male household members themselves. This is evident from the fact that for big farmers during this period from September to January, total hours of work per day are about the same for the male and the female members of the household. The data show that the relative position of the female members in regard to calorie consumption and work is worse for the big farmers than for the small ones.

VII Conclusion

The preceding analysis of micro-data at household and individual levels shows that while in terms of conventional definitions of economic activity and employment, women's share is significantly lower, the total work burden of women becomes larger than that of men when home production activities are taken into account. This turns out to be valid across locations, communities, economic statuses and seasons. When the work burden is set against food consumption, the male-female differential in family status and strategy becomes apparent through the index of equity in work-

A. Calorie Consumption per Head per Day by Male & Female Household Members
Small Farmers

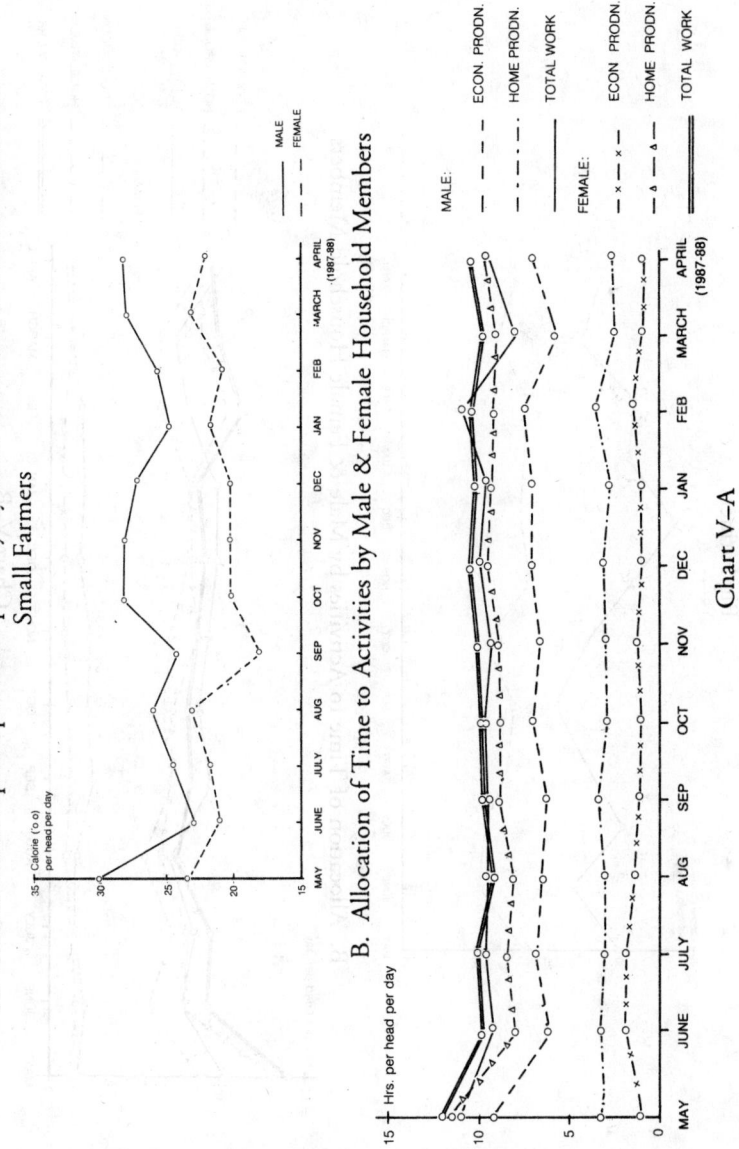

B. Allocation of Time to Activities by Male & Female Household Members

Chart V-A

286   *From the Seams of History*

A. Calorie Consumption per Head per Day by Male & Female Household Members
Big Farmers

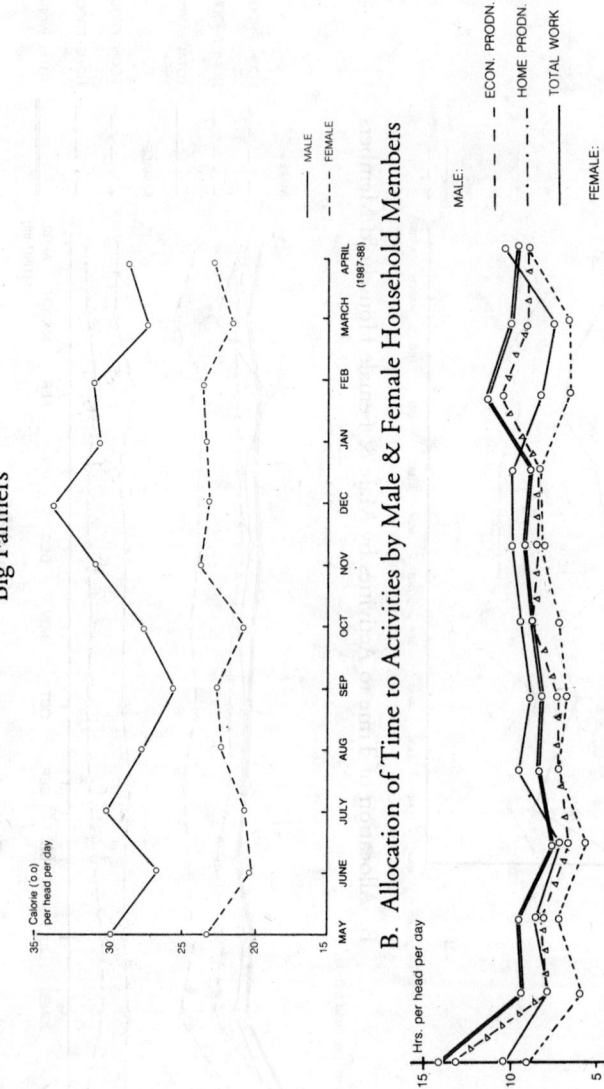

B. Allocation of Time to Activities by Male & Female Household Members

Chart V–B

Table 15
Work-Consumption Relation Between Male and
Female Members of Small and Big Farm Households

Farm-Households

Month	Small Consumption	Small Work	Big Consumption	Big Work
May	M > F	M = F	M > F	M > F
June	M > F	M < F	M > F	M < F
July	M > F	M < F	M > F	M < F
August	M > F	M < F	M > F	M = F
September	M > F	M > F	M > F	M = F
October	M > F	M > F	M > F	M = F
November	M > F	M > F	M > F	M < F
December	M > F	M > F	M > F	M < F
January	M > F	M > F	M > F	M < F
February	M > F	M < F	M > F	M < F
March	M > F	M < F	M > F	M < F
April	M > F	M < F	M > F	M < F

calorie distribution between men and women. The female works longer hours, consumes smaller quantities and sacrifices more during the harder days. This is also supported by the smaller proportion of consumer expenditure enjoyed by the female within the household. All this results in persistent inequities in the distribution of work and nutrition.

Analysis of the data on the impact of HYV technology gives rise to several interesting conclusions in regard to male-female differential in labour use in agriculture. First, in rice production there is an overall increase in the gross total female labour use and a marginal decrease in male labour. However, when the entire rice-based farming systems (that includes other crops and animal husbandry) are considered both female and male labour use increase by about the same proportions. Second, the bulk of the increase in female labour use is due to increase in processing and supervision activities. The isolated effects of the application of commercial fertilizer and plant treatment is negative on female labour use. The implication of this attribute of the new technology is higher inequity because processing and supervision are done mostly by family female labour of owner farmers, whereas weeding and other field operations are performed by hired female labour. The technology thus tends to displace the already poor hired female labour, while it generates increase in total female labour use.[16]

The implications for policy changes revealed in this study relate to the need for appropriate choice of technologies and work environment that augment women's share in employment, income and consumption, even if the current concepts and measurement are accepted. However, these concepts need to be revised and many of the social accounting systems should be changed accordingly. This would at least provide a fair index of the existing disparity and call attention to the need for its removal in the interest of the economy and society.

---

[16] Sudhin K. Mukhopadhyay, 'Adapting Household Behavior to Agricultural Technology in West Bengal, India: Wage Labor, Fertility and Child Schooling Determinants', Center Discussion Paper No. 631, Economic Growth Center (New Haven, 1991).

Index

Abala Bose 191, 205–6
Abarodh 112–3, 117–18, 121–2, 132, 138–40, 142, 144
Abdul Lateef 110, 115
Act of 1856 3, 4, 8, 40
Akhtar Imam 125–7
Akhtar Mahal Syeda Khatun 140, 142, 144–5
All India Women's Conference 208–9
Ambuja Sundari Dasgupta 186
Andarmahal 71–2, 84–5, 108, 112, 114, 128, 139, 141–8
Anindita Debi 214
Antahpur 77–8, 82, 185, 187, 211
Anusilan Samiti 129, 211
Arubala Sen Gupta 199
Arya Samaj 40–1
Ashalata Sen 185, 198, 202, 204, 207
Azizunnessa 133–4

Bamabodhini Patrika 12, 21, 29–30, 35, 74, 79–81, 83, 113, 125, 132–3, 186, 211
Bonalata Debi 187
Bangalakshmi 206–7
Bangiya Nari Samaj 192
Bankim Chandra Chattopadhyay 119, 133
Bankura Zilla Mahila Sammelan 207
Barthes, Ronald 67, 77

Basanti Debi 194–5, 197, 202
Bengal Census Reports 221, 236–7
  undernumeration of women in 221–3, 229, 233
Bengal Women's Education League 205–6
Bengali as language of resistance 5, 112–3, 119–21
Bernstein, Basil 157
Besant, Annie 181, 190–2
Bethune College/School 125–7, 130, 148, 197, 201
Bhadralok 12–13, 15, 108, 111, 135, 179, 189–90
  see also *Bhadramahila* and Muslim
Bhadramahila 4
  construction of 5, 71, 74–5, 83, 91–2, 97, 99–104
  dresses of 67–106
  morality of 75–6, 92–3, 100
  See also movement, Muslim and Women's journals.
Bharat Stri Mahamandal 204–5
Bharatamahila 211–3
Bharati 74, 184
Bibi Taherunnessa 132
Bina Das 200
Brahmo Samaj 72

Calcutta Girls' Madrassah 113
Campbell Medical School 132, 180

Caste 14–16, 25–7, 32, 34, 39–40, 62, 65
  Associations 24, 36
  Council and Raja 22–3, 31
  and *dal* 23–4, 30–1
Chandramukhi Bose 114
Chapman, Priscilla 113
Chhatri Sangha 200–1
Christian missionaries 105, 180
Cohn, Bernard 19
Cousins, Margaret 181, 190–1, 209

Dakshinaranjan Mukhopadhyay 15
Daulatunnessa Khatun 128
Debendranath Tagore 72, 95
Dhaka University 127–8
Dipali Sangha 128–9, 198–201, 207–8

Eden College/School 15, 124–31
Education 13, 19, 35–6, 72–4, 105
  for girls 6, 149–73
  for women 107–31, 179, 182, 205–6
  National Commission on 154

Faizunnessa Chaudhurani, Nawab 111–12, 114–16, 119–20, 133–4, 147–8
Faizunnessa College/School 115, 120, 131, 147
Family:
  Hindu 17, 21, 30, 35, 86
    condition of women in 17–18, 29, 49–50, 60, 69–70, 179, 213–14

discipline in 3, 21–2, 29–30
reproductive labour in 86
sexual exploitation within 38, 53–9
see also women's economic activity and widow-remarriage—
Muslim 110, 123, 134
see also *sharif*
Fazilatunnessa Zoha 127–8, 143
Firdaus Mahal, Nawab 113
Fort William College 118–19
Foucault, Michel 76
Freedom Movement 129
  girl students in 199–201
  participation of women in 128–9, 134, 138, 176–8, 182–201, 203, 211
  religious symbols in 183–4
  and linkage with women's movement 176–8, 181, 201–18
  see also Muslim, Swadeshi Movement and Suffrage movement
Friend of India 25, 31

Gandaria Mahila Samiti 198
Gandhi, M.K. 190
  and Bengali Women 193–4, 198, 202, 209
Gyanadanandini Debi 74

Hasmat Ara 125
Hemalata Tagore 206
Hemaprabha Majumdar 194–7, 204
  on clothes 77–8, 82, 86, 100
  political participation of 185

Index

Hemanta Kumari Chaudhury 77
Hindu Intelligencer 20, 27, 32
Hindu Patriot 9, 12, 15, 24, 33
Hiranmoyee Debi 82, 100

Indian National Congress 184, 189, 193, 196
Islam Pracharak 133
Iswarchandra Vidyasagar 110, 119, 122
and society 14–17, 20–6, 31–4
and the issue of remarriage of widows 3, 8–10, 17–18, 25–30, 33–5
reliance on Shastras 19–21, 27–8, 30–1
and on the State, 32–3
treatises by 27–9

Jayasree 207, 211–14
Jyotirmoyee Ganguly 94, 192, 196, 204, 206

Kadambini Ganguly 109, 114
Kailasbasini Debi 179
Kalpana Dutta 123, 200
Kalyani Bhattacharya 200–1
Kamala Das Gupta 200
Kamaladevi Chattopadhyaya 190, 196
Kamini Roy 192–3, 215
Kamrunnessa Girls' School 128–30
Karewa 38, 41, 50–2, 57–65
Keshab Chandra Sen 72, 110
Khairunnessa 134
Khujasta Akhter Bano 114
Krishnabhabini Das
concept of femininity of 83
in women's organization 205
on widow's costume 96, 100, 165
on women's work, 90
Kumudini Bose (neé Mitra) 187, 192, 204–6, 211–12

Lady Brabourne College 124, 147–8
Lakshmi Menon 196
Latika Ghosh 197, 199, 200, 204, 206
Levirate 51, 59–63
women's resistance to 63–4
see also karewa
Lila Roy (neé Nag) 127–9, 148, 198–9, 204, 247–8, 211
see also Dipali Sangha
Lilabati Mitra 185

Mahakali Pathshala 187–8
Mahila Rashtriya Sangha 199
Mahishya Mahila 18, 35–6
Mahmuda Khatun Siddiqua 120, 146–7
Maleka Begum 109
Mamlukul Fatema Khanam 109, 121, 140, 145–6
Mankumari Bose 109
Mill, James 30, 102, 104
Mrinalini Sen 192, 205
Muthulakshmi Reddy 192
Muslim
Bhadralok 108, 114, 136, 142
Bhadramahila, emergence of 5, 107–12, 128, 132, 136–7
creative writings of 107, 109, 111, 116–20, 124–7, 131–48
education of 5–6, 107–34, 138–9, 144, 147–8

participation in freedom
movement 128–9, 134, 138
sexuality of 140–1
identity 107–10, 114–20, 132–3, 144, 147
League 120
Suhrid Sammilani 114, 122, 137

Nagendrabala Mustafi 86
Nari Karma Mandir 195
Nazrul Islam 123–4, 127, 143, 146
Nivedita, Sister 187
Nurunnessa Khatun 109, 120, 141–5
Nutrition
Gender–differential in 280–4

Pandita Ramabai 204
Patriarchy 3, 5, 179–80
Classic 152–3
Polyandry 53–7, 110
Polygamy 17, 25, 30–1
Prabhabati Das Gupta 199
Pritilata Waddedar 203
Purdah 58, 110, 112, 117, 123, 126, 132, 138–9, 140, 146

Rabindranath Tagore 110, 133, 146, 212, 216–17
Radhakanta Deb 31
Rajnarayan Basu 103
Ramabai Ranade 191
Rammohan Roy 12, 110, 122
eradication of Sati 3, 8, 33
Rasasundari Debi 67
Raziya Khatun Chaudhuri 138–40

Renuka Ray 209
Rokeya Sakhawat Hossein 5, 109, 128, 140, 148
on bhadralok 135
and burqa 140
and suffrage movement 193
on women 11, 132 134–9
and women's education 113, 115–23

Sakhawat Memorial School 115, 118, 145, 121–2
Samachar Darpan 34
Samachar Sudhabashan 20, 27, 32
Sambad Prabhakar 27
Sanjivani 185–6
Santosh Kumari Gupta 199
Sarajubala Dutta 211–12
Sarala Ray 205, 209
Saraladebi Choudhurani 109
on clothes 95
political participation of 184–5, 187
in women's organization 204–5
writings of 205, 211
Sarat Chandra Chattopadhyay 133, 146–7, 216
Sarojini Naidu 109, 191–2, 196
Sarojnalini Dutt Memorial Association 206–7
Sati 37, 110 141
eradication of 3, 8, 33–4, 179
as an ideal 39–40, 99
Saudamini Khastagiri, Kumari 78–80, 85, 93–5
Savitri Debi 198
Schools
conformity within 164

Index

functions of 149, 157–8
and resistance 149–73
rituals in 160, 171–2
see also Bethune School, Eden School and Kamrunnessa School
Seclusion 5, 84–6, 148
see also abarodh, andarmahal and purdah
Sexuality 3–4, 29–30, 42–9, 59, 75–6, 80–1, 83, 87–8, 93–5, 97–9, 105, 140–1
Shaista Ikramullah 120
Shamsunnahar Mahmud 109, 117, 121–4, 128, 131, 137–9, 144, 148
Sharif 108, 112, 115, 118–19, 133, 141
Snehashila Chowdhury 185
Social Reform Movement 11, 12, 21, 30, 34–6, 40, 68–70, 74–5, 110, 111, 179–82
Subarnabanik Mahila Sammilani 35
Subhas Chandra Bose 197, 199
Suffrage Movement 190–3
Sufia Kamal 120, 146–7
Suniti Debi 194, 197
Suprabhat 187, 211–12
Surama Mitra 200
Swadeshi Movement 120, 129, 177, 182–90, 202, 213, 216
and Muslim women 134, 138
Swarnakumari Debi 71–2, 74, 85–6, 95, 103, 109, 184, 204
Syed Ahmed Khan 110, 115
Syed Ameer Ali 110–11

Tattvabodhini Patrika 12, 29–30

Urdu 5, 13, 118–21
Urmila Debi 194–5, 197, 200, 204

Victoria Institution 197

Widowers 30
Widows
remarriage of, in Bengal, 3, 8–15, 33–5, 110, 179
in Haryana 3–4, 34–66
women's views regarding 35–6, 38, 56–64
sexual exploitation of 53–9
Women's economic activity
definition of 219–23, 255–62
impact of technology on 237–9, 268, 274–80
invisibility of, see Census
in agriculture 225–39, 242, 256, 262–4, 273–5, 278
in industry 227–8, 235–9
in food processing and selling 237, 239
and allocation of time 257–73
and gender asymmetry 224–9, 240–52
and home production 226, 235–8, 258–62, 266–74
Women's India Association 192
Women's journals
see *Antahpur, Bamabodhini Patrika, Bangalakshmi, Bharatamahila, Jayasree, Mahishya Mahila* and *Suprabhat*
see also freedom movement
Women's Literary output 5, 71–4, 79–86, 93–6, 100, 174–6, 181, 184–5, 194, 211–15

see also Muslim and women's
    journals
Women's Movement 109, 122,
    129, 215–16, 218
    see also freedom
    movement

women's organizations 147, 192–
    3, 195–6, 198–9, 203–10

Young Bengal 12

Zemindars 22–4